WHY WE ARE NOT NIETZSCHEANS

WHY WE ARE *not* NIETZSCHEANS

Edited by

LUC FERRY *and*
ALAIN RENAUT

Translated by

ROBERT DE LOAIZA

THE UNIVERSITY OF CHICAGO PRESS   *Chicago & London*

LUC FERRY is professor of philosophy at the Sorbonne and at the University of Caen. Among his previous books published in translation by the University of Chicago Press is *The New Ecological Order.* ALAIN RENAUT is professor of political science at the Sorbonne and the author of *Sartre, le dernier philosophe.* FERRY and RENAUT are co-authors of *Heidegger and Modernity,* also published by the University of Chicago Press.

The University of Chicago Press, Chicago 60637
The University of Chicago Press Ltd., London
© 1997 by The University of Chicago
All rights reserved. Published 1997
Printed in the United States of America
05 04 03 02 01 00 99 98 97   1 2 3 4 5

ISBN 0-226-24480-6 (cloth)
      0-226-24481-4 (paper)

Originally published as *Pourquoi nous ne sommes pas nietzschéens,*
© Éditions Grasset & Fasquelle, 1991.

Library of Congress Cataloging-in-Publication Data

Pourquoi nous ne sommes pas Nietzschéens. English.
    Why we are not Nietzscheans / edited by Luc Ferry and Alain
Renaut ; translated by Robert de Loaiza.
      p. cm.
    Includes bibliographical references and index.
    ISBN 0-226-24480-6 (cloth : alk. paper). — ISBN 0-226-24481-4
(paper : alk. paper)
      1. Nietzsche, Friedrich Wilhelm, 1844–1900. I. Ferry, Luc.
II. Renaut, Alain. III. Title.
B3317.P58 1997
193—dc20   96-41718
                                                                 CIP

Contents

Preface to the
1991 French Edition

To think with Nietzsche against Nietzsche: that could be another title for this collection of essays the idea for which was suggested to us by our friend André Comte-Sponville a year ago. For most of the students of our generation—the one that began its course of studies in the 1960s—the ideals of the Enlightenment could not but be a bad joke, a somber mystification. That, anyhow, was what was taught to us. The master thinkers in those days were called Foucault, Deleuze, Derrida, Althusser, Lacan. Merleau-Ponty, the humanist, was old hat, and most of us no longer read Sartre. From the rue d'Ulm to the Collège de France we discovered the philosophers of suspicion: Marx, Freud, and Heidegger of course, but, above all, Nietzsche, the inventor of the "genealogy" in the name of which we had to treat every discourse as a symptom.

Retrospective illusion or ruse of history? Those who intended to be the heirs of this "philosophy with a hammer" with which Nietzsche wanted to smash the idols of metaphysics now look like the last creators of a philosophical tradition that has come to its exhaustion. This has become increasingly obvious to our generation. The essays gathered together here demonstrate, through their very diversity—no common dogma links them—that philosophy is not condemned to infinite deconstruction. In various forms, philosophy renews the ancestral desire for rationality, which the relativism of the modes of thought of difference invited us, too facilely, to renounce. Naturally, the scales have fallen from our eyes: no one today believes in Absolute Knowledge, in the meaning of history, or in the transparency of the Subject. That is precisely why it is together with Nietzsche that we have to think against Nietzsche.

Luc Ferry and Alain Renaut

1 *Hierarchy and Truth*

ALAIN BOYER

What have I to do with refutations . . .

F. Nietzsche

The *Foundations of Arithmetic* was published in Breslau in 1884. In Nice, at the same time, he who wrote such good books was finishing the fourth part of *Zarathustra*. Frege and Nietzsche. What, then, is philosophy, and, even, what is *German* philosophy, for these two books to be considered as belonging to the same "discipline"? The scission between *matheme* and *poem*, to speak as Alain Badiou does, never seemed greater. In the twentieth century, each of these two thinkers would, in fact, be considered the inventor of a new way of thinking. Frege's revolution would have such descendants as Russell, Wittgenstein, Carnap, Quine. The philosopher "with a hammer" will be a prophet for Heidegger and for the "French thought" of the 1960s and 1970s, but we should not forget his influence on men such as Georg Simmel and Max Weber. (Husserl's position is peculiar: he seems to ignore Nietzsche, but the impact of Frege's criticism of the former's first book in 1895 was apparently as decisive as Brentano's critique was).

The nineteenth century left us with at least three clusters of problems around which most of our preoccupations still turn: economic, political, and epistemological ones. The market, democracy, science (and technology) are still the objects we must constantly try to think out. Marx or Walras, Tocqueville or Pareto, Auguste Comte or Claude Bernard: there was no shortage of analysts at modernity's cradle. There were even authors such as Cournot or Mill who tried to understand the totality.

As for the market or, more broadly, the industrial economy, Nietzsche does not seem to have attached as much importance to it as did Marx his contemporary—an author Nietzsche never cites, in any case. But when it came to democracy, Nietzsche never stopped thinking about it: not to ground it, but to condemn it. Reading Nietzsche will no doubt long have a bracing effect on all those who do not want to make of philosophy a professional activity "like any other" and who see in it rather a vital activity, a passion. Works like *Human, All-Too-Human* or *The Dawn* hold many alarming[1] texts, worthy of being reread and meditated on even if you spend most of your time reflecting on the interpretation of scientific theories or on the meaning of Gödel's theorem. Yes, yes, reading Nietzsche, all very well, but that's not the problem. The question is: can one be a Nietzschean?

Nietzsche's central obsession is *hierarchy*. He says so and repeats it: "Given that it is the *problem of hierarchy* of which we must speak, that it is the problem for us, free spirits."[2] Hierarchy: meaning both the problem of the *hierarchy of values* and praise of the *values of the hierarchy*. To think is, of course, to judge, but this in the sense of the *value judgment*.[3] To situate oneself "beyond good and evil" does not in any way mean giving up judging, classifying, eliminating. On the contrary. It is to want to position oneself beyond traditional evaluations, simultaneously Christian and egalitarian. If the Enlightenment and the French Revolution were in conflict with the Church, it was in the name of egalitarian values whose origin was Christian.

But can we find an interesting *critique* of equality in Nietzsche beyond that lucid diagnosis? I'm not convinced of it. We do find an eternal recurrence of the antiegalitarian obsession. We have to stop *interpreting* Nietzsche and start taking him at his word. Christianity is, in his eyes, first of all the religion of the revolt of the weak, of the plebeian mind-set, of full-fledged egalitarianism. His admiration for the Indian caste system (in *The Antichrist*) is there to show us that Nietzsche goes over without hesitation to the side of the partisans of *Homo hierarchicus* against those of *Homo aequalis*. It could be objected that he never ceases to praise the historical person Jesus or the individual over against the crowd. But how does he do this?

AGAINST EQUALITY, HIERARCHY

Nietzsche-Callicles[4] is in revolt not so much against individualism as against democratic egalitarianism: "Democracy is naturalized Christianity."[5] Modernity is a "denaturalization of values . . . Contraries introduced in place of natural degree and rank. Hatred of hierarchy."[6]

To not interpret Nietzsche, to take him at his word, without commentaries:

> *The labor question.* The stupidity—at bottom, the degeneration of instinct, which is today the cause of *all* stupidities—is that there is a labor question at all. Certain things one does not question: that is the first imperative of instinct. I simply cannot see what one proposes to do with the European worker now that one has made a question of him. He is far too well off not to ask for more and more, not to ask more immodestly. In the end, he has numbers on his side. The hope is gone forever that a modest and self-sufficient kind of man, a Chinese type, might here develop as a class: and there would have been reason in that, it would almost have been a necessity. But what was done? Everything to nip in the bud even the preconditions for this: the instincts by virtue of which the worker becomes possible as a class, possible in his own eyes, have been destroyed through and through with the most irresponsible thoughtlessness. The worker was qualified for military service, granted the right to organize and to vote: is it any wonder that the worker today experiences his own existence as distressing—morally speaking, as an injustice? But what is *wanted*? I ask once more. If one wants an end, one must also want the means: if one wants slaves, then one is a fool if one educates them to be masters. (*Twilight of the Idols*, § 40).

The workers ask for a "just" wage where they should seek to carry out their end, their function, while remaining in their place: "Workers should learn to feel like soldiers. A fee, a salary, but not a wage! No relation between payment and performance! To instead place the individual, each one in his own way, so that he can achieve the most that lies within his field."[7]

More generally, the marching order is clear: for the categorical imperative, substitute the *natural imperative.*[8] The problem with all naturalisms is that one can make nature say more or less anything one wants. "Natural right" and "return to nature" are practically empty slogans, waiting to be filled. Nietzsche's nature is made up of forces, relations of force, results of force,[9] but these forces never stop giving rise to evaluations. If morality consists in evaluating, it is a mistake to think that Nietzsche puts himself beyond *all* morality. Quite the opposite. That is as big a blunder as seeing in the author of *Beyond Good and Evil* the propagator of a hedonistic, libertarian, and individualistic moral-ity.[10] That being said, when Nietzsche *judges,* his judgments can matter to us, even if we accept them *a contrario*. Generally speaking, his *intu-itions* are precious. We may simply add that the evaluations they imply are in effect only the inversion of "our" values:

"This inversion of values (following which "poor" became syn-onym of "sacred" and of "friend") is what makes the Jewish people im-portant: with it begins the *revolt of the slaves within morality*."[11] "Christianity is a rebellion of everything that crawls on the ground against that which has *height*: the evangel of the 'lowly' *makes* low."[12]

Where René Girard sees in Judaism, and then in the Gospels, the progressive overturning of archaic religion, in other words of the mech-anism of victimization, and, in this process, a liberation, Nietzsche—who in essence makes the same diagnosis—sees in it the sign of supreme decadence. Girard opposes the myth of Cain and Abel, which takes the victim's side, to that of Romulus and Remus, which sanctifies the mur-derer. Nietzsche would have liked that opposition—the better to *de-valorize* the Bible's vision.

In the same way, when Popper, before Castoriadis, accuses Plato of having "betrayed" Socrates and of having forgotten the latter's toler-ant and democratic wisdom, he is only taking up again Nietzsche's op-position and inverting it. For the author of "The Case of Socrates,"[13] Plato had "good" aristocratic tendencies, sadly corrupted by the "deca-dent" and "popular" Socrates: "with the dialectic the populace takes over."

Not that "our" liberal-democratic values blithely ignore anything that could resemble the idea of *culture,* of the furtherance of the arts, in a word *certain* "aristocratic" values. But it is clear that we are not pre-pared to make absolutes of these "perfections," to the detriment of jus-tice or liberty.[14]

Among the specifically Nietzschean concepts, which ones have an oper-ative or analytic, and not merely a prophetic, value? Those of overman, eternal recurrence, or even will to power seem to me, to be honest, rather poor. The concept of *genealogy,* on the other hand, is not without its seductions, in that it can give rise to a research program. It is there-fore hardly a mystery that it left its mark on Foucault's work: isn't the latter's project already written into this tentative plan from the autumn of 1887?:

Fundamental Innovations: In place of "moral values," purely naturalistic values. Naturalization of morality.

In place of "sociology," a theory of the forms of domination.

In place of "society," the culture complex, as my chief interest (as a whole or in its parts).

In place of "epistemology," a perspective theory of affects (to which belongs a hierarchy of the affects; the affects transfigured; their superior order, their "spirituality").

In place of "metaphysics" and religion, the theory of eternal recurrence (this as a means of breeding and selection). (*The Will to Power,* § 462).

Genealogy asks the question of origin. But, as Foucault demonstrated in an excellent article,[15] it does not inquire after origin in the essentialist way metaphysics (i.e., Platonism) does. It doesn't rest on the idea that the origin is the custodian of essence in its purity, or that history is the working out of an originary truth. The search for provenance (*Herkunft*) is not search for foundation, for origin (*Ursprung*) in the sense of "[the thing's] identity carefully folded in upon itself."[16] To break with essentialism is, moreover, to break with both the Origin and with the End, and to put forward the idea of *emergence* (*Entstehung*). In this, contemporary critics of any "philosophy of history" can claim Nietzsche as one of their own. Genealogy still has, despite everything, too much trust in origins. It is as though Nietzsche still gave the discovery of origin the value of an unveiling but this time one that cheapens: a concept's "populist" origin, as Foucault repeats without batting an eyebrow, would devalorize it.[17]

We can be skeptical about this procedure. The origin may be "low"—if one accepts this typically aristocratic characterization—yet the concept or institution can transform its sense and "be of value" in and of itself. Humanist morality could have been invented for reasons it itself might not accept yet present itself to us as a possible solution to the problems of living together. To measure the value of any human production by asking "who wanted it?" or, rather, "what kind of will produced it?" is to ignore every creation's transcendence with respect to its creator. Not that we should reject inquiry into origins as a causal, historical approach; but it is quite necessary to carefully distinguish questions about origin from questions about value, and in particular from questions about truth.[18]

"Perspectivism" is hardly Nietzsche's last word: behind the "perspective of affects" there is the *"hierarchy* of affects." Nothing could therefore be less Nietzschean than the (nihilist) idea that "all values are of equal value," that one can neither compare them nor judge them: to evaluate is to hierarchize. To evaluate the evaluations: to hierarchize the systems of values. Egalitarianism is a gregarious instinct, vile and low.

What we could find seductive in Nietzsche's obsessive condemnation of Christianity is his pathetic struggle against the "ascetic ideal," his ferocious denunciation of the "lie" of salvation "as a goal for life," or of sentiments/resentments such as hatred of the body, fear of sin, certain kinds of pity, etc. But it would be an illusion to see here the underlying reason for Nietzsche's ire. It is not, in a word, *virtue* that is being condemned but the pretention of making all men share in this privilege: "We must defend virtue against the preachers of virtue: they are its worst enemies. For they teach virtue as an ideal *for all*: they disrobe virtue of the attractiveness of its rarity, of the inimitable, of the exceptional and the extreme—of its *aristocratic charm*." There is in fact no argument of Nietzsche's that cannot be brought back, at least in part, to his hierarchical obsession.

SCIENCE AND TRUTH

Nietzsche's ambivalence towards science is well known: the latter is either praised for being a marvelous instrument for the critique of religion and of the prejudices of Christian morality, or accused of also relying on illusions and "moral" lies.

Science is excellent in that it is a school for skepticism, and "convictions are prisons" (*Antichrist*, § 54). Therefore "the priest knows one sole danger: science—the sane notion of cause and effect" (ibid., § 45). But science is also a modern idea and it participates in the illusion of progress: " 'Progress' is a modern idea, which is to say a false idea" (ibid., § 4).

At the time of *Daybreak* and of *Human, All-Too-Human,*[19] science is considered to be the anti-Christian, antimoralist weapon par excellence. But science's mortal sin is that it is at bottom of democratic essence: "Monsieur Renan's absolute lack of instinct, counting science and *noblesse* as one. Science is fundamentally democratic and anti-oligarchic."[20]

Despite these violent attacks on the idea of universal truth, Nietzsche cannot be thought of as a vulgar relativist. Relativism would, on the contrary, no doubt be in his eyes but an avatar of nihilism. It is natural to try to answer relativism by putting forward the Idea of objective Truth. It is true or false that the human being and the chimpanzee are "cousins" that evolved differently from a common ancestor; it is true or false that planets' orbits are circular; it is true (or false) that Napoleon was "short" and de Gaulle "tall," etc.[21]

It should be clear that using such an Idea of Truth does not presuppose that we dispose of a *criterion* permitting us to *recognize* the true. Kant used to say that the dialogue between him who asks for a criterion and him who suggests one resembles the dialogue between two men, one of whom asks for something with which to milk a goat while the other hands him a sieve. To believe that such a denial leads to skepticism is to be subject to a sort of blindness towards the actual epistemological situation.[22]

A second, no less serious error consists in suspecting the Idea of absolute Truth of all sorts of authoritarian and liberticide effects. A pragmatist and relativist conception would be better suited to our tolerant and pluralist democratic epoch.[23] Nonsense. That truth is, properly speaking, inhuman, meaning that it in no wise depends on human desire or will—any more than the *existence* of oil under the soil of Saudi Arabia depends on the desires it brings about—does not in and of itself have any dogmatic effects, quite the contrary. It is this inhumanity which permits the assertion that anyone, me, you, all of us perhaps are *wrong*,[24] because we have not arrived at a truth that does not depend on our means for getting to it. Truth is not an epistemological concept. Pragmatism, on the other hand, can lead to the notion that many incompatible ideas are true as long as they are "efficient" or "well confirmed." The predicate *true* becomes historical: what is true at t_0 can become false at t_1. We ought then to use another term, to state that what was *believed* X at to was revealed to be not X at t_1.

Nietzsche "flirts" with pragmatist and even with relativist conceptions of truth, but he doesn't stick with them. Why, then, does he not come over to the "objectivist" position? Because the idea of an objective, independent truth is still too nihilist for him: not hierarchical, not evaluating enough. Nietzsche is, in the end, not satisfied with modern science's "axiological neutrality," grounded on the logical impossibility, demonstrated by Hume, of going from the *is* to the *ought*, of drawing normative consequences from purely factual premises.

Value is not in Nature. Science, as Poincaré put it, is not written in
the imperative but in the indicative. Its imperatives can only be hypothetical, directed by an End determined elsewhere. I don't know why
some persist in seeing in this logical fact a weakness of modern science,
even a *specific* characteristic of positivist thought. It is, certainly, a *consequence* of positivism, but not one that defines it as such. (And let's
beware of the sophism through the negation of the antecedent: positivism brings about duality between facts and norms. Positivism is false.
Therefore, dualism is false.)

Jean Granier, summing up Nietzsche's arguments in *The Will to
Power,* writes: "The scientific will to knowledge is therefore but the subtle disguise of the old morality; it is the expression of the need leading
man to create the fable of an 'intelligible world' where change, pain,
contradiction, struggle, and becoming would be excluded."[25]

Science supposedly leads to "bringing existence down to the cal-
culus formula, to make of it a thought-object for mathematicians."[26]

The mathematization of physics, a vulgarization? I have to admit
to a certain fatigue at the idea of having to answer this kind of talk.
"Doltishness" and "naïveté" are not where many think they are. The
great contemporaries of the author of the *Gaya scienza,* Boltzmann,
Helmholtz, Maxwell . . . dolts and fools? The chapter "On the
Learned" in *Zarathustra* is edifying. The great aristocrat's contempt for
"the croaking of toads (of the learned)" is there expressed with particular violence. We should be able to croak with toads such as Einstein or
Poincaré.

The idea that "science" rules out change is a received idea. It is
true that Laplace's determinism seems to exclude the notion of a temporality that can create the new, but it does not *exclude* change as such, it
tries to *explain* it. Pain, "excluded" by science? What twaddle. Science
seeks, on the contrary, to *understand* pain, and we can moreover make
use of this knowledge to *reduce* suffering.

"Contradiction"? A delicate question. As usual, philosophizing
"with a hammer" can lead to confusing the aims, losing the nuances,
stiffening what are dynamic antagonisms. That the usual logic of scientists respects the principle of contradiction is due to the trivial fact that a
contradiction can imply just about anything.[27] If by "contradiction" is
understood the idea of forces in dynamic conflict, science as such sus-
tains nothing that rules out *a priori* such a possibility. The exclusion of

"struggle," of "becoming"? Isn't the theory of evolution scientific? The Nietzschean characterization of science is not quite convincing.

Jean Granier, perhaps influenced by Heidegger, and anticipating Michel Henry, wrote: "The generalized mathematization of the real indicates the reduction of Being to platitude" (op. cit.). What to say, except that old Plato would have here diagnosed an acute symptom of misology? Reducing science to the project of the domination of phenomena leads to granting thinkers like Nietzsche or Heidegger that "science does not think." Positivism paves the way for antiscience.

I'm not arguing for the idea that science could have the "last word" on Being, on Nature, on the Absolute: there never will be a "last word." But to believe that science comes down to a "paltry calculation" is inept. As for criticizing the "epistemological ideal of objectivity" by arguing that the *motivations* of scientists often belong to the register of pride "with an aftertaste of honors and daily bread,"[28] it is to ignore the real nature of scientific *objectivity,* founded not on the objectivity of scientists, flesh-and-blood beings, but on the institutional possibility of critical debate.[29] Genealogical questioning once again misses the interesting problem, which is not that of scientists' "human, all-too-human" motivations, but that of the institutional rules that make the objectivation of phenomena possible.

THE WILL TO TRUTH

How to resist the argument—old as the Sophists—that holds that since language is "nonnatural," understood as meaning that words have no necessary relation to their referent, sentences also are *conventional,* and therefore there are no truths "in themselves"? Nietzsche goes even further than the Ancients when, refusing to accept any myth of an original language whatever, he locates the origin of all language in the production of metaphors.[30] The human being doesn't *discover* any hidden truth or, if he does, it is because he forgets he himself hid it:

> When I supply the definition of a mammal and I state after examining a camel, "This is a mammal," a certain truth has certainly been brought to light, but it is a truth of limited value; I mean to say that it is anthropomorphic and does not contain a single point "true in itself," universally real and applicable

when man isn't taken into account. He who seeks such truths is in fact searching for the metamorphosis of the world within men; he aspires to an understanding of the world as a human object and, in the best of cases, obtains the feeling of an assimilation.[31]

The example is interesting in many ways, and Nietzsche here brilliantly anticipates many later theses, such as Le Roy's (and Bergson's) radical conventionalism, or the thesis about the existence of "variations of meaning" that render theories "incommensurable" (Kuhn, Feyerabend). Despite the seductive power of this line of argument, we have to respond here: no, the proposition "the camel is a mammal" is no less "true in itself" than the proposition "Friedrich Nietzsche wrote *The Birth of Tragedy*." The fact that the concept "mammal" is the product of a *classification* does not mean that the categorization is arbitrary, like a classification à la Borges, and does not imply that the proposition attributing such and such a quality to such and such an object is because of that very fact "anthropomorphic." If man had never existed, it could nevertheless have been true that the camel was, and the snake was not, an "animal bearing mammary glands" (among other characteristics defining the class of mammals).

What exactly is Nietzsche's *argument* against this? Instead of arguments, we most often find brilliant *metaphors,* infinitely seductive, as they should be, but of little rational weight. The idea that every sentence is false, or rather not true, because there are no identical "things," and that language, necessarily abstract and generalizing, cannot grasp meaning, is also, it seems to me, falsely profound.[32] "Nothing is identical," says Nietzsche. Certainly, identity is a relation every object entertains only with itself. But (1) it is possible to state nontrivial identities between referents with different designations: the fact that "the morning star = the evening star" is not obvious, it had to be discovered;[33] (2) it is possible to assert the identity of two objects *under some determinate aspect:* if two "objects"—selected out from the continuum of the real by some point of view—have the same price, or the same weight, their prices, or weights, *are identical.* There is of course no similitude absolutely speaking but only resemblances in *certain* aspects. But it is not absurd to think some propositions of identity true—stating a real identity—and some false. If the aspect under which the objects are compared is specified, then the proposition *can* be true or false, speaking absolutely (*simpliciter*).

As Aristotle would have taught, the fact that signs are arbitrary does not imply that the relations between judgments and their referents are also arbitrary. That there is no "own meaning," that very concept guards the trace of its metaphorical origin, does not imply that this trace effectively lives on in the *actual* use of the concept, nor that the stated relations between concepts depend on this (supposed) origin for their truth value.

Besides, as has often been pointed out, every challenge to the idea of (absolute) truth comes up against the problem of self-referentiality. If all truth is illusion, then what is the status of the discourse stating this "truth"?

If we are then told[34] that Nietzsche distinguishes between two kinds of truth, namely the metaphysicians' truth-illusion which, if it is a woman, turns out to be remarkably difficult to seduce, and the "philological integrity" kind of truth, the genealogist's one, a question comes up: on what is this saving distinction, the only one that allows Nietzsche not to submit his own utterances to generalized suspicion, based? Why would the discourse of science, as modern paradigm of the "quest for truth," not fall under this "philological integrity"?[35] Could it be because science, contaminated by the Socratic, and therefore "popular," virus, is of the order of the discussable, there where the aristocratic "master of truth" *poses* and *imposes* his truths? If that were the case, we could find some grounds for agreement with Nietzsche, except that for us nothing is more precious than the Socratic idea that everything can be submitted to argument, everything can be tirelessly brought into question, if we take truth and the validity of arguments as regulating Ideas. Absolute truth, of course, is not arguable: as Aristotle put it, we don't argue anymore to find out if the diagonal of a square is measurable. But as long as there is no *proof,* every attempt to state the true will be open to the criticism of others. Genealogy, as a matter of fact, does not exactly seem to be located within the (dogmatic) perspective of "indiscussable" truth. Nietzsche—and here resides the great interest of his best texts—offers hypotheses or drafts of research programs that can eventually be argued about (and it is one of the great qualities of Foucault's work that it presents itself in the form of refutable hypotheses, hypotheses which have, moreover, often been refuted).

As a consequence, the Nietzschean critique of the Socratic dialectic and, in general, of the idea of a search for objective truth through critical debate finds itself confronted with a dilemma: either (1) Nietzsche is forced to uphold a prerational conception of "the mastery of truth" and, so doing, look like a "dogmatist"; or (2) he locates the genealogical inquiry within the, all in all, traditional framework of the search for truth and puts forth explicative hypotheses that can possibly be contested.

Often, despite himself, Nietzsche *argues,* and most of his "aphorisms" are not simple apothegms. But his arguments should still not try to be in principle inaccessible to criticism. Genealogy *can* be used as a "vaccination strategy" when any dissent to the assertion imperiously put forth by Nietzsche is interpreted as itself proof of the difficulty of recognizing its truth: "The strongest knowledge (about the complete unfreedom of human will) is the poorest one in results, for it has always the strongest adversary: human vanity."[36]

Any doubting of the necessitarian thesis can be attributed only to foolish human vanity—which only reinforces the thesis.

Let us imagine a Nietzschean who has decided to stick with the idea that "there are no facts, only interpretations," and who states that the rationalist is mistaken in thinking his position universalizable. Someone, in other words, who maintains that rationality is *one* attitude among many others, and a weak, even negative one as far as the will goes. What should one answer? To begin with, nothing. There is no argumentative response to be made to someone who authorizes himself not to accept the other's arguments under the pretext that he does not consent to being dragged into the snares of logic. ("My poor friend," a "Nietzschean" to whom I dared to speak about coherence once answered me, "you're pushing me back to metaphysics"!) But, let us not forget, there is a third actor: the public of "young people" attentive to the jousts that will forever oppose Socrates and Euthydemus. The rationalist has lost in advance if he does not accept that he must *seduce* those who hesitate and are ripe for being charmed by the irrationalist sirens.

Should we attempt to *found* rationality in, obviously, an *ultimate* way (until the end of all time) while attempting thereby to *demonstrate* that the other contradicts himself? This project—Karl-Otto Apel's project—is impressive but not convincing. There are, first of all, excellent arguments to demonstrate that the idea of an ultimate foundation is a utopia; and, as the French saying goes, no one has a duty to attempt the impossible. Besides, it is not at all clear that such a strategy would shake the irrationalist, who is not someone who absolutely refuses to argue but someone who grants himself the right not to pay attention to a bothersome argument when it suits him. Someone, so to speak, who decides not to obey the categorical imperative. The theoretical immoralist isn't going to be convinced by a "typology of the practical judgment in rational discussion" that would enjoin him to try out the universalizable character of his maxim. If, on the other hand, he accepts the principle of coherence, of logic as the "*organon* of critical debate" (Popper), it is possible to show him that his position is weakly argued and is not without inconsistencies. But the crucial choice, between Reason or Violence, remains ungrounded.[37]

When Nietzsche *calls into question* the "will to truth," he, after all, brings up a legitimate problem. It is . . . *true* that many *false* beliefs are useful, in that knowing the truth can turn out to be harmful. Ignorance and insufficient information *can* be beneficial. But let us keep this in perspective. It would be an exaggeration to suppose that truth is useless and harmful "most of the time," as the philosopher from Stagira would have said. And, anyway, that is not what was said by Nietzsche, who on the contrary tended towards a pragmatist reduction of the idea of truth to that of utility: "All of our organs of knowledge were developed only as a function of conservation and of growth." We know, or we should know, the limits to any purely pragmatist conception of truth. But we should also recall what Spinoza already knew: that every idea is affirmative and thereby *claims* to be true. The proposition *a* is logically equivalent to the metalinguistic proposition "'*a*' *is true*" (Tarski). To say with Nietzsche that "there is no truth"[38] is to say "It is true that nothing is true," which is not, *stricto sensu*, paradoxical, but equivalent to statement *p*: "All sentences are false," which cannot be true (because if *p* is true, it is false). The "pretention of truth" is not exactly an unheard-of novelty, but it is consubstantial with language itself in that it manifests its descriptive function as described by Bühler and Jakobson.

We can, moreover, accept B. Constant's argument that veracity does not constitute an absolute imperative from a moral point of view: it is obviously *moral* to lie to a Gestapo man who asks me if I know where a Jew or a resistance fighter is hiding. As Kant himself would put it, a child would have no difficulty concluding that in that case one *has to* lie. That lying[39] could become nonexceptional is much more debatable, and we are aware by now of the mephitic swamps that abandoning the idea of historical ("factual") truth leads to: the gulag, or the gas chambers, never existed, etc.

But why want the true? Not want to *say* the true, but to want to *know* it? That this desire is not the effect of an instinct (*Trieb*), of an "epistemophilic drive" is perhaps . . . true, as Nietzsche suggests[40] against the opening statement of Aristotle's *Metaphysics*. Only the *belief* in truth might be instinctive.[41] We need to believe, says Nietzsche (and in this, we are still too pious!). Of course: how to act without anticipating, and how to anticipate without belief? The radical skeptic cannot even move, speak, eat . . . But *belief* can have many meanings, and "blind faith" is not necessary before acting. And certain beliefs, though not demonstrated, fallible, ungrounded, are more reasonable than others. So why want the truth? Nietzsche is no doubt partly right: science is not innate; it has historical conditions of production. But what makes science different from other human practices is not the will to truth that is so manifest in, for example, the various religions of the Book; it is, rather, its critical attitude, intersubjective debate, attempts at refutation, eternal nonsatisfaction. And all that is no doubt not "natural" and "instinctive." *So what?* Democracy, help given to the weakest, universal (nontribal) altruism: none of these is any more "natural." (But we should beware of falling into the opposite, antinaturalist, exaggeration and pretending that the human being has no instincts, that everything is learned, etc., which would obviously be false. Man overcomes, gets around, uses, trains, transcends his "instincts"; his "behavioral programs," unlike those of—the other—animals, are "open.") Every appeal to nature is to be doubted because, first of all, one can make nature say whatever one wants, and then because even if we were to suppose that nature prefers such and such a dynamic process, we always maintain the possibility of opposing it.

It does seem plausible to maintain, as a lot of biologists do, that the human being is in part characterized by a sort of innate tendency to explore its environment, by a kind of "curiosity instinct." This tendency may of course at times be dangerous, but to go on from there and conclude, as Nietzsche does, that the will to knowledge could in the end be harmful is to make a leap that is difficult to carry out without forcing the argument. Man has, it's true, taken fatal risks in his will to unveil, to discover, nature, and knowledge is not an *absolute* value (if it were, we would have no scruples about experimenting on human beings). But this infinite adventure of knowledge is not devoid of seductive power, and certain "heroic" values can even be redeployed in it.[42]

As for the idea that art is a "true lie," a veridical illusion, because it acknowledges being *illogical*:[43] there is an interesting paradox here whose importance should not be overestimated. It is clearly impossible to assign art *one* regulatory value such as the True or the Beautiful. But whereas certain arts manifestly produce their own worlds (architecture, music), other arts (literature, painting, cinema) *can* emit "truth effects": *Antigone* is as instructive as *The Peloponnesian War*. But why oppose art and science? Why want to *choose* between, say, Milton and Newton, Stendhal and Durkheim? Perhaps because Nietzsche, in refusing science any access to the truth of being[44] and assigning art the function of treating *appearance as appearance,* considers science to be misleading us by pretending to be what it is not, where art "doesn't want to mislead, it is true."[45]

What to make of such an argument? The debate between realism and phenomenism, not to speak of transcendental idealism,[46] is still open today, and it would be cavalier, to say the least, to treat "science" globally as being entirely devoted to "saving the phenomena" (Osiander, Duhem), or to the "explanation of the visible through the invisible" (Jean Perrin, Karl Popper). The problem is one of knowing whether the "laws" postulated to account for phenomena fall under the judgment of being true or false, or whether they are only convenient instruments for classifying and predicting appearances.

Instrumentalism is a stronger position than realism because its requirements are weaker. But it tends to grant critics of science that the latter is but a project for manipulation, for pure calculability, and that it "does not think." Realism maintains that the ideal of truth is absolutely regulatory, and that science seeks after the depths and not merely the "observable" surface. Paradoxically, as Duhem's position shows, antirealism is compatible with a theist metaphysical position. Realism should be more troublesome for the religious conception of the world, since it is less easily concordant with the theological theme of the incomprehensible mystery of Being.

But Nietzsche cannot accept realism, for that would lead him to accept the idea that, in order to cease being "pious," we must accept the infinite quest after objective truth.

As Heidegger pointed out, Nietzsche's doctrine of truth never stops being ambiguous.[47] One cannot simultaneously speak and refuse every conception of truth. One can only contest one conception of truth in the name of another one. That is, without a doubt, what it means to be unable to "step outside metaphysics." (It would be more coherent to fight against any moral idea in the name of an absolute amoralism. But that's not Nietzsche's case.)[48] But then it is not easy to avoid the habitual oppositions, or to "subvert" them. If, especially, we are not happy with reducing truth to coherence—there is an infinity of mutually incompatible coherent theories—we find it difficult not to have recourse, be it surreptitiously, to some sort of idea of correspondence or adequacy. But if language is characterized as a relation of language to beings, independent of the knowledge we have of them, it turns out that this relation is, de jure, the same for all: we argue because we differ as to the true, but we cannot modify it at will.

Truth is indomitable, unmasterable, transcendent. This transcendence of truth, joined to our inability to *demonstrate* our points of view, leads to an egalitarianism in principle.[49] And that is precisely what Nietzsche cannot accept: leveling. But there is a certain amount of exaggeration involved here. If anyone can, in principle, try to reach the truth, it is because the latter is in no way an imposition, a product of the will; it implies no sort of egalitarianism of ideas—on the contrary! Good ideas are rare and we should not stop trying to rank them in hierarchies, to measure them with the yardstick of veracity (an operation which can in no way be automated).

As for the practical domain, that of freedom, I don't believe that it's necessary, in order to struggle against both relativism and "decisionism," to try to bring into the debate the concept of truth itself. Naturally, if I say "Torture is an unacceptable method of police inquiry," my affirmation, being such, presents itself as a declaration, true or false. But it would be more interesting to formulate this proposition in a way that makes its normative nature clearly apparent: "You will not torture!" Such a sentence can be neither verified nor refuted by a counterexample. When we decide to adopt a normative proposition we *create* the norm in question, whereas when we decide—after a rational examination of the various possibilities—to adopt a factual proposition, we are not *creating* the corresponding fact.[50]

Every modifiable fact[51] can be *judged* with reference to norms. But no norm is deducible from facts. That said, we are not about to pretend that universalist morality—which may have many meanings—is *true,* and the morality of the Overman *false.* We shall not be able to *convince* an inegalitarian to accept "Human Rights." But we can make the objection to him that his ethics are not in *harmony* with certain epistemological positions he should be able to subscribe to, to a form of critical rationalism, for example. In other words, the choice of rationalism is an ethical choice.

If we feel so distanced from Nietzsche even when we wish we weren't, it is because we no longer believe that the "departure from religion" has to go by way of a "transvaluation of all values" or of a challenge to the "will to truth." We know, or believe we know, that the most interesting debates, the subtlest distinctions, the most fertile oppositions, are located nowadays *inside* the modern, rationalist, and universalist "transcendental."

Not that we have the leisure of not answering those who put it under radical questioning. The challenge is even in itself fertile. But our internal debates deserve, if I may say so, at least as much attention. The Nietzscheans can in any case feel reassured: the critique of equality and of truth is not about to cease returning, because "one can in fact state it: it isn't once that the same opinions appear among men, but an infinite number of times."[52]

NOTES

1. In both the good and the bad meanings of the term: certain cold praises of war for the sake of war (*Human, All-Too-Human,* § 477) are properly speaking "base."

2. *Human, All-Too-Human,* preface, § 7.

3. See Gilles Deleuze, *Nietzsche and Philosophy,* trans. Hugh Tomlinson (New York: Columbia University Press, 1983 [1962], p. 1): "Nietzsche's most general project is the introduction of the concepts of sense and value into

philosophy." As for sense, if "Nietzsche substitutes the correlation of sense and phenomenon for the metaphysical duality of appearance and essence and for the scientific relation of cause and effect" (ibid., p. 3), one wonders in what sense of the word *sense* natural phenomena "make sense"; on hierarchy, ibid., pp. 8, 59.

4. A comparison rejected by Jean Granier, *Le Problème de la vérité dans la philosophie de Nietzsche,* Éditions du Seuil, 1966, p. 419, but adopted by Deleuze, p. 58.

5. Posthumous fragments from fall 1887, in Friedrich Nietzsche, *"Nachgelassene Fragmente: Herbst 1887 bis März 1888."* In *Nietzsches Werke: Kritische Gesamtausgabe,* ed. Giorgio Colli and Mazzino Montinari, Berlin: Walter de Gruyter & Co., 1970, part 8, vol. 2, p. 166.

6. Ibid., p. 61.

7. Ibid., p. 14.

8. Ibid., p. 12.

9. See the beautiful aphorism 119 in *The Dawn,* "Experimenting and Imagining."

10. See Luc Ferry, *Homo Aestheticus: the Invention of Taste in the Democratic Age,* tr. Robert de Loaiza. University of Chicago Press, 1993 (Paris: Grasset, 1990).

11. *Beyond Good and Evil,* § 195. In *The Antichrist,* the term used is the Indian *Chandala* (untouchable). Democracy = Christianity = Judaism = revolt of the excluded.

12. *The Antichrist,* § 43.

13. In *Twilight of the Idols.*

14. See John Rawls, *A Theory of Justice* (Harvard University Press, 1971) on Nietzsche's "perfectionism."

15. "Nietzsche, la généalogie, l'histoire," in *Hommage à Jean Hyppolite* (Paris: Presses Universitaires de France, 1971). See, in this same collection of essays, Georges Canguilhem's article: "De la science et de la contre-science," p. 180: "Nietzsche . . . does not manage to give truth a positive meaning . . . [He] doesn't manage to produce a theory of science."

16. Ibid., p. 148.

17. See, for instance, "Philosophy in the Tragic Age of the Greeks": "The concept of Being! As if it didn't already show the poorest empirical origin in the etymology of the word! for *esse* means, at bottom, only 'breathe.' " *Nietzsches Werke: Kritische Gesamtausgabe,* ed. Giorgio Colli and Mazzino Montinari. Berlin: Walter de Gruyter, 1973. Part 3, vol. 2, p. 341.

18. Truth is not a value in the sense justice is, but they play a similar role in the economy of our judgments, in, respectively, our theories and our institutions. See John Rawls, pp. 12ff.

19. Without a doubt Nietzsche's most *seductive* texts, in the eyes at least of those for whom *Zarathustra*'s emphasis and the violence of the last writings are more irritating than anything else. See the excellent prefaces that Vincent Descombes and Philippe Raynaud have written for recent French editions of these two works. (Hachette, collection «Pluriel»).

20. *Nietzsches Werke,* ed. Colli and Montinari. Part 8, vol. 2, p. 13.

21. The fact that a concept may be vague does not imply that all its manifestations are "vague" and that all the propositions in which it is used are exempt of truth-conditions. It is false that Napoleon was "tall."

22. See Karl Popper, *The Open Society,* vol. 2, addendum 1, 11; the citation is from *Unmodern Observations.*

23. See Richard Rorty's ideas in, for example, *Contingency, Irony, and Solidarity.*

24. Every reader of Plato should know that it is possible to try to show that the other is wrong without oneself being "in possession" of the truth.

25. Granier, p. 84.

26. *The Gay Science,* V, § 373.

27. At least in "classical" systems of logic. There are "para-consistent" logics in which this theorem is not valid. I don't know whether Nietzsche would have liked this "logicalization" of dialectics.

28. *The Gay Science,* III, § 123.

29. Karl Popper, *The Open Society,* II, ch. 23.

30. "Über Wahrheit and Lüge im aussermoralischen Sinne" (On truth and lying in the extramoral sense): "Truths are illusions about which we have forgotten that that's what they are; metaphors, used up and sensually without force." *Werke,* vol. 3, part 2, pp. 374–75.

31. Ibid., p. 377.

32. *Human, All-Too-Human,* § 11. It would be interesting to compare these positions with Bergson's; see also *Mixed Opinions and Maxims,* § 9 (*H a-H* II): " 'The Law of Nature' as superstition's expression." It is probable that this, as well as aphorisms 12 and 17, aims at Kant in particular.

33. See Gottlieb Frege's essay on "Meaning and Denotation." It goes without saying that the problem of identity is extremely complex. But nothing in this area seems to lead us to maintain without further ado that "nothing is identical."

34. Jean Granier, op. cit., p. 498. See also p. 604 ff.

35. Thus, when Nietzsche opposes his own concepts to Darwin's, we fail to see where the difference in "truth régimes" is located (Granier, p. 407). It seems clear, besides, that Nietzsche doesn't grasp the extent of the Darwinian mechanism when he reduces it to "Lamarck plus Hegel."

36. *Sed contra:* "What makes for Nietzsche's force is his affirmation of things that are immediately refutable, but only by he himself." Pierre Klossowski, in *Nietzsche aujourd'hui?* Paris: 10/18, 1973, vol. 1, p. 121.

37. *Human, All-Too-Human II: Mixed Opinions and Maxims,* § 50. We can see yet again why the "libertarian" interpretation of Nietzsche is not possible.

38. See chapter 25 of Popper's *The Open Society* (1945), but also Eric Weil's theses in *Logique de la philosophie* (1947) and Lucien Sebag's arguments in *Marxisme et structuralisme* (Paris: Payot, 1962). The Popperian Bartley has developed the idea that this fundamental choice is rational in that it remains

open to criticism: see *The Retreat to Commitment,* Open Court, 1986 (1st ed. 1962).

39. *Nachgelassene Fragmente.*

40. Including the "lie . . . with which one lies to oneself" (*The Antichrist,* § 55), or Sartre's "bad faith," whose very possibility is troublesome (more so than the idea of "unconscious desire"). See also the delicate problem of "self-creating utterances" (A. Boyer: "Effets pervers et effets Œdipe," *Revue philosophique,* 1989. no. 1).

41. "On Truth and Lying": "Es gibt keinen Trieb nach Erkenntnis und Wahrheit, sondern nur einen Trieb nach Glauben an die Wahrheit; die reine Erkenntnis ist trieblos" (There is no drive towards knowledge and truth, only a drive to belief in truth; pure knowledge has no drives).

42. Cf. *Daybreak,* V, § 450.

43. Ibid., § 177.

44. Ibid., § 187.

45. Ibid., § 184.

46. See the *Critique of Pure Reason,* the passage about the iron filings preceding the "Refutation of Idealism."

47. Heidegger, *Nietzsche,* Pfullingen: Verlag Günther Neske, 1961, vol. 2, p. 184.

48. On the importance in Nietzsche of the idea of justice, see *ibid.,* p. 198, with the surprising example of Mers el-Kébir.

49. Karl Popper, *Conjectures and Refutations,* introduction.

50. Karl Popper, *The Open Society,* vol. 2, addendum I, § 13.

51. An always *interpreted* fact, of course. There are no wholly uninterpreted facts, which does not mean that there are only interpretations.

52. Aristotle, *Meteorology,* 339b 27.

2 The Brute, the Sophist, and the Aesthete: "Art in the Service of Illusion"

ANDRÉ COMTE-SPONVILLE

To the memory of Etty Hillesum

For every philosopher of our time the confrontation with Nietzsche is a necessity. That fact, which signals his greatness, is also, be it said in passing, the justification for the present work. Confronting Nietzsche means being faithful to him—more faithful perhaps than are all the little Nietzscheans who are going to accuse us of pettiness or of resentment. But what do the Nietzscheans matter?

To think Nietzsche: with him, against him. The same thing in the end. We know, all the commentators have pointed it out, that more than anyone else he practiced *self-contradiction;* as Jaspers put it, "For nearly every single one of Nietzsche's judgments, one can also find an opposite. He gives the impression of having two opinions about everything."[1] That which would have gone against him in other times today rather doubles his glory. Here is a philosopher for all tastes and distastes! And, which is quite convenient, useful for justifying your contradictions, recantations, and denials in advance.

How to put it better? What, inversely, more boring, more suspicious than a coherent philosophy? What does this fear of contradiction, of turnarounds, of unreason betray? What is it the symptom of? Whose mask is it? Interpretation and genealogy can have a field day here, can consider logic, as Nietzsche himself did, as a sign of weakness[2] and brandish as a weapon all that is most manifestly unreasonable—all that is illogical, passion-bound, at times mad—in our author's thought.

But such a "proliferation of contradictions,"[3] such a "contradictory duplicity,"[4] though a windfall for the commentator, renders any

21

attempt at serious discussion very difficult. Whatever the position you wish to criticize, the first Nietzschean around, and they are legion, will always be able to object that Nietzsche said exactly the contrary—and the worst is that the Nietzschean will be right almost all the time: not that you credited Nietzsche with a position that wasn't his, but that he always, or almost always, also defended the opposite argument, so that, "leaving the task of contradicting him to no one else" as François George so prettily put it,[5] Nietzsche makes the position of whoever would do it in his stead or after him most uncomfortable!

But, for all that, do we need to give up debate and to contend—whether out of submission or lassitude, fascination or rejection—that Nietzsche makes the examination of reasons impossible or obsolete, that we have to take him as a whole or not at all and that we are always wrong to argue with geniuses and with sophists (and even more so with a sophist of genius!)? We could do so if all that were at stake were Nietzsche, or even only philosophy. All these books are, in the end, not that important—since they are only books—and there is something silly about the way first Nietzsche and then the Nietzscheans wanted to see in them the beginning of a new era, of a new humanity even. Marx, in his day, had the same pretention, and history, after seeming to bear him out, made a liar out of him too. History hasn't been so kind to Nietzsche: it has gone on without taking notice of him, and the only historical movement which could have claimed Nietzsche for itself, and did so in fact, would have been for our author—if such a claim even merited being taken seriously—a terrible, an apocalyptic refutation.

We have to stop here for a moment to rule out some false trails and one false conclusion. We know that the Nazis often claimed to be inspired by Nietzsche and that, for example, Hitler made a gift to Mussolini of a luxury edition (that the former had had printed in 1935) of our author's *Complete Works*. Such facts, and others one could cite, prove nothing. It is doubtful that Hitler ever read Nietzsche, or read more anyway than scattered quotes. And that Nietzsche is in no way suspect of Nazism is a certainty to which both chronology and the reading of the texts are enough to lead us. But the disciples are a little hasty when they conclude that therefore there is no problem and that anyone would definitely have to be ill intentioned to see the least relation between Nietzsche and Hitler.

Without, obviously, being one of Nazism's causes, or even one of its real sources, Nietzsche belongs nevertheless to the same spiritual

world—antidemocratic, anti-Jewish, antirationalist German thought—
that will *also* produce Nazism, and that fact explains to some extent the
Nietzschean pretentions of this or that Nazi as well as the Nazi strayings
of this or that Nietzschean without in any way authorizing them. "A
doctrine," Jankélévitch said about Nazism, "in which Heidegger immediately found himself and which so visibly carries Nietzsche's mark."6
In both cases, that's going too far. Maybe. But it would not be going far
enough—in both cases—to attribute to chance or to misunderstanding
the monstrous proximity that made of Heidegger a Nazi and seemed,
though erroneously, to give the Nazis Nietzsche's blessing.

"The porks will wallow in my doctrine" the latter had foreseen,
and that, indeed, is what happened. But why? We can hardly imagine
the Nazis laying claim to Kant or Husserl in the same way, and every
doctrine, we may say, has the porks it deserves. "There will be wars the
like of which have never yet been seen on earth," Nietzsche also announced, bragging about it. "It is only beginning with me that the earth
knows *great politics.*"7 It is of course clear that there is a great deal of
derision in these swaggerings. But a philosopher turns prophet at his
own risk. Whose fault is it if, now that history has gone on further down
the road, we have the choice only between the ridiculous and the
odious?

Reading Nietzsche, since that is our common lot, after Auschwitz,
I for one have never been able to turn that subsequent history into a
total abstraction, and on this subject I have always found the Nietzscheans to be rather lightweight. It is true that "all that is good is light,
all that is divine runs on delicate feet." (*CW*, 1). Dear dancers! Go run
lightly on the ruins of Oradour, go dance *divinely* at Auschwitz or
Mauthausen! I'm like everybody else: I prefer lightness to heaviness. But
I also like what is weighty and serious (Jankélévitch: "It is not a case of
having to be sublime, it is enough to be faithful and serious").8 And
even if this lightness were, as Nietzsche sometimes claimed, specifically
Greek, or French, or Italian—and God knows that I, like Nietzsche,
love those three countries and three cultures!—it cannot make us forget
the great seriousness, the profound gravity, the infinite suffering and the
irreplaceable fidelity of the Jewish people.

You may say that I'm mixing everything up. It's that I've read a lot
of Nietzsche in the last few months, and that's not a school for serene
clarity or rigorous order. Besides, he explicitly claimed to invert all the
values "Judea," as he writes (and that concept for him includes the Ref-

ormation, the French Revolution, and socialism!) brought to the world (*GM*, I, 16), fan up the "old fire" (*GM*, I, 17) against them, shatter the ancient tablets of the law, and in the end *overcome man* (*Z*, passim)—and that is what has to be stopped. Possibly I put too much passion into it, but that itself is Nietzschean—and not exclusively Nietzschean.

I have never been able to speak calmly about Nietzsche. That is no doubt due to his genius, to that in him that is wrought up, explosive—"I am not a human being, I am dynamite," he said in *Ecce Homo*—to his talent for provocation, and always to his proximity despite all risks to the essential and the unfathomable. He was not one to think just to pass the time. He goes to the extremes, to the deepest depths, where he places his bomb or his laughter, and there also we have to confront him.

But there is something else. It is that I feel so close to Nietzsche in so many ways: not to the man, of course, but, all questions of genius to one side, to the philosopher. Of all the authors in this collection, I am perhaps the only one who can say it: my agreements with Nietzsche, if we could be satisfied with a merely quantitative approach, are much more numerous than my disagreements. Which explains why certain journalists placed me "in Nietzsche's wake"⁹ when my first book was published, and why certain authors were surprised that I should speak in the end so little (in *Le mythe d'Icare*) or so disparagingly (in *Vivre*) of an author to whom I seemed indeed close.

These agreements, these encounters, these convergences with Nietzsche had not gone unnoticed. There was of course atheism, even materialism (or quasi materialism, to which I'll come back), but also the rejection of nihilism and of spinelessness, the search for a philosophy that helps us to live—and not only to think—the critique of religion, of idealism, of freedom of the will, the rejection derived from all this of any morality that pretends to be absolute, yet accompanied nevertheless (or precisely because?) by a certain exaltation of willing, of the *determination* to will, leading to an "affirmative," "creative," "ascendant" ethic with no other world but this one, with no other reward but itself; then there was the attempt to think against the subject, to unmask its illusions (beginning with it itself!), a distrust, finally, of speculation and of systems, which led me more and more to prefer Montaigne to Kant, Pascal to Hegel. Not to mention that, like Nietzsche (anyway the late Nietzsche), I can't stand Wagner and the Wagnerians, and know nothing more beautiful than the "cheerful, enthusiastic, tender, enamored spirit of Mozart" (*NCW*, "Wagner As a Danger," 2).

To stay with philosophy, and to simplify, let us say that I shared with Nietzsche (though arriving there by entirely different roads: Marxism and the critique of Marxism) most of his rejections: anti-Platonism (against the intelligible world), anti-Cartesianism (against the *cogito*), anti-Kantianism (against the thing-in-itself and the absoluteness of the moral law), anti-Hegelianism (against the dialectic). That's a lot for one philosopher, and even though in fact Nietzsche did not influence me much—I only read him rather late and always with many reservations—I could not but be struck by this so frequent nearness to him, all the more so since, as I mentioned, had I ignored him critics and readers would have made me amply aware of it.

I read, then, Nietzsche, when I read him—and that was drawn out over fifteen years and isn't over—with a feeling the inverse of the Freudian formula: of *disquieting familiarity*, as the most dangerous of my friends or, increasingly, as the closest enemy. Not that, having read him, I feared being less original. That has never been my concern and today less so than ever. Quite simply, I perceived in Nietzsche, despite all our points of agreement, an obscure background that bothered me for a long time and which made me take a dim view of him when I thought I made out its content. What does it consist of? Of what is no doubt most especially Nietzschean. Most of the convergences I just cited I also shared, and to a greater degree, with Epicure or Spinoza, Marx or Freud. There is no need to be a Nietzschean to reject freedom of the will, idealism, or religion. But there was, on the other hand, all the grand guignol of *Zarathustra*, all of the Nietzschean hardware—and how kitsch! how German!—that I found only there and which I decidedly could not accept: the Overman, the Eternal Recurrence, the Will to Power, the Transvaluation of All Values. For a long time, I thought of all that as being between parentheses, as it were. I even invented, for my own use, a system of rough but useful equivalences between Nietzsche and Spinoza. The Overman was something of a Nietzschean version of the wise man, the Eternal Recurrence could pass for a metaphor for eternity, and the Will to Power was not without resemblances, I thought, to the *conatus*. As for the transvaluation (or inversion, or revaluation, as you will) of all values, I thought I saw there something like an echo of Spinozist immoralism; God knows I was led along this path by several good books.[10]

Let me here take the risk of telling an anecdote. When I was a young philosophy teacher, just after the French *agrégation*, I professed like all my friends, or nearly all, and though we were quite kind and pleasant about it, a vehement immoralism. It was the spirit of the times, and after all a disillusion with morality is also something we all go through. I based myself on Epicure, on Spinoza, on Marx, on Freud. And, of course, on Nietzsche, essentially the Nietzsche of the *Gay Science* and the *Genealogy of Morals*. But I needed to find examples.

With Spinoza, and with Nietzsche, I explained that humility, repentance, and shame are nefarious errors (I had not yet discovered, even though it is explicitly explained by Spinoza, that they are nevertheless less nefarious than their contraries, and that only virtue allows you to do without them). And since I had adolescents in front of me, I added— with a lively sense of my liberating audacity—that we had to get rid of the guilt in sexuality, and that, for instance, masturbation was only guilty in the eyes of a morality itself worthy of being despised. I must have repeated the example in front of different classes once, twice, thrice—no teacher likes to repeat himself. I tried to vary my examples. Masturbation is not a fault, and neither is . . . neither is *what,* come to think of it? I could have said: neither is homosexuality, fellation, sodomy.

Of course, and I still agree. But I could also see that I remained within the same small gamut—of what is commonly called "sexual morals"—in which it was much too easy for someone of my generation to be right. Smash the idols: sure, but why bother with ruins? Most of all I could see that though masturbation and homosexuality are no crimes, rape is, and a very clear one, and this sole example was enough to put my immoralism ill at ease. If I had no morality, as I so haughtily claimed, then in the name of what did I condemn rape or forbid it to myself? In the name of what could I decide what was *wrong* or not? In the name of what, for instance, fight against racism, injustice, or barbarity? In the name of what should I even prefer sincerity to mendacity or sweetness to cruelty? For a time I tried to answer: "In the name of an *ethic.*" But this kind of purely verbal solution is satisfactory only for a while. This ethic still had to be thought out, and the strange fact accounted for that a supposedly amoral ethic most often corresponds quite well, and this on all the serious problems, to what any honest man would call *morality.*

So I took up my Spinoza again, and what I saw there is that there is no Spinozist immoralism, or rather only a theoretical immoralism,[11] and that . . . but let's get back to Nietzsche. There is a Nietzschean immoralism, not only theoretical but practical, and the more I got to know it, the more I found it—I barely dare to write the word, so much does it go without saying, and so much will it make our great wits smile. The more I got to know this immoralism, the more I found it *immoral*. Simply, stupidly, inadmissibly immoral. I beg pardon for such a platitude. The most elegant thing to do would be to go on my way, as the Nietzscheans do. Go on, mortals. But morality is more important to me than elegance: that platitude—the immorality of Nietzsche's immoralism— is the first point on which I would like to dwell for a while. The point is not to try to be sublime or original. The point is to be faithful and serious.

THE BRUTE

It is a question I once asked the philosopher Clément Rosset, and which, to my knowledge, he has never answered: a tragic, or Dionysiac, bastard—in what way is he less of a bastard? Not, to be perfectly clear, that I in any way suspect—assuming I even had the right to do so!—the warm and obvious good nature of the author of *La force majeure*. That is what strikes me so often about the Nietzscheans when they are likable: they go off against morality as if with a chip on their shoulders, they claim to invert all values, to begin a new area for humanity, to live beyond good and evil, etc., and in the end they behave like you and I do, more or less honestly, more or less virtuously, being good fathers and husbands if they're married, and in any case the best friends in the world. Like the singer Georges Brassens, and like most of us, they could sing

> *Je n'ai jamais tué, jamais violé non plus,*
> *Y a déjà quelque temps que je ne vole plus . . .*
> [*I've never killed, never raped either,*
> *It's been a while since I last stole . . .*]

And even if they still steal or abstain only out of prudence, which one among them would not prefer, even if the loot were the same, to steal from a rich man or from a real crook? Which one would consent to despoil a poor man or an orphan, to oppress the weak or betray a friend's trust? And which one, conversely, would be shocked by the obvious morality—so very Christian at bottom—of Brassen's *"Chanson pour l'Auvergnant"* or *"La Jeanne"*? But then: Why pretend to invert all values? Why call oneself an immoralist? And what could their "beyond good and evil" mean? I came to tell myself that they must be better than I am, and that only their spontaneous morals or the mildness of their instincts permitted them to do without morality. Maybe. As for myself, who am not so lucky, who carry within myself, as Socrates did, "all the bad vices"[12] (I wish to God masturbation were the only thing I had to reproach myself with!), who would willingly kill, who would even more willingly rape, I truly do need, again like Socrates, that voice that says *no*[13]—I truly need a morality!

That paradox (the very moral life of many of our immoralists) already no doubt applied to Nietzsche and partly explains his aggressiveness. We only really insist on attacking the idols we can't quite get rid of. As E. M. Cioran so well put it, Nietzsche "draws his enemies from within himself, as he does the vices he denounces. Does he inveigh against the weak? He is being introspective; and when he attacks decadence, he is describing his own state. All his hatreds are directed against himself . . . He took revenge on others for *what he himself was.*"[14] That makes him rather more likable (even, almost, touching, as when he evokes health or strength), more alive, perhaps even more creative. More plausible? As a man, no doubt. As a philosopher, we'll have to see.

At least he had the excuse of having to fight a morality that was in effect crushing—the very one Freud also had to confront—against which it made sense to say that it condemned life, the body, sensuality, a morality, in a word, that leaned on sexual prohibitions and which seemed to find in them the essential part of its energies and perhaps of its themes. But today? Who can seriously think that morality aims at regulating our little erotic affairs, or worries, in order to fight against them, about this or that one among our preferences, or even (on condition of everyone else's free consent) about our perversions? There is some sort of bad faith in attacking morality in the name of sexual freedom at a time—ours—when morality has decidedly, and happily, ceased to concern itself with it. And that is also for us a lesson about horrors. Who, after Auschwitz, and outside of a few Catholic bishops, still cares about the alleged immorality of wearing condoms or sexual liberation? Who does not see—in the century of Auschwitz, of Hiroshima, of genetic manipulation, and of world hunger—that morality decidedly has other sharks to fry, more fearsome, and more urgent, than this or that person's puny fantasies? Who does not see that it isn't sexual freedom that is the problem today, but freedom period, the refusal of barbarism, of infamy, of abandonment? Are we going to keep on mixing up morality and the moral order, honest citizens and bluenoses? And isn't that committing the same error, dear anti-Christians, as the Christian moralists you so detest?

The ancient Greeks were more sensible about this. We know that the Cynics, for example, and even several Stoics, justified masturbation, sodomy, and incest, seeing no wrong in them not because of immoralism (there is no more rigorous morality than that of Diogenes or Chrysippus) but because morality seemed to them to bear upon much more serious subjects, forbidding not this or that morally indifferent pleasure but only that—cruelty, dishonesty, egoism—which hurts what is human in another being or in oneself. Yes, because egoism also damages the egoist, and Epictetus knew more about that than Nietzsche. But let us get back to the tragic bastard.

What is the tragic? Against Aristotle, Nietzsche answers that it is neither terror nor pity—nor, he adds aiming at Schopenhauer, resignation (*WP*, 851). The tragic is, on the contrary, the joyous approval of the real, of all that is real, even the worst, that is the "*yes* to all that is problematic and terrible" (*CI*, 107); it is the Dyonisiac approval "of life in its entirety, of which we deny nothing, from which we take nothing away (*WP*, 1052); it is, in a word, the affirmation of "the global economy of the universe, which justifies, and more than justifies, fearful, evil, equivocal things" (*VP*, IV, 462). In this the tragic, according to Nietzsche, is opposed to morality: every morality says *no* to something living (that is surely undeniable!), every morality condemns life, denies it, never ceases trying to make it poorer, to suffocate it, to accuse it. Thus immoralism: "To the extent to which we believe in morality we *condemn* life" (*VP*, I, 303); we therefore have to unmask the former to render the latter innocent. "Morality is life's negative instinct. We have to destroy it in order to liberate life" (*VP*, I, 299). Morality is "the danger par excellence" (*GM*, foreword, 6), the "peril of perils" (*BT*, 5). It is the "idiosyncrasy of *decadents,* with the ulterior motive of avenging oneself against life" (*EH*, "Why I Am a Destiny," 7). The tragic is the opposite: the idiosyncrasy of the strong, the loving and amoral affirmation of life, which condemns nothing, which forbids nothing, which says *yes* to everything, even to the worst, and which dances over the precipice. The tragic turns "*against* morality" (*BT*, 5) from the start: the goal is to make man "stronger, wickeder, profounder" (*BGE*, 295). That is Dionysus's lesson: to live tragically is to live beyond good and evil.

I have always been perplexed by the supposed coherence of this thinking. If the Dionysiac ideal consists in "the affirmation of life as a whole, from which we deny nothing, from which we take nothing away" (*VP*, IV, 464), then why wish to *deny* morality, why wish to *roll back* two thousand years of, as Nietzsche says, *Judeo-Christian* culture? In the name of the real? In the name of life? In the name of affirmation? But in what way is "the Crucified One" less real than Dionysus? In what way are the good people less alive than the bastards? In what way is respect for others less affirmative than violence or contempt? The real Nietzschean response is: in the name of power and the will to power! But why should we always "defend the strong against the weak" (*WP*, F.v., I, 395) since in Nietzsche's own opinion (which is here the opposite of Darwin's) the strong never stop being defeated—where here is strength, where weakness, and by what standards does one decide? By the amount of joy? But where do we find more real joy: in power or in love? In Nietzsche or in Spinoza?

Let's not go too fast. More than these theoretical objections, having to do with the doctrine's coherence or decidability, it was practical reticences which at first distanced me from Nietzscheanism. *Beyond Good and Evil*, that "scandalous book,"[15] played a special role. I refer the reader to it. Clément Rosset, in his remarkable attempt to make Nietzsche acceptable—*his* Nietzsche I'm quite happy to accept!—is forced to put aside not only all the texts collected in *The Will to Power* and nearly all of *Zarathustra*, which is already considerable, but also all of the properly immoral or immoralist content of *Beyond Good and Evil* or *The Genealogy of Morals*.[16] As a matter of fact, if we stick with *The Gay Science* or *Daybreak*, if from the later texts we keep only the passages dealing with music or with joy, we get a very plausible and attractive Nietzsche—realist, rationalist, a merry demystifier—in truth quite close to Spinoza or, for good reason, to Clément Rosset.

But there is *Zarathustra, The Will to Power, The Genealogy of Morals;* there is *Beyond Good and Evil*. The very idea that there are "master morality and slave morality" (*BGE*, 260) seems to me, as you might guess, suspect; but even if it were the case, how could we grant Nietzsche that slave morality is contemptible—the morality that teaches "pity, the complaisant and obliging hand, the warm heart, patience, industry, humility, and friendliness" (ibid.)—and that, on the contrary, we must worship master morality, for "such a morality is self-glorification" and imposes the maxim that "one has duties only to one's peers; that against beings of a lower rank, against everything alien, one may behave as one pleases or 'as the heart desires,' and in any case 'beyond good and evil'" (ibid.)? Should we be surprised that the Nazis loved this book so much? And how, with such a morality, can we fight against French nationalist leader Jean-Marie Le Pen and his ilk?

We would have to multiply the quotations here, which would quickly get boring. Nietzsche is one of the rare philosophers, the only one perhaps (unless one considers Sade to be a philosopher!) who at the same time, and nearly systematically, advocated force against law,[17] violence or cruelty against gentleness,[18] war against peace;[19] who defended egoism,[20] who considered the instincts to be higher than reason[21] and intoxication or the passions higher than serenity,[22] nutritional rules higher than philosophy and hygiene higher than morality;[23] who preferred Pontius Pilate to Christ or to Saint John,[24] Cesare Borgia (a "man of prey," "a kind of superhuman"!) to Giordano Bruno[25] and Napoleon to Rousseau;[26] who claimed there are "neither moral nor immoral actions"[27] (while declaring himself "the friend of the evil" and the adversary of the "good"!);[28] who justified castes,[29] eugenics,[30] racism,[31] and slavery;[32] who openly advocated or celebrated barbarity,[33] contempt for the greater number,[34] the oppression of the weak,[35] and the extermination of the sick[36]—and all this, as we know, a century after the French Revolution, and while keeping up statements about women[37] and about democracy[38] that are, though less absolutely exceptional, no less distressing.

We would have to quote everything, and we can't. Only a few examples. Advocacy of warlike virility: "Man must be trained for war and woman for the diversion of the warrior: all else is foolishness . . . Go you to women? Do not forget your whip!" (Z, I, "On Little Old and Young Women"). Contempt (always virile, and racially pure!) for the greater number: "What is female, what issues from servility and from the rabble's hodgepodge: *that* is what now wishes to become the lord over human destiny—oh horror! horror! horror!" (Z, IV, "On Higher Men"). Stupid elitism: "That everyone is allowed to learn to read at length spoils not only writing but also thinking" (Z, I, "On Reading and Writing"). Eugenics: "In many cases it is society's duty to impede procreation; to do this it has the right, without regard for origins, rank, or intellectual qualities, to plan for the most rigorous coercive measures,

all kinds of hindrances to freedom, castration in certain cases . . . Neither the sick man nor the criminal should be acknowledged as being apt
for reproduction . . . Marriages have to become rarer! Walk around the
great cities and ask yourself if this population should reproduce!" (*VP,*
IV, 252, 253, 258). Extermination of the weak: "The weak and the defective should disappear. First maxim of *our* love for men. And they
should be helped to it" (*AC,* 2).

Justification of slavery: "Every enhancement of the type 'man' has
so far been the work of an aristocratic society—and it will be so again
and again: a society that believes in the long ladder of an order of rank
and differences in value between man and man, and that needs slavery
in some sense or other" (*BGE,* 257). Advocacy of oppression: "The essential characteristic of a good and healthy aristocracy . . . is that it . . .
accepts with a good conscience the sacrifice of untold human beings
who, *for its sake,* must be reduced and lowered to incomplete human
beings, to slaves, to instruments" (*BGE,* 258). Explanation of the—
naturally, regrettable—progress of socialist ideas as stemming from the
fact that the "lower orders have been too well treated" (*WP,* 209). Contempt for democracy, messianism of the leader:

We have a different faith; to us the democratic movement is not only a form of
the decay of political organization but a form of the decay, namely the diminution, of man, making him mediocre and lowering his value. Where, then, must
we reach with our hopes? Toward *new philosophers;* there is no choice . . . at
the same time new types of philosophers and commanders will be necessary for
that, and whatever has existed on earth of concealed, terrible, and benevolent
spirits, will look pale and dwarfed by comparison. It is the image of such leaders
that we envisage: may I say this out loud, you free spirits? (*BGE,* 203)

Finally, and at greater length, racism. I won't dwell, because I have
spoken elsewhere about it,[39] on the question of antisemitism, from
which Nietzsche is supposed to be exempt because he *also* detested the
anti-Semites! Beautiful! As if a man like Nietzsche couldn't detest Jews
and anti-Semites at the same time! Everybody talks about *jüdischer
Selbsthaß* (Jewish self-hatred); why wouldn't there be an *antisemitischer
Selbsthaß* (anti-Semitic self-hatred)? I will grant that Nietzsche's position concerning the Jews is ambivalent and above all that it is hard to
distinguish from anti-Judaism and anti-Christianism.

Just one example. We know that, in *The Genealogy of Morals,*

Nietzsche affirms that it was the Jews, "the priestly nation of *ressentiment par excellence*," who were the first to invert aristocratic values, "and to hang on to this inversion with their teeth, the teeth of the most abysmal hatred (the hatred of impotence)," thus taking a "tremendous and immeasurably fateful initiative" (*GM*, I, 7, 16). Thus, Nietzsche goes on, it is "with the Jews [that] there begins *the slave revolt in morality*" (*GM*, I, 7) revolt that triumphs in Christianity and to which we owe what Nietzsche, in *The Antichrist* (§ 25), calls the "*denaturing* of natural values." Here, we can certainly speak about anti-Judaism or anti-Christianism; anti-Semitism may still seem doubtful.

What, on the other hand, can one think of aphorism 46 in, again, *The Antichrist*?:

What follows from this? That one does well to put on gloves when reading the New Testament. The proximity of so much uncleanliness almost forces one to do this. We would no more choose the "first Christians" to associate with than Polish Jews—not that one even required any objection to them: they both do not smell good.

How can one deny that anti-Christianism and anti-Judaism are mixed here? And what does one say about the conclusion to the same aphorism: "Need I add that in the whole New Testament there is only a *single* figure who commands respect? Pilate, the Roman governor. To take a Jewish affair *seriously*—he does not persuade himself to do that. One Jew more or less—what does it matter?"

I only bring this up in passing, to remind us that the problem, after all, exists, and that it is not enough to evoke Nietzsche's hatred towards his brother-in-law, the anti-Semite Bernhardt Förster, to cancel such statements and others of this type. Nor do I wish to discuss the few admiring passages—themselves almost always fearfully equivocal— Nietzsche has consecrated to the Jews (*HAH*, 475; *D*, 205; *BGE*, 250–51; *AC*, 24–25). Once again, I grant that Nietzsche's is an ambivalent position, and that anti-Judaism and anti-Semitism are in him joined to a no doubt sincere admiration. But can the latter annul the former? And of the former, can the first justify the second?

But there is something more serious that goes beyond biographical or psychological givens. Nietzsche's thinking is racist in its essence through its conjunction (under cover of heredity) of elitism with biologism. "One pays a price for being the child of one's parents," Nietzsche wrote in *The Gay Science* (§ 348), but he is more precise in *Beyond Good and Evil* (§ 264): "It is simply not possible that a human being should *not* have the qualities and preferences of his parents and ancestors in his body, whatever appearances may suggest to the contrary. This is the problem of race. If one knows something about the parents, an inference about the child is permissible." For Nietzsche, because of that every human activity depends on what he calls "blood" (*Geblüt*), and even philosophy doesn't escape from this:

For every high world one must be born; or to speak more clearly, one must be *cultivated* for it: a right to philosophy—taking that word in its great sense—one has only by virtue of one's origins; one's ancestors, one's "blood" decide here, too. Many generations must have labored to prepare the origin of the philosopher; every one of his virtues must have been acquired, nurtured, inherited, and digested singly. (*BGE*, 213)

The same illumination is, as we might have supposed, also valid for the general history of humanity. In *The Genealogy of Morals* (I, 4, 5), after having noted that the "veritable method to follow" was the genealogical one, Nietzsche writes:

In the Latin *malus* (which I place next to Greek *mélas*) could indicate the common man as the dark one, especially as the black-haired one (*"hic niger est* ——"), as the pre-Aryan dweller of the Italian soil which distinguished itself most clearly through his color from blonds who became their masters, namely the Aryan conquering race.

And then he adds this remark (whose status in a philosophy book leads one to wonder): "The Celts, by the way, were definitely a blond race." And he gravely asks himself:

Who can say whether modern democracy, even more modern anarchism and especially that inclination for "*commune,*" for the most primitive form of society, which is now shared by all the socialists of Europe, does not signify in the main a tremendous *counterattack*—and that the conqueror and *master race*, the Aryan, is not succumbing physiologically, too? (*GM*, I, 5)

And he drives the nail in the wall: "These carriers of the most humiliating and vengeance-seeking instincts, the descendants of all European and non-European slavery, especially of the pre-Aryan people—they represent mankind's regression! These 'instruments of culture' are a shame for human beings, and a cause for suspicion, a counterargument against 'culture' in general!" (*GM*, I, 11). And he praises, on the contrary, "the blond beast at the bottom of all the predominant races," all the "jubilant monsters, who perhaps came out of a terrible sequence of murders, burnings, rapes, tortures with high spirits and tranquility of soul, as if it had all been a case of student high jinks; convinced that the poets would now have something to sing and to praise for a long time" (ibid.)! And, perhaps influenced by Gobineau, whom he greatly admired:[40]

At heart in these predominant races we cannot mistake the beast of prey, the *blond beast* who lusts after booty and victory . . . The deep, icy mistrust the German brings forth when he comes to power, even today, is an echo of the indelible outrage with which Europe looked on the rage of the blond Germanic beast for hundreds of years.[41]

All of these texts, and many others one could quote, justify my title, or at least its first qualifier. Not of course that Nietzsche was a brute as an individual (the poor man didn't have the means!); but he is the philosopher—and the only one to my knowledge (for though Machiavelli legitimizes immorality *politically,* he doesn't thereby condemn morality as such)—who justifies brutes and consciously makes models out of them. At this point it will be said—the Nietzscheans will say— that these texts should not be taken literally, that they have but a metaphorical meaning, that the "force" they extol is of an intellectual kind, and finally that (as Heidegger is supposed to have demonstrated!) there is in Nietzsche no biologism, and that therefore the "races" he evokes are not really races.

Unfortunately, if metaphor there is, it works the other way. Nietzsche often explained himself about this, and it touches the heart of his doctrine: far from the body being the metaphor of the spirit, it is on the contrary the spirit that is the metaphor of the body, its sign or symptom,[42] and all philosophy is in that sense "an interpretation of the body and a *misunderstanding of the body*" (*GS*, preface). Nietzsche adds:

Behind the highest value judgments that have hitherto guided the history of thought, there are concealed misunderstandings of the physical constitution—

of individuals or classes or even whole races. All those bold insanities of meta-physics, especially answers to the question about the *value* of existence, may always be considered first of all as the symptoms of certain bodies.

To want to absolve Nietzsche of his barbaric or racist remarks on the pretext that, in his case (and contrary, it is specified, to what we see in *Mein Kampf* or among the theoreticians of national socialism), *it is metaphysics*[43] is to be mistaken from beginning to end about the status of Nietzschean metaphysics, which, far from escaping from the body's vital order (and therefore from biologism), is but one of its expressions (a "symptom"), neither the most dignified nor the most important one, and one, most of all, that remains de facto and de jure dependent on the body. This is put clearly in one of the posthumously published notes:

All our religions and philosophies are the symptoms of our bodily state: that Christianity achieved victory was the result of a generalized feeling of listless-ness and of a mixture of races (that is, of conflict and disarray in the organism). (*Kröner,* XIII, § 600)

Thus we must take "the body and physiology [as] the starting point" (*WP,* § 492); consider "all that is 'conscious' . . . only of secondary im-portance" (*Kröner,* XIII, § 382), and consequently revise "our beliefs and our very principle of evaluation" and only hold on to the intellect (*das Geistige*) as "the body's sign language" (ibid.; see also *WP,* § 707, 676). This is where Nietzsche is closest to materialism—and where the materialist must therefore be the most vigilant. If "in man there is mate-rial" (*BGE,* 225), if the soul is only the symptom of the body and if this symptomatology is itself, as Nietzsche never ceases to repeat, biolog-ically determined, how can we not proceed from physical differences (those that result from heredity) to intellectual differences—and what is that called if not racism?

The most radical materialisms escape, or can escape, from this by subordinating life to something other than itself, from a point of view either theoretical (the true is not a symptom) or physical (matter is nei-ther racist nor racial), or practical (it is not morality which must subor-dinate itself to life; it is life, in human beings, which must subordinate itself to morality: even if the notion of race were biologically pertinent, racism would still be morally damnable). Racism is, in a word, a her-meneutics of the epidermis (that is its theoretical error) that mistakes heredity for a morality (that is its practical flaw). It is a barbarous and superficial materialism.

I can't draw out the analysis of all this to the extent the topic demands. But it will already be understood at this point that, rejecting as he does both idealism (which is a nonsense for the body) and, in the end, materialism itself (because, he makes clear, "I do not believe in 'matter'"),[44] Nietzsche can only fall into vitalism (in a large sense: he doesn't believe in the existence of any kind of vital principle either) or, if you prefer, into biologism. That is his ontology, what separates him from materialism: "Being—we have no idea of it apart from the idea of 'living.'—How can anything dead 'be'?"[45] But "the organic was not generated" (*Kröner*, XIII, § 560). Organic life is essentially will to power, as Nietzsche hammers on repeatedly, and will to power is, as we know, the basis of reality.

Nietzsche is here, as often—perhaps by way of Boscovich?—closer to Leibniz than to Epicurus or to Lucretius, and his vitalist monism remains prisoner of the "perspective," as he puts it, of the living; which is to say (because anthropomorphism also has to be avoided!) of the animal.[46] Human, all-too-human . . . To take life as norm and model is to fall into all the naturalist traps (critique of culture, rejection of morality, apology for the instinct and animality) and, in consequence—since there is no humanity except through culture—to cease viewing humanity as an irreducible fact (theoretical antihumanism: "To translate man back into nature")[47] and, above all, as a value (practical antihumanism: "Man is something that shall be overcome").[48] Therefore the justification of the worst, beginning in *The Gay Science*:

He that is richest in the fullness of life, the Dionysian god and man, cannot only afford the right of the terrible deed and any luxury of destruction, decomposition, and negation. In his case, what is evil, absurd, and ugly seems, as it were, permissible, owing to an excess of procreating, fertilizing energies that can still turn any desert into lush farmland. (*GS*, 370)

Nietzsche, or the scorched earth policy.

The conclusion of all this is that the force extolled by Nietzsche is well and truly first of all a *physical* force and that the *brute*, far from being a metaphor for the aristocrat or for the hero of the spirit, is both their model and origin. That is what is illustrated by aphorism 257 of *Beyond Good and Evil*, among many others: "In the beginning, the noble caste was always the barbarian caste: their predominance did not lie mainly in physical strength but in strength of the soul—they were more whole human beings (which also means, at every level, 'more whole beasts')." And that is also what is confirmed in *The Will to Power* (§ 942):

There is only nobility of birth, only nobility of blood. (I am not speaking here of the little word *"von"* or of the Almanach de Gotha: parenthesis for asses.) When one speaks of "aristocrats of the spirit," reasons are usually not lacking for concealing something; as is well known, it is a favorite term among ambitious Jews. For spirit alone does not make noble; rather, there must be something to ennoble the spirit.—What then is required? Blood.

It is, finally, what gives the "overman" and the "revaluation of all values" their meaning. The goal is, against the "denaturing of natural values" the Jews have been guilty of (*AC,* 25), to rediscover the amoral spontaneity of the living. Thus the biblical commandments "Thou shalt not steal" and "Thou shalt not kill" are condemned in the name of life:

Is there not in all life itself robbing and killing? And that such words are called holy—was not truth itself killed thereby? Or was it the preaching of death that was called holy, which contradicted and contravened all life? O my brothers, break, break the old tablets! (*Z,* III, "On Old and New Tablets," 10)

This is what Nietzsche calls his *"Fundamental Innovations:* In place of 'moral values,' purely naturalistic values. Naturalization of morality" (*WP,* 462). These "naturalistic values" are, of course, of vitalist inspiration:

Every naturalism in morality—that is, every healthy morality—is dominated by an instinct of life . . . *Anti-natural* morality—that is, almost every morality which has so far been taught, revered, and preached—turns, conversely, *against* the instincts of life. (*TI,* "Morality as Anti-Nature," 4)

We can see here that Nietzsche was right to feel himself singular: all philosophers, more or less, have affirmed that morality should conquer the instincts or, at the very least, dominate them; Nietzsche teaches that the instincts should conquer morality. Spinoza would have said: *Ultimi barbarorum!*

Besides, if all the texts I have just quoted or to which I referred were only metaphors and nonliteral discourse, we could not very well see how Nietzsche could flatter himself, as he does so often, for being "the first immoralist," for undertaking "a radical overturning of values," an "inversion of all values," to the point of announcing— beyond good and evil!—the coming of a new era, prodigious and terrible. And what, in that case, about this philosophy put forward for our benefit, that advocates an overturning that overturns nothing, an overman who isn't one, a will to power that doesn't will power, an immoralism that is not immoral, and, at last, an eternal recurrence where nothing recurs? Is it really doing Nietzsche a favor, is it really being faithful to him, to transform this philosopher-dynamite into a poor little firecracker, just good enough—much ado about nothing!—to liven up a Parisian dinner table?

But let us leave aside polemics and experts' quarrels. Whatever may be done to eliminate Nietzsche's most spectacular or most troubling texts, what there is in him of barbarity remains visible at one precise point, the core of his immoralism. Which is? Nietzsche explained himself on this point a thousand times, and it would become the subtitle to *The Will to Power*: all of Nietzscheanism is intended as *an attempt at a transmutation* (or an *overturning*, or an *inversion*, or a *transvaluation* . . .) of all values. Such a project presupposes that we wipe the slate clean of past values—and that is what I call barbarity.

"That nothing formerly held is true . . . This entire old morality concerns us no more: there is not a concept in it that still deserves respect" (*WP*, 459). Barbarity is in this respect the opposite of fidelity.[49] It thus willingly vindicates the future against the past or the present— hope against memory or respect. It is ever the logic of life ("impossible," observes Nietzsche in the second untimely meditation, "to live without forgetting"), and it is to life only that Nietzsche wishes to be faithful: faithful to unfaithful life, to forgetful life, to bloodthirsty life, full of hope and disrespect! No doubt, when it comes to life, Nietzsche is not entirely in the wrong. But is it life that we should take as a model? Wouldn't it be, out of fidelity to life, to betray the fidelity we also owe to man, I mean to man's humanity, to that long chain of struggles and refusals we call history? Why say *yes* to nature rather than to culture? What is a human being, in fact, if not this living creature in revolt against life itself, who refuses to follow life's pitiless logic to the end? What is man if he isn't, to speak like the French novelist Vercors, a *de-*

natured animal who only creates himself as a human being by refusing the given naturality of the world and of the instincts?

The spirit denies always. Wasn't that the meaning of Socrates' *daimon*? And, before Socrates, wasn't that the essential thing Judaism contributed, over against all the paganisms, over against all the naturalisms? "Naturalization of morality": wasn't that precisely what Judaism taught us to stop doing? Didn't it permit us to *humanize* morality, to *spiritualize* it? Isn't that what we have kept, even without God (especially without God!), from Christianity?

Nietzsche would no doubt agree, but to deplore it. Therefrom his constant will—he, the new prophet and the enemy of the old ones!—to side with the future against the past and against the present. He does not change at all on this point. As late as *Ecce Homo* he confesses he cannot improve on "the end of the fifth book of *la Gaya Scienza*":

Being new, nameless, hard to understand, we premature births of an as yet unproven future need for a new goal also a new means—namely, a new health, stronger, more seasoned, tougher, more audacious, and gayer than any previous health . . . After such vistas and with such a burning hunger in our conscience and science, how could we still be satisfied with *present-day man*? (*EH*, "Thus Spoke Zarathustra," and *GS*, 382)

Genealogy culminates in a new prophetism: "I am a bringer of glad tidings like no one before me; I know tasks of such elevation that any notion of them has been lacking so far; only beginning with me are there hopes again" (*EH*, "Why I Am a Destiny"). Therefore *Zarathustra*'s haughty tone, condemning man in the name of the overhuman, the present in the name of the future and—like any self-respecting prophet—the real (and especially real men!) in the name of meaning. "The now and the past on earth—alas, my friends, that is what *I* find most unendurable; and I should not know how to live if I were not also a seer of that which must come" (*Z*, II, "On Redemption"). What must come? The meaning: "The overman is the meaning of the earth" (*Z*, prologue, 3).

Grandiloquence, as Clément Rosset has shown, always betrays "resentment and hatred [. . .], the desire to cross out the real itself when it becomes unendurable and indigestible"; it is a "fundamental denial of the real" that includes an "indictment of the other."[50] One could hardly put it better. But what is more *grandiloquent,* dear Clément Rosset, than Zarathustra? It is because he is disgusted with men, as he explains ("O nausea! Nausea! Nausea!"), even with the best of them (the "superior men"!), that he longs "to get up, out, and away to the overman," that he is "prophet and imbued with the prophetic spirit that wanders on the ridge between two seas," that he is "he who is destined to light the torch of the future" and fly off "to the far distant futures" (Z, II, "On Human Prudence," III, "The Seven Seals [or: The Yes and Amen song]"). And to canonize his own laughter (Z, IV, "On the Higher Man," passim).

Clément Rosset elsewhere mentions "the neurotic character of hope," which always betrays "a lack of force, a failure, a weakness."[51] Very well. But what, then, could be more neurotic than Zarathustra, who teaches "the greatest hope," "the highest hope," that of the overman, and calmly announces: "In my children I want to make up for being the child of my fathers—and to all the future, for *this* today" (Z, II, "On the Land of Education")? Here, Nietzsche remains a philosopher of meaning, of otherness, of elsewhereness, even if—through the fiction of the eternal recurrence—this otherness remains included in the same, this elsewhere in the here and this meaning within immanence. The overman must become "the meaning of the earth," and this meaning still has to be fought for: "over the whole of humanity there has ruled so far only non-sense—no sense. Let your spirit and your virtue serve the sense of the earth, my brothers" (Z, I, "On the Gift-Giving Virtue", 2). And he must wait ("I am here, waiting," Z, III, xx) for "he who must yet come" (Z, III, "On the Vision and the Riddle").

This kind of messianism resembles all the others. It teaches nothing but contempt. For Karl Marx, all of history was condemned to being but the shadow of itself, it had not even begun, it was only the "prehistory," he said, of the communism to come:[52] we know what that led to. For Nietzsche, it is man that is but an "experiment" (Z, I, "On the Gift-Giving Virtue", 2), "something that shall be overcome" (Z, prologue, 3 and passim) to become, compared to the overman, "a laughingstock or a painful embarrassment" (ibid.). We can imagine what that could have led to. Those "glad tidings" have a price, as always:

The most concerned ask today: "How is man to be preserved?" But Zarathustra is the first and only one to ask: "How is man to be overcome?"

I have the overman at heart, that is my first and only concern—and *not* man: not the neighbor, not the poorest, not the most ailing, not the best . . .

the greatest evil is necessary for the overman's best. (Z, IV, "On the Higher Man," 3)

But what does the cost matter, since "the mountain of man's future" must give birth . . . to the overman!

We can better understand what in Nietzsche's stance, if we compare it to that of most philosophers, and especially to those philosophers he is the least distant from and who are closest to us (Epicurus, Montaigne, Spinoza), is unique, and especially what in it is inadmissible: not because he said *yes* to reality or to life, something they also did and with a different kind of gentleness, but because he said *no* to actual men and, especially, *no* to morality, *no* to culture, *no* to history, *no* to man's humanity—inadmissible, then, less for what he affirms than for what he denies! Nietzsche, or the resentment *against* morality . . .

That wisdom is on the side of the *yes*, of affirmation, of the joyous acceptance of everything—I obviously agree. Perhaps that is the main objection one can make to the idea of wisdom (can one, should one accept *everything*?). I have explained myself about this elsewhere.[53] Between wisdom's *yes* and morality's *no* there is always, if not a contradiction (wisdom is not immoral: see Epicurus, Montaigne, Spinoza), at least a perhaps irreducible tension (morality is, no doubt, never wise) that can be overcome only, if at all, from the point of view of the *yes*—that is, for it is the only veritable *yes*, from the point of view of love, of quite pure and quite respectful love. All right. But are we capable of it? Can we hope to become capable? We need morality only due to a lack of love: I agree and perhaps Nietzsche would too.[54] But—and here is where Nietzsche and I part company—I conclude from this that we are terribly in need of morality. For, in truth, we are so little capable of love!

But, all right, very well: let us say that it's not like that, that we are quite wise. Now we are on the side of the *yes* without reserve, of love without limits. What happens then? Here, we must ask the teachers. What they teach, in the Orient as in the West, is that acceptance of everything accepts also morality—that to say *yes* to everything is also to say *yes* to man, to man's humanity and therefore to his rejections: to say *yes* to everything is also to say *yes* to *no*! That in the end the 'no' ends up being absorbed again, dissolved again, that, in other words, in the end morality ceases to be necessary, is understood, and Christianity itself has never taught anything else. Love is enough, and it is from that aspect that true morality can do without morality.

That is also the teaching of the wise. Everyone can see how, with Epicurus, with Montaigne, with Spinoza (as, in the East, with Buddha or, in the twentieth century, with Swami Prajnânpad), the most radical wisdoms, the most liberated from all moralism, those which are most faithful to nature (and to the human being *within* nature), lead to a life which, far from being in any way immoral, fulfills on the contrary—but joyously, without constraint or resentment—the most rigorous demands of traditional morality. *Love, and do what you will . . .* Beyond good and evil? That would be saying too much, because love is the good in itself (what would be the meaning of saying that the good is beyond good and evil? Wouldn't that be excessively Platonist?), since there is no other good than to love.

The formulation of all this—I'm forced to go very fast—was best furnished by Spinoza in a decisive sentence that deals with the Christ (yes, for Spinoza saw himself quite explicitly as the contrary of an Antichrist!) and with what he brought to his most enlightened disciples: "He freed them from servitude to the law yet nevertheless confirmed it and wrote for all time on the bottom of their hearts."[55] To free, to confirm. It's the second moment (which in fact is but one with the first) that is lacking in Nietzsche, through which fact he is the opposite of Spinoza at the very point where the latter feels himself to be the heir of Christ and the friend of decent people. And we don't find in Spinoza any overturning of values, any inversion of traditional hierarchies either. On the contrary: he never ceased to affirm that, once the dogmas and superstitions of the churches have been rejected, the double requirements of justice and of charity continue to be valid—and that goes for the wise as well as for the ignorant.

Compare the point of view in chapter 14 of the *Theological-Political Treatise* with the first dissertation in *The Genealogy of Morals*, and especially with its eleventh paragraph. Nietzsche there opposes, as is well known, two pairs of evaluations, one aristocratic and affirmative (*good/bad*), the other servile and reactive (*evil/good*). The concept "good," even if it takes first place in the first system and second place in the second, seems to be common to both, but that is in fact not the case: this concept, Nietzsche explains, is itself double. To be convinced of this, he writes, one should ask rather precisely *who* is "evil" in the sense of the morality of *ressentiment*. The answer, in all strictness, is: *precisely* the "good man" of the other morality, precisely the noble, powerful man, the ruler, but dyed in another color, interpreted in another fashion, seen in another way by the venomous eye of *ressentiment*. (*GM*, I, 11; see also *BGE*, 260)

So that our pair of opposites (good/bad, evil/good) correspond in bi-univocal fashion, as long as we criss-cross the terms: what is good for the aristocrat is what is evil for the slave, and the good for the slave is the bad for the aristocrat! There is thus well and truly—Nietzsche never claimed anything else—a strict inversion of values, and even two successive inversions, Judeo-Christian morality (reactive, slave morality) having overturned Aryan morality (affirmative, master morality), Nietzsche explicitly aims at overturning Judeo-Christian morality to give aristocratic morality a new chance. Since it is "with the Jews that the slave rebellion in morality" begins, "monstrous" expression of "Jewish hate" (*GM*, I, 7–8), since "Judea" still triumphs through Catholicism, Reformation, and French Revolution (I, 16), the "old fire" must be revived against it (I, 17), all its values must be overturned so as to put natural hierarchies back in their place. It is the last word in *The Antichrist* ("Inversion of all values!") and Nietzsche's last word, so to speak (since it is in the last lines of *Ecce Homo*):

The concept of the *good* man signifies that one sides with all that is weak, sick, failure, suffering of itself—all that ought to perish: the principle of selection is crossed—an ideal is fabricated from the contradiction against the proud and well-turned-out human being who says Yes, who is sure of the future, who guarantees the future—and he is now called *evil*. And all this was believed, *as morality! Écrasez l'infâme!*
Have I been understood? Dionysus versus the Crucified.

We know that Spinoza, though he also rejected all churches and all superstitions, wished on the contrary to remain *faithful*—it's the word he uses—to the scriptures ("whose entire law consists in the sole commandment: love your neighbor")[56] and to the traditional moral teachings (which "remain salutary").[57] He also considered that "he truly possesses God's spirit who practices charity" (even if he is an unbeliever!), whereas, inversely, "he is in reality anti-Christian who persecutes men of honest life and friends of justice because their opinions differ from his."[58] Spinoza was here thinking of religious dogmatisms, of inquisitors, and of fanatics of every stripe. But the formula would also be valid, and is valid, against the *blond beasts* who would overturn values. "For," Spinoza also said, "We know that to love justice and charity is enough to make one a believer, and to persecute believers is to be anti-Christian."[59] Have I been understood?—*Spinoza against the Antichrist!*

THE SOPHIST

Thus it is—and life certainly forced me to it more than Spinoza did!—that I had to give up living *beyond good and evil*, just as in politics (but for reasons which are inseparably practical and theoretical) I gave up, as the "Internationale" sings it, making a "clean slate" out of "the past." That is another story, but it is significant that they should come together. "To be a Nietzschean," we were saying above, "is to be a Marxist without quite daring to be one completely." It may be that we should be saying the contrary, but it doesn't matter. For a long time Marx protected me from Nietzsche; the effort I made to free myself from the first also liberated me, in advance so to speak, from the second.

One can imagine the role Spinoza played in both cases. It is true that the moral (but therefore also philosophical!) reticences that contributed to distancing me from Nietzsche never ceased to increase—due both to my own evolution and because I came to know him better and better—to the extent of making the Spinoza-Nietzsche opposition (and no longer, as an entire part of our modernity does, their parallelism) into a structural axis of my philosophical universe. I understand that Nietzsche is not merely an immoralist and that there is some injustice in thus gathering together his most brutal, his most inadmissible texts to the detriment of certain others. One can read almost all of *The Gay Science* without being shocked by anything, or practically anything; how, on the contrary, can one not be seduced by so much lucid clarity, so much joyous depth, so much philosophizing alacrity? Yes. But we are here, let me repeat, explaining why we are not Nietzscheans, and not why or under what conditions we could have become adepts. And in this decision—that is what I wanted to explain first of all—Nietzsche's immoralism played a decisive role: if I am not a Nietzschean, if I neither can nor want to be one, it is because I don't want to live beyond good and evil, nor revaluate all values, nor even put an end to Judeo-Christian morality. That, from both Nietzsche's and my own point of view, is a crucial difference, one that would have been enough.

But another thing soon came up. The more I penetrated into this difficult and transparent, crystalline and labyrinthine oeuvre (and the more I saw its effects on our modernity), the more I was bothered by another aspect that, though not morally innocent, was above all of a theoretical nature: a certain indifference to truth or, more exactly, an overly occasional and loose relation to the true, to logic (therefore, among other things, the innumerable contradictions), to what Spinoza would call "the norm of the true given idea." But, it will be objected, there can't be any trace of a *true given idea*: Nietzsche is a skeptic, and his integral relativism—which is the source of his very own force and coherence—prohibits us from submitting him to the test of a norm (truth) he made every effort to critique and destroy. If "the concept 'truth' is nonsensical" (*WP*, 625), if "there is no truth" (*WP*, 540) nor any "state of things" (*WP*, 604), how then to scold an author for playing fast and loose with a truth . . . that doesn't exist?

Fine. But Nietzsche cannot then escape from the aporia of logical nihilism: if there is no truth, the proposition that states that there is no truth is not true. We must therefore conclude either that there is a truth (in which case the proposition "there is no truth" is false, and Nietzsche is mistaken), or that we cannot think at all any more (since the proposition "there is no truth" is simultaneously true and false, which violates the principle of noncontradiction, or neither true nor false, which transgresses the principle of the excluded third). In a word: we have either to save logic and give up Nietzsche or to save Nietzsche and give up on logic. The genealogists may ask us: "Why are you so attached to logic?" We have our reasons, to which I will come back. But we also have to return the question to them: and you, why are you *so little* attached to it?

Nietzsche claims that attachment to logic is a sign of weakness, that it betrays a plebeian or Jewish origin (*WP*, 431 ff.; *GS*, 348, 370). Should we then conclude that every illogicality is a sign of aristocratic or Aryan force? Or would this conclusion be itself too *logical*? Too plebeian? Too Jewish? Or are logic and genealogy legitimate only when coming from Nietzschean pens?

But let's leave that aside. Another, more solid objection that could be made against me is that the aporia I have just evoked (the self-contradiction of logical nihilism) is that of any radical skepticism, and that I can't take Nietzsche to task for it more than I would Pyrrhon, Montaigne, or Hume, whom I nevertheless profess to admire.

We can admit the fact where Pyrrhon is concerned. But it would seem that that led him to absolute nihilism (for the Pyrrhonian, explained Enesidemus, "there is neither true nor false, neither probable nor improbable, neither being nor nonbeing . . . The Pyrrhonian determines nothing, not even that nothing is determined"),[60] which in turn led—rather logically!—to indifference (since everything is the same and equally indifferent) and to silence (since all discourse remains the prisoner of the illusions of being and of truth). "For those who find themselves within these attitudes," Timon specified on his side, "what will result will be first of all aphasia, then ataraxia."[61] And in this Pyrrho, writing nothing and demonstrating the greatest possible equanimity, remained faithful to his thinking—if the word still fits—and at least coherent with himself. But Nietzsche? The least that can be said is that neither aphasia nor ataraxia were among his talents, and that blocks us from making him, who specifically denied it anyway, into a disciple or continuator of Pyrrho. The latter is, as seen by Nietzsche, and not without reason, a nihilist, "a Buddhist in Greece," certainly attractive but expressing nothing more than the "wise fatigue" of the "latecomer," and who only constitutes—as did Epicurus!—a form of "Greek decadence" (*WP*, 437). How could Nietzsche be a Pyrrhonian? He has to find a way to *affirm*, to *teach*, to *prophesy*—and how, if nothing is true?

The problem is entirely different as far as Montaigne and Hume are concerned. We know that Nietzsche admired Montaigne and that, though he kept his distance from Hume due to his stupid Anglophobia, he nonetheless defends, sometimes explicitly, more often without saying it or perceiving it, positions in many ways quite close to those of the author of *A Treatise of Human Nature*. Nevertheless, Nietzsche always, or almost always, refused to consider himself a skeptic; his criticism of the idea of truth goes far beyond Montaigne's and Hume's critiques, and for good reason: Montaigne and Hume never critique truth as such! What they question—and what they criticize *in the name of truth*—is the pertinence and ontological reliability of our knowledge: their skepticism is negation not of knowledge but of dogmatism, not of truth but of certitude. They are both at bottom empiricists, seeing the limits of experience too well to raise the innumerable—but always doubtful and relative—knowledges it permits into a dogmatic metaphysics. They loved truth too much to purely and simply identify it with what we think we know of it.

Such skepticism, though radical (in many ways more radical than Nietzsche's), remains, as both thinkers congratulated themselves, a moderate skepticism: they do not state as Nietzsche does that "nothing is true" (which would be contradictory: if nothing is true, it cannot be true that nothing is true) nor that "everything is false" (which would be equally contradictory: if everything were false, it would be false to say that everything is false), but—something very different—that *everything is uncertain,* which is not contradictory (it only follows from it, as Pascal, reading Montaigne, had seen, that "it is not certain that everything is uncertain,"[62] but that fact, far from refuting skepticism, confirms it, to "Pyrrhonism's greater glory")[63] and consequently allows for the elaboration of a discourse that remains rational and even rationalist because capable of accounting for its own truth (as uncertain truth) to the degree that it remains subject to what could be called the *norm of the apparent true idea* (and this more honestly in Hume and Montaigne than in anyone else!)—and in this the skeptics are philosophers, and of a high order, and not sophists or rhetoricians.

But Nietzsche? He can't resign himself to silence or indifference, as Pyrrhon did; nor can he merely question, as Montaigne and Hume did, our knowledge or our certainty. On the contrary! He pretends to both know the true ("It is truth which speaks through my mouth," he says in *Ecce Homo*) and point out its absence ("There is no truth," *WP,* 540), to critique knowledge ("Nothing can be known," *Werke,* XVI, § 1076) and to claim it for himself ("knowledge at the service of the higher life," ibid., X, 118, § 37):[64] to destroy, in short, truth with hammer blows—with the hammer of truth! *Héautontimorouménos?* That would indeed be his name if he only dealt his blows to himself, as he sometimes does, and forbade himself all pretension to the truth or any superiority over the other philosophers. But from the moment he pretends—from the heights of his position, impregnable *because nonexistent:* the truth of nontruth!—to refute the affirmations others have made and to hold all alone the correct interpretation of the past, the present, and the future, then it is not "executioner of himself" that we have to call him but, quite simply, *sophist,* and the designation would no doubt not have displeased him.

What is a sophist? We know that the word designates a philosophical school in antiquity, one that Nietzsche, against Socrates, claims to
be near to,[65] and one he indeed approaches by way of perspectivism or
relativism. But it isn't history of philosophy that concerns me here. We
can more generally call *sophistical* any manner of thinking that subordinates itself to something other than truth or that subordinates truth to
something other than itself. Sophistry is a logical relativism, the temptation towards which may be borne, to put it in a nutshell, from the following syllogism: every value is relative; truth is a value; therefore, truth
is relative. It is a temptation that is quite strong today, since the major
premise is incontrovertibly part of the legacy of our modernity (and
that, since Montaigne); and a temptation that is quite dangerous, since
the conclusion runs the risk of dissolving even the idea of truth (all truth
is relative—therefore there is no truth!).

Since the major premise and the conclusion are equally indisputa-
ble, at least from my point of view, we can only escape this chain of reasoning by rejecting the minor premise: that truth is a value, which is
what I contest. Not, of course, that it cannot be of value to such and
such a person. But it is not because it is of value that it has worth, that it
is true: value defines not its essence but our subjective relation to it
(truth is true, de jure, for all; it is of value only for whoever loves truth).
That is why I have elsewhere suggested calling *sophistic,* in a more precise sense, any manner of thought which assimilates truth to value *under the domination of value* (in other words, any thinking for which the
true is true the way the just is just or the beautiful beautiful: subjectively,
from a certain point of view or relative to a certain interest), sophism
being in that the opposite of practical dogmatism (which assimilates
value to truth *under the domination of truth*: the just is just, the beautiful beautiful, etc., as the true is true: absolutely or objectively) and of
what I have called, thinking about both Diogenes and Machiavelli, *cyn-
icism* (which on the contrary disconnects these two orders: all truth is
objective, all value is subjective, which leads to supposing that no value
is true in itself and that no truth has value in itself).[66] The word is, in
this sense, of technical use and is not meant to insult. But I have to admit
that, when it comes to Nietzsche, I am also sensitive to the pejorative
content it carries in everyday usage, and I can't help myself from also
using it in this sense, one neither historical (the Sophists of ancient
times) nor technical (the subjectivist, or relativist, conjunction of truth
and value), but well and truly polemical (the sophist then being he who

is ready to use anything—even at the cost of logic or of truth—to win the argument). Besides, these last two meanings are not really separable, as we could easily show (if all truth is subjective, why submit oneself to truth?), and, most of all, they both fit Nietzsche. How otherwise to designate a philosopher who calmly writes the following: "That a judgment be false is not, in our opinion, an objection against that judgment" (*BGE*, 4). How admirable: this, indeed, makes Nietzscheanism irrefutable. For what objections can one then make against it? And why would it care?

Nietzsche specifies his own viewpoint in the same aphorism: "Everything hinges on knowing the extent to which this judgment promotes life, entertains life, maintains, even improves, the species." Vitalism always commands. But, at that point, Nietzsche's thought is not only beyond good and evil but also, as has been often remarked, *beyond true and false* (what François George calls "sanitary thinking"!)[67] and thereby breaks—and Nietzsche was aware of this—with the near totality of the philosophical tradition. That kind of thinking is truly sophistical in the sense I use the word: it subordinates truth to value, that is, *to life*. What Eugen Fink designated as "Nietzsche's fundamental equation," namely "Being = value,"[68] thus derives—as does immoralism—from his vitalism and confirms it. But—and Fink had also seen this—Nietzschean sophistics remain in that in paradoxical solidarity with Platonic dogmatism ("with metaphysics," says Fink), precisely because, like the latter, they "interpret Being essentially as value," thereby remaining prisoner of the equation cited above, whose "origin is also to be found in Plato"[69]—though, I would add, in symmetrical or inverse fashion.

Indeed, just as Plato erects values into truths (the Good in itself, the Beautiful in itself, the Just in itself), Nietzsche reduces truth to value and therefore denies it as truth: "*Truth is the kind of error* without which a certain type of living creature could not live. Value for life is what decides in the end" (*WP*, 493).

From there, perspectivism: "There are many kinds of eyes. The Sphinx also has eyes: therefore, there are many kinds of 'truth.' and therefore there is no truth" (*WP*, 540). Reason is but a "useful *falsification*" (*WP*, 584), knowledge only a self-interested evaluation (*Kröner*, XII, 2, § 13: "To know is to understand everything as it best serves our interests"!). It is nonetheless the case that, as in Plato, *Being and value are on the same side*—on the side of Being for Plato, on the side of value for Nietzsche. Nietzscheanism is indeed an "inverted Platonism,"[70] but not only, as Nietzsche thought, because it values what Plato devalues (the sensible world) to the disadvantage of what was essential for him (the intelligible world). If Nietzscheanism is an inverted Platonism, it is also—from our point of view, it is above all—because it takes up again the Platonic joining of Being and value, merely inverting its terms: where Plato thought that value *is* (this conjunction constituting for Plato the very essence of truth), Nietzsche affirms that Being *has value,* in other words that it is only a value, which leads in effect to thinking that there is no truth or, what comes down to the same thing, that the *value of truth,* as logicians say, is only a value like any other and as such subordinate to life, to desire, or to the will.

For Plato, to evaluate is to know (intellectualism), and one can only know that which is (dogmatism). For Nietzsche, to know is to evaluate (sophistry), and one can only evaluate in accord with one's desires (perspectivism). The two thinkers meet there where they are opposed, in the joining of Being and value that dominates the being of the Good (Plato) or in the value-making creativity of the Will to Power (Nietzsche). Dogmatism and sophistry are in that way as inseparable as they are symmetrical. Which explains why they feed off of their mutual criticism: we fall into Plato's arms in order to escape Nietzsche, or into Nietzsche's to escape Plato. I have put forth another possibility, but this is not the place to go into it.[71] It remains to be said that, on the basis of an indeed truly radical critique of truth (so radical that it destroys itself), Nietzschean sophistry expands and has effects up to our own days that Nietzsche himself had desired should be destructive.

I don't have the time to go into details. The problem is all the more confusing in that Nietzsche, here as elsewhere, doesn't hesitate to contradict himself. Thus he can state, as we have seen, that "the falseness of a judgment is for us not necessarily an objection to [that] judgment" since, he specifies, "untruth is the condition of life" (*BGE,* 4), though writing elsewhere that "life is not an argument, for error could be one of the conditions for life" (*GS,* 121). The two affirmations certainly do have a common core (the solidarity between life and error); but where in *The Gay Science* Nietzsche had argued against life, in *Beyond Good and Evil* he instead argues against truth. An evolution? Perhaps. Nietzsche, growing old, seems to have loved life more and more and truth less and less. *The Gay Science* was a *science,* as Rosset put it, and a "science of disillusionment,"[72] where the books that follow proclaim above all—and I'll come back to this—the vital and aesthetic necessity of illusion.

But nothing is simple in Nietzsche. The two themes are sometimes simultaneous, and we would never be finished unraveling the threads. It is sure that Nietzsche goes so far as to reject even the idea of truth ("there is no truth," "the concept 'truth' is nonsensical," etc.: *WP*, 540, 625, and passim), even the possibility of any knowledge, *not only absolute, but also relative* (*Kröner*, XVI, § 1076), to the extent that he believes that "the will to know the true is already a symptom of degeneration" (ibid., XIV, 3, § 239) and presents on the contrary as his "Dionysus ideal—The perspective of all organic functions, all the strongest instincts of life: the force in all life that *wills* error; error as the precondition even of thought" (*WP*, 544). From there the absoluteness, if one can say so, of Nietzsche's relativism, which is resumed in the well-known formula (at the heart of his sophism in the same way that the revaluation of all values is at the heart of his immoralism): *"There are no facts, only interpretations"* (*WP*, 481).

Such a formula is obviously problematic (that there are no facts: is that a fact, or an interpretation?) or even nonthinkable: what can we interpret, if there are no facts? Other interpretations? But what is an interpretation if it isn't the fact of interpreting? Nietzsche doesn't enlighten us at all about any of this. He does see that his affirmation can be taken only as an interpretation, and that is how his perspectivism, as Jean Granier put it referring to another text, "ruins the foundation of his own discourse."[73] Like a good sophist, Nietzsche gets out of this with a bit of acrobatics: "Supposing that this also is only interpretation—and you will be eager enough to make this objection?—well, so much the better" (*BGE*, 22).

So much the better, or too bad, but the objection remains. And it isn't the most serious one. That the statement "there is nothing but interpretations" is itself an interpretation makes its value very relative but does not yet make it nonthinkable. But, on the other hand, such a statement is itself a *fact,* and its very existence (as fact) therefore refutes its content (as interpretation). Or else we have to consider, as certain commentators do, Nietzscheanism to be only a thought without content or reality, a mere play of simulacra, of value only for what it destroys and which remains deliberately—like a work of art, it's been said!—at the surface of its own discourse. Clément Rosset, in his "Notes on Nietzsche," has pinned down marvelously well this type of reading, which consists in pretending that Nietzsche never, so to speak, thought nor wrote *any-thing*, but that in this lack is found, paradoxically, the essential part of his force and his finesse, and the reason for his present-day influence. A curious appreciation, but a confirmed and persistent one, that reminds one of Mademoiselle Anaïs's judgments on matters of literature and modern art in Marcel Aymé's satire, *Le confort intellectuel* (Intellectual Comfort, 1947): "Her preferences went, in literature, to Picasso, and, in painting, to Jean Paulhan, who, not being a painter, nevertheless was one and in fact even more so." In the same way, Nietzsche is today happily celebrated as he who, not being a philosopher, "nevertheless is one and in fact even more so": a great interpreter precisely because he interpreted nothing, as Foucault put it in the Royaumont Nietzsche colloquium (1964), a great thinker precisely because he failed to think anything up, as Pierre Klossowski has repeated on various occasions. Such disinfection of what Nietzsche had to say is also manifest in the texts dealing with him by Bataille, Blanchot, Derrida.[74]

Nietzsche would seem to deserve better than this philosophy for chatterers, but how can we escape from it? If there are no facts, Nietzsche himself is not a fact, and from that point on anyone can replace him to his own advantage through his own interpretation of Nietzsche, which itself will be nothing more than the interpretation of an interpretation, and so on into infinity. If there is no truth, it is not true that Nietzsche wrote what he wrote, nor that he wrote something else, nor that he didn't write anything. We therefore can say nothing about him, or rather we can say anything we like, which is nice and convenient: it isn't Pyrrho's aphasia, it's the indefinite chatter of the sophists! It is a fortiori an illusion, and anti-Nietzschean, to think that one knows what Nietzsche *really* thought! That of course makes him irrefutable, and irrefutable any interpretation we may wish to make of him. But what is the point, since at that point there is nothing more to refute or to interpret?

And what's with this *affirmative* philosophy that leads only to the negation of everything ("there is no truth, no truth, no truth . . . "), to the subjectivist rejection of reality ("no facts, no facts, no facts . . . ")? Interpretation as the exclusion of the real. There are no facts: nothing but meaning! No truths: only evaluations! It is what Nietzsche calls "the supreme negation" (*Kröner*, XII, p. 406) and the triumph of nihilism: "That there is *no truth*; no qualities to things, no 'thing-in-itself.'— *This itself is a nihilism, in fact the extremest*" (*WP*, 13). Nietzsche, or sophistics in the service of nihilism.

Nothing remains then but the subjective evaluation (without a subject, of course!) of the *creator of value*: this nihilism, Nietzsche goes on, "places the value of things precisely in this, that these values correspond and corresponded to *no* reality, but only to a symptom of strength on the side of the *value-giver*, a simplification for the *purpose of life*" (*WP*, 13). And, so, from affirmation to affirmation, all anyone affirms anymore is—himself! Heidegger was right at least on this point: Nietzscheanism really is a monadology without God,[75] without monads even. It is also a subjectivism with neither subject nor object (or, what comes down to the same thing, an absolute relativism), and because of that without limits: "Nothing is true, everything is permitted" (*Kröner*, XII, p. 406).

And from this we can conclude that Nietzscheanism is not true, yet that it is possible to be a Nietzschean—and we are certainly not going to dispute either one of these conclusions!

But there is something more serious. The formulation in question is not only problematic from a logical and philosophical point of view, it is above all dangerous and—you will forgive me for coming back to this—*morally* dangerous. If there is no truth, how are you going to resist lies? What would be the sense of asking, for instance, whether Dreyfus was *really* guilty or who *really* set the Reichstag on fire? If there is no knowledge, how will you fight obscurantism and ignorance? If there are no facts but only interpretations, what objections will you make to the revisionists who maintain that the gas chambers are not, precisely, *a fact*, only a point of view, a mere hypothesis, a mere *interpretation* by certain historians connected to the Jewish lobby?

It may be objected that that was not Nietzsche's point of view. Certainly, those were not his examples. As for his point of view, I wouldn't know. In *The Antichrist*, after having praised Pontius Pilate's attitude ("One Jew more or less—what does it matter?"), Nietzsche adds:

The noble scorn of a Roman, confronted with an impudent abuse of the word "truth," has enriched the New Testament with the only saying *that has value*— one which is its criticism, even its *annihilation*: "What is truth?" (*AC*, § 46).

Indeed, any judge can say that when he needs to condemn an innocent man. But can we accept that? Should we accept it? And how do we prevent it, if there are neither facts nor truths? In aphorism 4 of *Beyond*

Good and Evil, after having announced, you will recall, that the falseness of a judgment was not for him an objection against that judgment
since the only thing that counts is its vital utility, Nietzsche concludes:

To recognize untruth as a condition of life—that certainly means resisting ac-
customed value feelings in a dangerous way; and a philosophy that risks this
would by that token alone place itself beyond good and evil.

   Logic and morality go together. Nietzsche never pretended otherwise, and that is also what French philosopher Jean Cavaillès taught
before being shot by the Nazis.[76] But the latter drew diametrically opposite conclusions, remaining faithful to both logic and morality even
unto death, where Nietzsche wished to get rid of both ("Everything is
false! Everything is permitted!": *WP*, § 602) even unto madness. It
would be somewhat impudent to claim to be an Cavaillès side—heroes
belong to no one. But I would feel I was insulting his memory if I
pretended— supposing I were even capable of doing so—to be on
Nietzsche's side.

THE AESTHETE

I would like to go quickly here, having been, thanks to anger, too long in
the preceding sections.
   What is an aesthete? Someone who loves beauty? If it were only
that, we would all be aesthetes and the word would lose its usefulness.
The aesthete is not he who loves beauty but he who loves only beauty;
he who, as the French *Petit Robert* dictionary specifies, demonstrates
his "skepticism towards other values." To be an aesthete is to love the
beautiful more than the true or the good, and even *instead* of the true
and the good. The aesthete is he for whom aesthetics takes the place of
logic and of morality!
   (An artist's ideology? Hardly. What creator, among the great ones
in any case, has not also had to deal with the good and the true? Could
we imagine Rembrandt or Beethoven, Rodin or Proust, being uninter-
ested in the truth of what they have to express? Can we believe that their
message isn't moral [even if, happily, it isn't moralizing!] as much as it is
aesthetic? Can we imagine that the only thing art is good for is to make
pretty things? Aestheticism is not an artist's ideology; it is an art *lover's*

ideology—when he no longer can love anything but the beautiful, when everything else frightens, bores, or tires him. Not, then, an artist's ideology, but art—amputated of its ethical function and of its knowledge-content—*as ideology!*)

That Nietzsche was an aesthete in that sense is hardly to be doubted. "For us, only the aesthetic judgment is law" (*WP,* French edition, III, 59). I will not insist on the moral and political dangers of that attitude: go fight Nazism by merely arguing how inaesthetic it is! Walter Benjamin, on the contrary, saw in Nazism the first political movement to have explicitly seen itself *as aesthetic,* and that was surely not entirely false. But can anyone believe that to fight against that *aesthetic* another one would be enough? Don't we have any better reason to disapprove of the death camps than that they were ugly?

But let us get back to Nietzsche. Aestheticism is his destiny. Leading his thought not only beyond good and evil but, as we have just seen, beyond true and false, he cannot escape nihilistic indifference—the night of the world in which all the cows are gray—except by not also thinking *beyond beautiful and ugly.* He thereby enters exactly into our definition: he affirms his cult of the beautiful or of art at the same time, as the *Petit Robert* would put it, as his "skepticism towards other values." To which it could be objected that it is not entirely true, since Nietzsche, though he thinks beyond good and evil, does not place his thought "beyond good and bad" (*GM,* I, 17), and that life is a normative universe of reference for him at least as much as art is, which fact gives his evaluations a content if not a foundation. Certainly. But that does not weaken his aestheticism, since *life itself is justified aesthetically.* Aestheticism and vitalism go together, as we will now try to demonstrate.

We remember Nietzsche's beautiful formulation in *Twilight of the Idols:* "Without music, life would be an error" ("Maxims and Arrows," 33). Proof enough that life is not in itself of value, and that it would be to betray Nietzsche to make of him, against Schopenhauerian pessimism, just another simple optimistic philosopher, an advocate of joie de vivre and of the pleasures of this world. Nietzsche is neither a hedonist nor a eudaemonist: neither pleasure nor happiness is the goal. Even his vitalism cannot provide him with an ethic. If life is good, it is not of itself nor for itself: it is good only through the evaluation that we make of it, it is good only to be beautiful! It is one occurrence of the tragic affirmation ("'That is beautiful' is an affirmation": *WP,* § 852), in truth it is the only one. For how can one *affirm* anything else. By celebrating Being, reality, the present moment? Impossible for Nietzsche, since Being is but an illusion (*WP,* 708), since there is no reality but only interpretations, since "present being does not exist" (*WP,* 570).

All affirmation is, in that sense, inseparable from an affirmative interpretation, and this interpretation is art. "Existence and the universe are eternally justified only as aesthetic phenomena," Nietzsche had written in 1871 (*The Birth of Tragedy,* 5), and he would repeat it in 1886, before adding:

There is an abyss between the purely aesthetic interpretation and justification of the world that appear in this work and Christian teaching which is, which only wishes to be, moral, and which, because of its absolute principles—be it only, for instance, its God of truth—rejects art, any art, into the domain of mendacity. (*BT,* preface, 5)

One has to choose: moralism or aestheticism. Truth (since truth is, for Nietzsche, only a moral value!) or the artist's "beautiful lie," as Mallarmé put it. Nietzsche chooses, obviously, the lie (that is what is called reversing values), and that is why he is an aesthete: he prefers a *beautiful lie* to a truth which is "ugly" (*WP,* 822). Whereas science and the ascetic ideal meet "in a common exaggeration of the value of truth," Nietzsche on the contrary chooses creative artifice: "art, in which precisely the *lie* is sanctified and the *will to deception* has a good conscience, is much more fundamentally opposed to the ascetic ideal than is science" (*GM,* III, 25). And we know that he aimed to make of life a work of art.

All of which is of course one with the celebration of appearance so beautifully expressed in the preface to *The Gay Science,* when Nietzsche praises the ancient Greeks' determination "to stop courageously at the surface, the fold, the skin, to adore appearance, to believe in forms, tones, words, in the whole Olympus of appearance. Those Greeks were superficial—*out of profundity.*" And Nietzsche adds: "Are we not, precisely in this respect, Greeks? Adorers of forms, of tones, of words? And therefore—*artists?*" But there is a long way from appearance to lying—as far as from nature to art! For one shouldn't believe that the aesthetic justification of the world is happy merely appreciating an objective, already real beauty—even at its surface—in the world or in nature: to think that would be to forget that all evaluation is *creation* of value (*Z,* I, "On the Thousand and One Goals": "Through esteeming alone is there value: and without esteeming, the nut of existence would be hollow") and that nothing is less aesthetic than nature merely observed. It is of this that Nietzsche acerbically reminds naturalists and realists of every stripe: "Nature, estimated artistically, is no model. It exaggerates, it distorts, it leaves gaps. Nature is *chance*" (*TI*, "Skirmishes of an Untimely Man," 7). And what could be less artistic than chance? The "artist god" is only a metaphor. If the world were a work of art, it would be enough to imitate it, and that would justify realism. But, Nietzsche goes on, on the contrary, "To study 'from nature' seems to me to be a bad sign: it betrays submission, weakness, fatalism; this lying in the dust before *petits faits* is unworthy of a *whole* artist" (ibid.).

"The famous modern 'objectivity,'" he specifies in the same book, "is bad taste, is *ignoble* par excellence" (*TI*, "What the Germans Lack," 6). Only the "antiartistic" spirit wishes "to see *what is*" (*TI*, "Skirmishes" 7); the artist *creates what has value*.

The "aesthetic justification" of the world is thus not its contemplation as if it were a work of art, but its transmutation *into* an artwork. Chance can be an artist only for artists and through artists. "Our sovereign right as artists could exult at the idea of having *created* this world," Nietzsche wrote (*Kröner,* XIV, 1, § 21)—but only artistic spirits have this right. "That the artist esteems appearance higher than reality is no objection to this proposition. For 'appearance' in this case means reality *once more,* only by way of selection, reinforcement, and correction" (*TI,* "'Reason' in Philosophy," 6). The world is not a work of art but it becomes one through artists: the aesthetic justification of the world is, for Nietzsche, nothing else than art itself. It isn't the world that is a work of art, it is art that makes a world!

Therefore the extreme importance of art, about which we can say that it has no equal either in Nietzsche (nothing is as important as art for him) or in the history of philosophy (no other philosopher has given it as much importance). It may be argued against me that, all the same, life . . . No. Life has no value in and of itself. Without art it would be ghastly and insipid. I have already quoted "Without music, life would be an error," which statement says a lot about the man Nietzsche: we can only imagine the kind of suffering it took to come to think this way. But it is not a casual confession; Nietzsche never stops confirming it: "Only possible life: in art. Otherwise, we turn away from life" (*Fragments divers,* ed. G. Bianquis [Paris: Gallimard, 1940], p. 231). And somewhat later: "Art and nothing but art! It is the great means of making life possible, the great seduction to life; the great stimulant to life" (*WP*, 853).

Only the *beautiful lie* makes truth bearable: "How is art born? As an antidote to knowledge. Life is only possible thanks to *art's illusions*" (*Fragments divers,* op. cit., p. 208). Art is the antidote to science, all the more necessary in that the latter keeps developing and ruining its own foundations:

Our ultimate gratitude to art. If we had not welcomed the arts and invented this kind of cult of the untrue, then the realization of general untruth and mendaciousness that now comes to us through science—the realization that delusion and error are conditions of human knowledge and sensation—would be utterly unbearable. *Honesty* would lead to nausea and suicide. But now there is a counterforce against our honesty that helps us to avoid such consequences: art as the *good* will to appearance . . . As an aesthetic phenomenon existence is still *bearable* for us, and art furnishes us with eyes and hands and above all the good conscience to be *able* to turn ourselves into such a phenomenon. (*GS,* 107)

Aestheticism and vitalism go together, as I was saying, and now we can see how: art is in the service of life, it is there to justify it and render it bearable. The aim is still to "transform the world so we can tolerate living in it" (*Kröner,* XII, 1, § 271). But we have to add: aestheticism and vitalism are in that inseparable from sophism. If art is "the great stimulant of life" (*WP,* § 851) it is because it is the power of illusion that intoxicates us. In Nietzsche, Gilles Deleuze has observed, "art is the highest power of the false, it magnifies 'the world as error,' it sanctifies lying, it makes of the will to delusion a superior ideal."[77] That is indeed, from its inception, Nietzsche's way of thinking. As he recalled in 1888,

The relation between art and truth is the first one I reflected on. Even today their enmity fills me with a sacred dread. My first book was devoted to this fact; *The Birth of Tragedy* believes in art, with, at the background, another belief, that *we cannot live with the truth;* that the will to know the true is already a symptom of degeneracy. (*Kröner,* XIV, 3 § 239)

Here is where we find immoralism once again:

For a philosopher to say, "the good and the beautiful are one," is infamy; if he goes on to add, "also the true," one ought to thrash him. Truth is ugly. We possess *art* lest we *perish of the truth*. (*WP*, 822)

The formula is aimed against Socrates ("It is Socratic to want to tell the truth at any price": *Kröner*, X, p. 139, § 70), but it also holds against every realist and, whatever Nietzsche may have thought, against all the classicists (Boileau: "Rien n'est beau que le vrai, le vrai seul est aimable."). But enough of that. We have, according to Nietzsche, entered the age of aesthetics, which must overcome science the same way science overcame religion: "History and the natural sciences were useful in conquering the Middle Ages; knowledge against faith. Now we put up art against scholarship. Return to life!" (*Fragments divers,* op. cit., p. 191). It all comes together. Life is, for Nietzsche, on the side of error, of mendacity, of artifice, of illusion, and morality is on the other side. And so is logic. He therefore opts for art against logic (against science, against reason, against knowledge) and against morality. "Our religion, our morality, our philosophy are only forms of decadence of humanity— the countermovement: art."[78] Dionysus against Socrates, aesthestics against reason and against morality: "art is *worth more* than truth" (*WP*, § 853, IV).

As always with Nietzsche, the problem comes from the fact that he *also* said the opposite, or nearly, in, for example, reproaching Wagner's music for "never being true" (*CW*, 8), in celebrating the psychological penetration of a Stendhal or a Dostoyevsky, in praising no end the classics' "ludicity" and "logic"—against the lies of romanticism! But then, why not, since "truth does not indicate a contrary to error, but the position of certain errors relative to other ones" (*Kröner*, XIII, § 204)? If life feeds on illusion ("error, mother of what is alive": *Kröner*, XII, § 44), if error is present "in all life" (*WP*, § 544), if truth itself is a "type of error" (*WP*, § 493), then a "truth" can stay possible (even if it is yet another error!) at least as adequacy to the flow of vital illusions, as faithfulness to the great lie of the living.

　　Perhaps. There is a knot here, that between knowledge and life: "Life is the condition of knowledge; error is the condition of life, I mean to say fundamental error" (*Kröner*, XII, § 89). Thus error is the precondition for knowledge and (since truth is never anything other than an error we believe in; cf. *WP*, §§ 493, 520) its only content. Concerning aesthetics, Luc Ferry has untangled this knot more or less well: I refer the reader to him.[79] But I will not follow Ferry when, apropos of Nietzsche, he speaks of a *hyperclassicism*—even if he then adds that it is a "hyperclassicism of difference." It is partly a quarrel about words, but I love the classics too much to compromise when it comes to this word. What is classicism, if it isn't, in art, the cult of reason, of truth, of measure? And what are Dionysian aesthetics, if not, on the contrary, the cult of intoxication, of illusion and unmeasure?

In his book on *Classical Art,* François-Georges Pariset distinguishes between "two options," one common to the Baroque and to romanticism, the other characteristic of classicism: "On one side élan vital, irrational forces, instinct, the subconscious, disquiet, anguish, jubilation, ecstasy . . . on the opposite side, classicism."[80] And he naturally, and legitimately, calls up the Nietzschean distinction between "Dionysian fervor" and "Apollonian balance."[81] That Nietzsche's taste may have often—in fact, more and more so—been contrary to his aesthetics is his problem; his love of the "great style" can't cancel out his repeated celebration of art as the "cult of error" (*GS,* 107) and antidote to truth (*WP,* § 822). I have already cited his terrible formulation: "We possess *art* lest we *perish of the truth.*"[82] A classicist would evidently say the opposite: we have art in order to *live* from the truth!

It may be objected to this that these two formulations come together in the end; but that is only apparently so. For Nietzsche, art is the illusion that protects from the true; for the classics and classicists, it is that little piece of truth that leads to the large one—not what protects us from the true, but what reveals it. The problem is not merely an aesthetic one, or else this aesthetics includes philosophy. If philosophy is an art, as Nietzsche taught and as I believe, its destiny is to be found in this choice between mendaciousness and truth, between illusion and knowledge. Philosophers, if they want to live up to their name, can only choose truth.

And if life itself were at stake? Even if that were the case, philosophy is philosophy (and not sophistics) only if it keeps up its requirements: better a truth that kills (under the condition, need it be made explicit, that it kill only me) than a lie that makes us live. But, fortunately, the choice does not always, nor often, present itself in those terms. What art reminds us of so magnificently, against disillusionment, dread, or fatigue, is that truth can also make us live—that is what classics and classicists called beauty.

In a fragment I have already referred to, Nietzsche, having evoked the solidarity between life and error, throws out his big formula, which could perhaps do as maxim for a Baroque aesthetics but that a classicist could never accept: *"Art in the service of illusion—that is our cult"* (*Kröner,* XII, § 89). There it is. Aesthetes are the sophists of the beautiful—philosophers, the artists of the true. Nietzsche is an aesthete.

Just one more word. A name.

This text is dedicated to the memory of Etty Hillesum, who had every quality to make Nietzsche dislike her: woman, Jew, democrat, a little bit socialist no doubt, and, at the end, almost Christian. But, to love life, to find it beautiful, she didn't need art or lies. Love and truth were enough for her. How she got that way is what she relates in her *Diary,*[83] for which I would unhesitatingly exchange *Ecce Homo, The Antichrist,* and all of *The Will to Power.* She kept her *Diary* from 1941 to 1943 in occupied Holland, as close as possible to the horror, as close as possible also to the sublime, to the only sublime: courage without hatred and love without hope. This woman revalued no values, did not live beyond good and evil, did not will power. She died at Auschwitz on November 30, 1943. "One Jew more or less," the Nazis used to say, "what does it matter?"

And I could also have dedicated this text to the memory—as if it still needed holding up!—of Jean Cavaillès, the "philosopher packed with explosives, this intrepid lucid man, this committed man without optimism."[84] How ridiculous Nietzsche's ramblings about cowardly and plebeian logic look, next to a single true hero, who knew what *thinking* means, who knew that one does not kid with logic or with morality! Everyone chooses his masters. I, who am not a logician, I, who am not Jewish, I, who am not Christian (and I, who am not a hero!), I've chosen—against Nietzsche and, even more so, against the blond or brown brutes—these two gentle intransigents as patrons: the Jewish saint and the logician hero.

Do we need to come back to Nietzsche? The question was: why aren't you a Nietzschean? The answer—but I needed all these pages to make it intelligible—is: because I like neither brutes, nor sophists, nor aesthetes. Nietzsche is no doubt not only that: he is *also* a philosopher, and an artist, and he is full of an exquisite delicacy. My goal was not to exhaust Nietzsche's thought—like any great manner of thinking, it is inexhaustible—nor to invalidate it completely. On the contrary. With him I have, as I have said, many points of agreement, perhaps more numerous (but less decisive) than our differences, and I contest neither his genius nor his greatness. But is that enough?

For the rest, every philosophy is irrefutable, and especially when it is a sophistical one. Anyone who wants to is thus free to be a Nietzschean—and I don't doubt that one can want this for good reasons. It is up to the Nietzscheans to explain themselves about this if they wish. But we who believe in neither prophets nor overmen, we who admire neither Cesare Borgia nor Napoléon (but Rousseau, oh yes!), we who hate the "men after prey," we, the disciples of Etty Hillesum and of Jean Cavaillès, those "committed . . . without optimism," those human beings of strength without hardness ("to become inured," Etty said, "not to become hardened"), we the faithful—and, let it be said in passing, entirely *philo*-Semitic!   we who know nothing more human than the Christ (which is why we are atheists: what would a God have to do with it?), nothing more praiseworthy than the morality of the Gospels, we who are neither barbaric nor brutal (and it isn't our fault if some of us are blond), we the gentle, we the merciful, we the peaceful (but certainly not nonviolent), we who love the woman within us more than the warrior, we who have not *canonized* our laughter—and who therefore laugh even better!—we who believe in an eternity without recurrence and without parallel (in becoming), we who are not the premature births of any future but are the children of the entire past, we who do not confuse value and truth (we who have renounced believing true everything we desire but have not renounced the desire for truth!), we who love the true more than the beautiful, the real more than art and art more than the aesthetes, we who believe in science and in reason, we the classicists (art in the service of truth: that is our cult!), we the rationalists, we who continue from Socrates and the Enlightenment—and, especially, we, disciples of Epicurus and of Spinoza!—we who prefer knowledge to interpretation, history to genealogy (and the question *"What is . . . ?"* to the question *"Who . . . ?"*), we who never find ourselves to be *too* human, we who seek to overturn no values (and especially not the Judeo-Christian ones), we who came not to abolish but to accomplish, not to destroy but to continue, we who do not philosophize with a hammer (or only against those who wield them!), we who want not power but love, not force but justice, we the *superior men,* as he would have said, and who don't care what he would have said (we who are not terrified by despair, nor reassured by contempt), we who can stand élitism only if it is a republican one, we democrats, we progressives, we who are—who want to be!—on the side of the weak and of the slaves, we who respect foreigners even more than we do our compatriots, we *good Europeans* but also citizens of the world, we who do not want to *overcome* man—especially not that—we who are wary of intoxication and the passions, we the Apollonians, we the civilized, who try to be more or less moral (always *between* good and evil), we the enemies of the wicked and of sophists, we the friends of wisdom and of good people, we who try to be good, just, and truthful—why would we be Nietzschean?

NOTES

Bibliographical note. References to Nietzsche's works are most often given within the text itself. They refer, as far as possible, to the works' internal divisions (books, parts, paragraphs) and, as far as the quotations are concerned, to English translations or editions. Where published English translations are unacceptable or misleading in context, translations here are from, and citations are to, the French editions used by the author. Unattributed translations are by Robert de Loaiza.

AC   *The Antichrist.* Trans. Walter Kaufmann. In *The Portable Nietzsche.* New York: Penguin Books, 1968 (1st ed. 1954).

BT   *The Birth of Tragedy.* Trans. Walter Kaufmann. In *Basic Writings of Nietzsche.* New York: Random House, Modern Library Giant, 1968.

BGE   *Beyond Good and Evil.* Trans. Walter Kaufmann. New York: Random House, 1966.

CI   *Le crépuscute des idoles.* Trans. H. Albert. Paris: Mercure de France, 1970.

CW   *The Case of Wagner.*

D   *Daybreak (Morgenröte).* In Friedrich Nietzsche, *Sämtliche Werke. Kritische Studienausgabe,* vol. 3. Ed. Giorgio Colli and Mazzino Montinari. Berlin: Walter de Gruyter, 1967–77 and 1988.

EH   *Ecce Homo.* Trans. Walter Kaufmann. In *The Genealogy of Morals and Ecce Homo.* New York: Vintage Books, 1967.

GM   *The Genealogy of Morals.* Trans. Walter Kaufmann. See *EH.*

GS   *The Gay Science.* Trans. Walter Kaufmann. New York: Vintage Books, 1974.

HAH   *Human, All-Too-Human.* In *Sämtliche Werke,* vol. 3 (see *D*).
Kröner   *Nietzsches Werke.* Leipzig: C. G. Naumann/A. Kröner Verlag, 1895–1913. First collection of Nietzsche's works.
NCW   *"Nietzsche contra Wagner."* In *The Portable Nietzsche* (see *AC*).
PTE   "Philosophy in the Tragic Epoch of the Greeks." In *Sämtliche Werke,* vol. 1 (see *D*).
TI   *Twilight of the Idols.* Trans. Walter Kaufmann. In *The Portable Nietzsche* (see *AC*).
VP   *La volonté de puissance.* Trans. G. Bianquis, 2 vols.
WP   *The Will to Power.* Trans. Walter Kaufmann and R. J. Hollingdale. New York: Random House, 1967.
Z   *Thus Spoke Zarathustra.* Trans. Walter Kaufmann. In *The Portable Nietzsche* (see *AC*).

1. Karl Jaspers, *Nietzsche: An Introduction to the Understanding of his Philosophical Activity.* Tr. Charles F. Wallraff and Frederich J. Schmitz, Tucson: University of Arizona Press, 1965 [1935], p. 10. Cioran makes the same remark: Nietzsche "manages to vary his unbalances. On everything, he has upheld the for and the against" (*Syllogisme de l'amertume,* Paris: Gallimard, coll. "Idées," 1976, p. 45).

2. See, for instance, *TI,* "The Problem of Socrates"; *GS,* 348, 370; and *WP,* § 431 ff. See also my article, "Nietzsche et Spinoza," in the published colloquium *Nietzsche et le judaïsme,* under the direction of D. Bourel and J. Le Rider, Paris: Le Cerf, 1991.

3. Jean Granier, *Le problème de la vérité dans la philosophie de Nietzsche,* Paris: Éditions du Seuil, 1966, new ed. 1969, p. 11.

4. Jacques Derrida, *Otobiographies: L'enseignement de Nietzsche et la politique du nom propre.* Paris: Galilée, 1984, p. 60. ("Otobiographies: The Teaching of Nietzsche and the Politics of the Proper Name." In *The Ear of the Other: Otobiography, Transference, Translation.* Ed. Christie McDonald. Lincoln: University of Nebraska Press, 1988).

5. François George, "D'un critère nouveau en philosophie," *L'Ame et le corps.* Collective work under the direction of M.-P. Haroche, Paris: Plon, 1990.

6. Vladimir Jankélévitch, *L'imprescriptible,* Paris: Éditions du Seuil, 1986, p. 52.

7. *EH,* "Why I Am a Destiny," 1. References to Nietzsche's works will from now on be given in the text itself, using the abbreviations given above in the bibliographical note. Unless otherwise stated, italics are by Nietzsche.

8. V. Jankélévitch, p. 55.

9. C. Widmer, in *Le journal de Genève.*

10. Especially Gilles Deleuze's: see for example *Nietzsche and Philosophy,* trans. Hugh Tomlinson. New York, Columbia University Press, 1983 [1962], and *Spinoza: Philosophie pratique,* Paris: Éditions de Minuit, 1981 which includes the material of the small *Spinoza* (Paris: Presses Universitaires de France, 1970).

11. On the sense of this expression, see my *Traité du désespoir et de la béatitude* (Treatise on despair and beatitude), vol. II, *Vivre*. Paris: Presses Universitaires de France, 1988, ch. 4, pp. 93–101 (and especially p. 97).

12. See *TI*, "The Case of Socrates," 3.

13. On Socrates' *daimon,* cf. *BT,* 13.

14. *Syllogisme de l'amertume,* p. 45.

15. As Nietzsche himself put it, in a letter to Peter Gast, April 21, 1886.

16. See Clément Rosset, "Notes sur Nietzsche," *La force majeure,* Paris: Éditions de Minuit, 1983, p. 31 ff.

17. For example *GS,* 377; *BGE,* 257 ff.; *GM,* II, 17.

18. For example *GM,* I, 13, and II, 6–7, or *WP,* 684.

19. *HAH,* I, 444; *AC,* 2; *TI,* "Skirmishes of an Untimely Man," 38; *Z,* I, "On War and Warriors" and "On Little Old and Young Women."

20. *BGE,* 265; *TI,* "Skirmishes of an Untimely Man," 35, 37; *EH,* "Why I Am a Destiny," 7.

21. *ET,* 13; *TI,* "The Case of Socrates"; *EH,* "Birth of Tragedy," 1; *WP,* 430, 440.

22. *BT,* passim; *GS,* 370; *BGE,* 198.

23. *EH,* "Why I Am So Clever," 1, and "Why I Am a Destiny," 8. See also Michel Onfray, *Le ventre des philosophes,* Paris: Grasset, 1989, ch. 6.

24. *AC,* 46. I am speaking here about the Christ of the Gospels; Nietzsche does occasionally dream about another one, who would have nothing to do with the Gospels or with Christianity but would be a sort of Nietzschean forerunner.

25. Compare *BGE,* 197, *AC,* 61, and *TI,* "Skirmishes of an Untimely Man," 37 (about Cesare Borgia), with *BGE,* 25 (about Giordano Bruno).

26. *TI,* "Skirmishes," 48. See also, on Napoleon ("the incarnate noble ideal par excellence, synthesis of the inhuman and the superhuman"), *GM,* I, 16, *D,* 245, and *BGE,* 199. On Rousseau ("This miscarriage, couched on the threshold of modern times"): *TI,* ibid.; *WP,* 98, 100, 1021.

27. *WP,* 685.

28. *EH,* "Why I Am a Destiny," 5 ff., and *Z,* passim. See also *WP,* § 98.

29. *HAH,* I, 439–40; *TI,* "The 'Improvers' of Mankind," 3; *Kröner,* XIV, 1st part, § 459; *WP,* 960.

30. *WP,* 732–34, *Kröner,* XI, 2d part, § 510, and XII, 1st part, § 404.

31. *BGE,* 200, 208, 213, 264; *GM,* I, 5 and 11; *TI,* "The 'Improvers' of Mankind," 4.

32. *GS,* 377; *BGE,* 257, 258.

33. *GM,* I, 11; *HAH,* I, 444.

34. *HAH,* I, 438; *BGE,* 202; *Z,* IV, "On the Higher Man".

35. *BGE,* 258–59; *GM,* III, 14; *WP,* 209.

36. *BGE,* 62; *AC.*

37. *BGE,* 232, 238, 239; *Z,* I, "On Little Old and Young Women."

38. *BGE,* 202, 203, 242, 261; *GM,* I, 5 and 16.

39. "Nietzsche et Spinoza" (cf. n. 2).

40. See S. Goyard-Fabre, *Nietzsche et la question politique*. Paris: Sirey, 1977, pp. 19–22, especially nn. 16 and 31: "When Nietzsche came across the *Essay on the Inequality of Human Races* (published, for its first part, in 1853, its second in 1855), he became enthusiastic about Gobineau's ideas." See also p. 50, n. 62.

41. *GM*, I, 11. After hoping (in *The Birth of Tragedy*) that the German genius would be "strong enough and pure enough to shake off the foreign elements it has been penetrated with and that it will remember its own nature" (*BT*, 23), Nietzsche came to despair of modern Germans (who decidedly had nothing in common with the "ancient Germanic tribes": *GM*, I, 11) and to put hope in nothing outside the selective effects of his own thought (*WP*, 1053–58) and eugenics (ibid., 732–34).

42. See for instance *Z*, II, "On Poets": " 'Since I have come to know the body better,' Zarathustra said to one of his disciples, 'the spirit is to me only quasi-spirit; and all that is "permanent" is also a mere parable.' "

43. That is, following Heidegger, the spirit of Mme. Goyard-Fabre's book (which is nonetheless quite rich and useful): see especially, op. cit., prologue, pp. 30–35, 156–68. See also, in Heidegger's inexhaustible book, the disappointing passage on "Nietzsche's supposed biologism" (*Nietzsche*, xxx): "When Nietzsche conceives of beings in their totality and before that Being as 'life,' and he determines man in particular as rapacious, he is not thinking biologically but grounding this apparently biological image of the world metaphysically." Heidegger did recognize that this indication "does not do away with the appearance that Nietzsche thinks strongly and exclusively in a biological sense."

44. *Kröner*, XIV, 2, § 215. See also *WP*, 582, as well as *GM*, III, 16. What Y. Quiniou writes in his *Problèmes du matérialisme* (Paris: Méridiens Klincksieck, 1987), ch. 6 ("Nietzsche matérialiste") needs to be greatly nuanced.

45. *WP*, 582. What I call Nietzsche's *vitalism* is thus characterized by the fact that, as Heidegger writes (*Nietzsche*): " 'Life' according to Nietzsche is a term equivalent to that of Being." I have elsewhere shown that materialism, in its most radical tradition, teaches on the contrary that Being is on the side of death, or, to speak more precisely, that life is not its essence but its accident (not the rule but the exception): see my article "Qu'est-ce que le matérialisme?" in *Une education philosophique*, Paris: Presses Universitaires de France, 1989, p. 86 ff.

46. On Boscovitch, see *Kröner*, XIV, 2, § 215. On animality in Nietzsche, see Heidegger's pertinent remarks in *Nietzsche*. Interpreting, as is well known, Nietzsche's philosophy as a "metaphysics of subjectivity," Heidegger notes that "for Nietzsche, subjectivity is absolute insofar as it is a subjectivity of the body, meaning of impulsions and affects, meaning of the Will to Power," from which it follows that "in Nietzsche's metaphysics it is *animalitas* that becomes the guiding thread." Heidegger adds: "The unconditional essence of subjectivity therefore necessarily develops as the *brutalitas* of the *bestialitas*. At the end of metaphysics we find the proposition: *Homo est brutum bestiale*. Nietzsche's ex-

pression 'the blond brute' is not a fortuitous exaggeration, but the term that characterizes a sequence in which Nietzsche consciously places himself without thereby discerning its relations of a historical nature."

47. *BGE,* 230. This project, which was already taken up by Spinoza and will be again by the social sciences (we find the same or very similar expressions in Durkheim, Freud, Lévi-Strauss) seems to me obviously legitimate, but it is a purely theoretical project (it has to do only with the true) from which we cannot consequently draw a morality—or an immoralism.

48. *Z,* I, prologue, 3 and passim. On the notion of practical humanism, and the opposition from this point of view between Nietzsche and Spinoza, see my *Traité du désespoir et de la béatitude,* II, *Vivre,* ch. 4, p. 135 ff.

49. On what I mean by *fidelity,* see my article in the publication *Autrement* ("La fidélité"), Paris, 1990.

50. Clément Rosset, *Le réel (Traité de l'idiotie),* Paris: Éditions de Minuit, 1977, p. 81 ff. (p. 99 for the quoted expressions).

51. *La force majeure,* p. 28.

52. In the famous preface to the *Contribution to a Critique of Political Economy.*

53. In the preface I wrote for the French edition of the correspondence of an Indian sage of this century: S. Prajnânpad, *Les yeux ouverts,* L'Originel, 1989.

54. See *BGE,* 153: "What is done out of love is always beyond good and evil."

55. Spinoza, *Theologico-Political Treatise,* chap. 4. See my *Vivre,* p. 138 and n. 1.

56. *Theologico-Political Treatise,* chap. 14.

57. Spinoza, letter 43 to J. Osten.

58. *Theologico-Political Treatise,* chap. 14.

59. Ibid. On the role of the Christic model in Spinoza, we must once again refer to the troubling and magisterial work by A. Matheron, *Le Christ et le salut des ignorants chez Spinoza.* Paris: Aubier-Montaigne, 1971.

60. Quoted by M. Conche, *Pyrrhon ou l'apparence.* Villers-sur-Mer: Éditions de Mégare, 1973, p. 112.

61. Quoted by M. Conche, p. 31.

62. Pascal, *Pensées,* 521–387, ed. Lafuma.

63. Ibid.

64. See also, we could say, *The Gay Science* in its entirety, for, as Clément Rosset has remarked, *The Gay Science* "is a *science,*" and "Nietzschean gaiety" implies therefore "a form of knowledge in the most intellectual and theoretical sense of the expression" (*La force majeure,* p. 67). But how, if nothing is true and nothing can be known?

65. See for example *WP,* §§ 428–29. The praise of the Sophists culminates in this charming appreciation: "The Sophists were Greeks: when Socrates and Plato took up the cause of virtue and justice, they were *Jews* or I know not what" (§ 429).

66. See my exposé on "La volonté cynique" (Cynical will), Actes du colloque de Caen, *L'aethique et le droit à l'age démocratique*, "Cahiers de philosophie politique et juridique," 1991.

67. *L'âme et le corps*, p. 185. But, as F. George remarks, "reason of health is not reason any more than 'reason of State' is."

68. Eugen Fink, *Nietzsches Philosophie*, Stuttgart: Kohlhammer Verlag, 1979, esp. pp. 14, 185–86.

69. Ibid., p. 185.

70. "My philosophy is an *inverted Platonism*," Nietzsche claimed back in the 1870–71 period, in a fragment cited by Heidegger.

71. "La volonté cynique" (see note 66).

72. *La force majeure*, p. 69.

73. *Le problème de la vérité*, p. 606.

74. *La force majeure*, pp. 32–33.

75. *Nietzsche*. See, on this subject, the outstanding analyses by Alain Renaut, *L'ère de l'individu*, Paris: Gallimard, 1989, p. 210 ff.; and by Luc Ferry, *Homo Aestheticus*. Paris: Grasset, 1990, ch. 5.

76. On Cavaillès, see the moving pamphlet by Georges Canguilhem, *Vie et mort de Jean Cavaillès*, Les carnets de Baudasser, 81340 Ambialet, 1984. See also my article "Jean Cavaillès ou l'héroïsme de la raison" (Jean Cavaillès, or the heroism of reason), *Une éducation philosophique*, p. 287 ff.

77. *Nietzsche et la philosophie*, p. 117. The same observation is made by Jean Granier: for Nietzsche, "art is, in effect, nothing other than the sanctification of illusion and lying" (*Le problème de la vérité*, p. 521).

78. Fragment 794, cited by Heidegger.

79. *Homo Aestheticus*, chap. 5.

80. F.-G. Pariset, *L'art classique*, Paris: Presses Universitaires de Frances, 1965, p. 15.

81. Ibid., p. 16.

82. *WP*, § 822.

83. Etty Hillesum, *Une vie bouleversée, Journal* (1941–1943), Paris: Éditions du Seuil, 1985. I have already had the opportunity to say a few words about this book in the preface I wrote for S. Prajnânpad's correspondence (see note 53), pp. 27–29.

84. As George Conguilhem says, p. 38.

3 Nietzsche's French Moment

VINCENT DESCOMBES

NIETZSCHE IN PARIS

There has thrice been a French moment for Nietzsche: among writers at the end of the last century, among certain "nonconformist" intellectuals of the period between the wars, and, lately, among philosophers at the time of the decline of the currents of thought that had dominated the postwar period (such as existentialism and Marxism, and, later on, structuralism). I use the word *moment* here in its etymological sense of a potential to move or displace things and not in that of a small period of time. I am very far from reducing Nietzsche's influence in France to a limited episode. As a remark of Lachelier's, reproduced by André Lalande,[1] informs us, the confusion in French between the temporal and the mechanical senses of *moment* comes from the "misinterpretation that, during the winter of 1870–71, Parisians made of the expression attributed to M. de Bismarck: *psychological moment of bombardment* (that is to say the bombardment as acting upon the morale of the besieged, leading to capitulation)." That is, I believe, the use made of Nietzsche's work by French writers, intellectuals, and philosophers. This oeuvre, so often intent on treating problems internal to German culture, does indeed have a French moment. When our authors call upon it, it is less to cite its analyses or hypotheses than to produce some effect on the reader's morale. Unlike the bombardment of Paris by "M. de Bismarck," the goal here is not to terrify individuals: it is, on the contrary, to mobilize them and exalt them. One could say, to be more exact, that the expected effect of the Nietzschean moment on the French reader should be to "subvert the morale" of instituted bodies (churches, institutions) and mass organizations (political parties) in order to "buck up" the morale of individuals, thereby liberated from all subjection to transcendent laws or authorities.

We can already foresee what the inevitable limit will be of this moment of "Nietzscheanism" *à la française*. The public engagements inspired by it emanate from intellectuals and mobilize the cultured milieu above all. They take place in avant-garde publications, preferably confidential, or in colloquia, willingly esoteric. We are obviously very far from the "great politics" and the "strategic thinking" on a planetary scale that had been announced.

An ideal portrait of the French "Nietzschean" should include the following traits: an intense awareness of the era's conflictual background; awareness also of the moral and spiritual dangers inherent in the different militant positions among which his historical period is torn; external signs, finally, of a resolute commitment within the ongoing conflict, but a commitment that must be called paradoxical because it reveals itself to be intransitive or undecidable. It is a militant (or "warrior") pose, but one that is outside any identifiable camp. Indeed, the external signs of participation in combat issued by the French Nietzschean are all negative as long as the subject is politics. They become positive only when one has to take a stand not on a political line but on principles of individual morality. Thus, the intellectual touched by the Nietzschean moment will be *against* fascist movements, without for all that accepting being *for* one of their adversaries, liberal democracy or the communist movement. Affirmation can only declare itself in an entirely different sphere, that of a pure freedom of thought against a background of utopian community.

We can here point to the case of the now celebrated group around the Collège de sociologie. When this group, in a declaration on the Munich accords, lets it be known that it aspires to be a "source of energy" and not a mere "society of thought," it gives the forces it wishes to mobilize no point of application except the refusal of everything. This declaration, meant to be political, ends on a surrealist gesture of inaugural rupture. The Collège, we read,

invites those to whom anguish has revealed that the only answer is the creation of a vital bond among men to join it, excluding any determination other than the consciousness of the *absolute mendaciousness* of current political forms and of the need to reconstitute through principle a collective mode of existence that ignores all geographical and social constraints and which permits a little dignity when death threatens.[2]

This appeal, as we can see, is directed to people brought together by the perspective of death but not of the tomb. It is sent by pure "existents" to other "existents." Following existentialist doctrines, one dies alone, where we would have to accept a community too obviously limited in its humanity to be able to lie with one's own. Death is no doubt the common lot, but it affects only particular beings. The abstract universality of the *self,* to be radically affirmed, demands that death be despoiled of its human, but particularistic, meanings (funeral rites, cult of the dead). The Collège de sociologie's political stance is here reduced to a sort of millenarian existentialism, whose echo is still found after the war in certain of Maurice Blanchot's writings.[3]

Philosophy and Rhetoric

In what follows I will deal only with the contemporary Nietzschean moment. It is different from the preceding ones because of the place philosophers have within it. The high point of what can be called French-style "Nietzscheanism" was the ten-day colloquium at Cerisy-la-Salle in 1972.[4]

With this labeling as an ism, in quotation marks, I describe here neither Nietzsche's own thinking, richer and more varied, nor the particular elaboration of this or that interpreter, often more complexly articulated, but a general configuration of common axioms and typical moods making up this basis, this background, this terrain on which the philosophical sects eager not to be confused with the others will thereafter confront each other. I shall not go into the disputes, internal to "Nietzscheanism," between Nietzscheans of Heideggerian obedience, Nietzscheans arriving from Marxism, Romantic Nietzscheans, Nietzschean men of the pen, Nietzschean metaphysicians, etc.

The "Nietzscheanism" that concerns me here is a philosophy that intends to count as such. It seems, therefore, if we are to speak of it properly, that we should leave intellectual history (or history of ideas) to one side and proceed to philosophical examination. The problem is that it's obvious that the movement from history to philosophy is precisely what the "Nietzschean" philosophers call into question. For them, the method to be followed in a philosophical examination is exactly that of intellectual history: Who said that? Who speaks in this text—the individual author, or the institution? Who is seeking to assert himself by saying this? And against whom? What sentiments underlie this or that way of reasoning?

Nevertheless, the "Nietzschean" philosophers do not intend to purely and simply give up philosophical questions and dedicate themselves from now on only to historical studies. They intend to pursue philosophy by way of and with the means of history. In other words, they invite us to translate questions about the *meaning* of human thoughts into questions about the *origin* and the *value* of assertions made within the vital combat. The point should be stressed, because this movement from the philosophical towards the "genealogical" and "strategic" is too often presented as an opening certain philosophers are supposedly making towards the historians. There is indeed here a movement of philosophers towards history, one that, more generally, partakes of modern historicism, but it is a movement of conquest and not of acknowledgment. The historicist philosophers are not inviting us to read the works of historians (work probably written by authors full of the traditional prejudice according to which historiography is not to be confused with philosophy). They are announcing that philosophy books must from now on be written like history books.

It would be a mistake to see here a vulgar little corporatist quarrel about borders between learned societies. The point is well and truly philosophical. If a distinction is to be maintained between history of ideas and philosophy, it is so that we can make a distinction between an argument's success and its content. The distinction passes between two meanings of what is called an argument's *force:* (1) the power it has, under certain conditions, to mobilize the mental forces of the public it is presented to (power which is, precisely, its "psychological moment"); and (2) the power it has to logically generate diverse consequences (the power that its "meaning" consists of, in the philosophical use of the term).

Now: the "Nietzschean" philosophers object that this distinction amounts to denying the fact of rhetoric. For, say they, rhetoric is a fact. There is, for every discourse, an *ethos* and a *pathos,* a polemical aim and a psychological moment. That there is a rhetoric to every discourse, including philosophical discourse, cannot be denied by "Platonist" philosophers at the level of fact, only at the level of value. They decide, out of idealization, that we should abstract it out, that we should act as if philosophy could be purified of every effect of seduction and theatralization.

Plato, of course, is himself the greatest of rhetoricians and men of theater. But the "Platonists" have decided to ignore that. They are therefore authentic philosophers when it comes to their psychological type (this abstraction, this idealization, is indeed what we expect to find in philosophers). Yet they are, at the same time, inauthentic philosophers or philosophers divided against themselves: for the psychological type of the philosopher, characterized, if we wish to admit it, by the "will to truth," should lead him to accept that the truth of philosophy resides in rhetoric.

The objection is, apparently, a strong one. Who would want to deny that there is indeed a rhetoric of philosophy? That there is, in other words, a veritable *history* of philosophical ideas, something entirely different, therefore, from a mere "temporal manifestation" of the timeless articulation of the Logos. But the objection draws its force from the intense dispute between "Platonists" and "Nietzscheans." The two camps accept as a given a degrading, *immoralist,* definition of rhetoric. If arguments have something rhetorical about them, then they are masks for the will to win. Either it is reason that speaks (without rhetoric), or else it is the reign of persuasion through seduction, emotion, and prejudices disguised as "reasons." But why shouldn't reason speak in the forms of rhetoric? "Platonism" and "Nietzscheanism," hostile brothers, forget this: that there exists a *philosophy of rhetoric.* Its principle, as we can see in Aristotle, is to examine discourses of justification from the point of view of their rationality (thus, philosophically). The rhetorical art, conceived of this way, is quite different from the semblance of art that smooth talkers pretend to have, conceiving of rhetoric as they do as the assured production of *effects* by way of signs ("meaning effect," "truth effect," etc.). False semblance of art, authentic practical nonknowledge, since the efficiency of its recipes is doubtful.

The philosophy of rhetoric reestablishes the difference between a good and a bad oratorical proof, so that we see, on the terrain of rhetoric itself, the antithesis cited earlier between reason as argument and reason as instrument, between meaning and moment, come up again. We find thus once again the need to distinguish between the historical production of effects and the logical generation of consequences.

The refusal to make this distinction leads to positing an equivalence between effects and consequences. Every equivalence is, of course, read both ways. Consequences will be spoken of in terms of effects: logic will be made historical, will be interrogated for its "genealogy." But, inevitably, effects will also be spoken of in terms of consequences, so that history will be rendered logical. The philosophers of "Nietzscheanism" had declared that they were going to introduce *force* and *effect* within the *concept* (program to "overturn Platonism"). They had not said that this would amount to introducing the logic of concepts into the physics of forces and into the psychology of affects. But, as we shall see further on, this is what would happen. The a priori philosophy of history has never been in finer shape than in the age of "Nietzscheanism."

A FALSE GOOD IDEA

"Nietzscheanism" comes about as the attempt to solve within the forms of philosophy certain modern-day problems, problems that will be called *ideological* if we wish to emphasize their political dimension and *cultural* if we stress rather the ends and values at stake. But it isn't necessary to subscribe to the philosophy of "Nietzscheanism" in order to judge these problems to be serious ones. I believe the answers given by French-style "Nietzscheanism" should be rejected because they are philosophically incoherent. But I do not thereby conclude that they are answers to false questions—only that they are badly conceived answers, in uselessly mannered or desperately confused terms. It is appropriate that we recognize the presence of these problems behind the formulations of French "Nietzscheanism."

As is generally known, this family of ideas made its official debut on the philosophical scene when Nietzsche's name was joined to those of Marx and Freud to create the corpus of reference of philosophers opposed to what has been called "philosophy of consciousness." This last label covers, in practice, the doctrines of traditional idealism and those of the more recent schools of phenomenology. Sartre as well as Alain, Merleau-Ponty as well as Léon Brunschvicg, are philosophers of consciousness. To these philosophers of consciousness were opposed the philosophers of interpretation, those whom Ricoeur has called the "masters of suspicion" and who are united by a vague general orientation expressed by formulas such as the "decentering of the subject," the "symptomal" reading of language, and the critique of "false consciousness."

But, to be honest, this grouping of three thinkers into one three-headed authority looks like the very example of the false good idea. Thinking is, from its very starting point, committed to following a false track, that of a supposed antithesis between the viewpoint of the *cogito* and that of a *critique of consciousness (critique de la conscience)*. The only conceivable reason for such an opposition is to be found in the French word *conscience*. It so happens that the French tongue does not make a distinction—as English and German do—between moral conscience (*Gewissen, conscience*) and "consciensiosity" (*Bewußtsein, consciousness*).[5]

The suspiciousness of the philosophers of interpretation has to do with the motives for human behavior, motives Nietzsche calls "sentiments" when he sets out to find their origins. And Nietzsche here only takes up again, as he himself says, the theme of moralists (in particular French ones) clever at unmasking the self-conceit (*amour-propre*) behind our generous feelings. What is doubtful, what is the object of suspicion, is that the official motivation, the one the agent himself puts forward, is the real one. Contrary to what *moralizing* authors (such as Sartre) maintain, it is not necessary for the agent to be in *bad faith* for his self-interested motives to be disguised as the pure spirit of justice and benevolence. From the point of view of *moralist* writers, authors of "characters" in comedies or novels, it is more truthful to present a character convinced of the nobility of his sentiments at the very moment he is moved by jealousy, envy, or vanity. A moral swindle is psychologically more perfect and truer when it is practiced, if one may say so, in good faith.

But a moral subject who receives no reproach from his (moral) conscience is not for all that the subject of a Cartesian consciousness, of a *cogito*. When we speak of an agent's conscious motivations, we do not mean that these motivations are present to his consciousness in a Cartesian mode, as *cogitationes*. It is not a requirement that the motive be a mental datum, an event in the subject's psychological life. In a Cartesian philosophy of mind, I cannot have a conscious motive of consciousness without the feeling that moves me being immediately offered up to the "regard of the mind" (*regard de l'esprit*). If I act out of anger, I must at every instant *know* that I am angry. My anger must even, in all rigor, be the object of a knowledge even more certain than my action itself. Between my action and my anger there is indeed this difference: my action is, in the final analysis, a movement of my body, whereas my anger is a *cogitatio,* a thought.

Remarkably, there is in Nietzsche himself a critique of the *ego cogito* philosophy, but it isn't a part of what Nietzsche calls "psychology." It is, as it should be, purely philosophical and consists in a discussion of the prejudice according to which thinking presupposes a thinker, therefore a *res cogitans.* What is for Descartes a self-evident first notion is disqualified by Nietzsche as a mere grammatical fact. Whatever may be thought about this point in metaphysics, we need only note that it calls for no "suspicion" in the sense discussed above. It is not a problem here of unmasking an agent's true sentiments, but of clearing up a problem of first philosophy.

But, then, is the whole quarrel between "philosophers of consciousness" and "philosophers of suspicion" based on an ambiguous use of the French word *conscience?* There is no doubt something else, namely the continuation of an ethical and political dispute *as if* it had to do with Descartes's *cogito,* with, precisely, metaphysics. We have to take into account here the presence within many minds of an eclectic combination of classic themes of modern philosophy (*cogito* principle, principle of the equivalence of Being and meaning in consciousness) and of human ideals that inspire the progressivist philosophy of history. This alliance is not based on a logical connection between speculative and practical positions, as if the formulation of the *cogito* should be seen as the first article in a doctrine of human rights and the universal Republic. It corresponds rather to the encounter, within the heads of French philosophers, between their preferences as philosophers and the values they share as citizens.

Where does the very idea of a Marx-Nietzsche-Freud triad come from? To find out, we can consult the proceedings of the first colloquium to have brought together "Nietzscheanism's" main representatives: the Nietzsche colloquium at Royaumont, held 4 through 8 July 1964.[6] At this colloquium, Michel Foucault dealt with this very subject, which had been suggested to him: Marx, Nietzsche, Freud. Why put them together? In his presentation, Foucault avoided the excessively easy *topos* of mystified consciousness and chose to present Marx, Nietzsche, and Freud as technicians of interpretation. Anticipating the argument of *The Order of Things,* he sought to find in the nineteenth century a mutation in the notion of signs to which the three authors had been witnesses.

We notice two things when reading Foucault's communication and the discussion that followed it. The three names that have been put forward do not have, for one thing, the same historical weight. Marx and, in certain ways, Freud are founders of an order. Their writings are used as references and legitimations by collective movements. Nietzsche, on the other hand, has remained a solitary figure. If you declare yourself to be a Marxist, you are expected to have not only opinions but also a political party. Psychoanalysts are in the same way quite right in pointing out that they have a practice within the framework of various associations, and not only ideas.

The quality of being a "Nietzschean," by contrast, allows one to take up a position on a contemporary scene characterized by what Foucault himself calls the "war of interpretations" without being subjected to the discipline of a political party or professional guild. A major difference will likewise distinguish Nietzschean interpretation from the ones that can be carried out in a Marxist or Freudian mode. In the two latter cases, there is inevitably a canonical interpretation, one that fixes the party "line" or the therapeutic practice's "orthodoxy." The Nietzschean interpretative mode radicalizes instead the hermeneutical idea, since it replaces the notion of correct or just interpretation by that of dominant interpretation.

A second, remarkable, point comes out of this. Gathering the three names together in a triumvirate of suspicion does not result in any equality. If we accept the idea of a war of interpretations we exclude the possibility of being Marxist *and* Freudian *and* Nietzschean. As Jean Wahl quite correctly pointed out after Foucault's presentation, "If Marx is right, Nietzsche should be interpreted as a phenomenon of the bourgeoisie at such and such a time. If Freud is right, we need to know Nietzsche's unconscious. So I see a sort of war between Nietzsche and the two others."[7]

But in reducing Marxist or Freudian science to the level of interpretations Nietzsche has already been given the advantage. In this trio, Marx and Freud look like hermeneutic clodhoppers. They interpret, just as Nietzsche does, but they still believe like the positivists that a true interpretation exists. And despite Foucault's efforts to make out in Marx and Freud an awareness of interpretation's *interminable* character, he doesn't really succeed in dissolving the robust realities of sex and of the class struggle into an infinite play of signs. He can at best discern, in Marx the historian and Freud the analyst of his own dreams, a presentiment of the thesis that only comes into its own in Nietzsche. This central thesis of French "Nietzscheanism" is expressed in three propositions in Foucault's text: 1) "Interpretation has become an infinite task"; 2) "If interpretation can never end, it is quite simple because there is nothing to interpret"; and 3) "Interpretation finds itself obligated to interpret itself infinitely."

Why does Foucault put this thesis forward as if indicating a joyful liberation, news about a "life of interpretation"? We could, at first, see worrying news here. What's so gay about announcing the epistemological impotence of the human sciences compared to natural sciences? Why should we feel freer to learn that the meaning we look for will never be found, that this meaning was not that of signs *given* to interpretation anyway (nothing is given) but nothing other than violence against older interpretations, meaning older cases of violence?

The motive for Foucault's jubilant reaction is to be found in the opposition he makes, in the vocabulary used in those years, between *hermeneutics* and *semiology*. Hermeneutics, by which he means the activity of infinite interpretation, represents the "life of interpretation." Semiology, which for him consists in interrupting the indefinite play of signs, is its death. According to Foucault, semiology is guilty of exercising a reign of terror on signs because it seeks to give a status of authority to what is only one interpretation. The ultimate aim of his presentation was therefore to find a way to escape dogmatism, to escape the "terror" of truth laid down by organizations given the power to do so. Behind Foucault's rather abstract variations on the theme, we end up hearing the political vocabulary of the 1950s: *dogmatism, orthodoxy, right to revisionism, exclusion.* A specific political experience (that of the cold war and of the de-Stalinization of opinions) has strangely set once and for all the sense of the word *truth*. To use the word *truth* would be dogmatic.

The radicalization of the notion of interpretation thus permits chasing the Marxist and the Freudian out of their critical positions. The accusers are accused in turn. They have, like inquisitors or police detectives, changed *signs* into *clues* or *indices* (to take up Foucault's opposition between signs offered up to endless interpretation and indices of a reality external to the play of signs). This distinction between a hermeneutics and a semiology truly does seem to draw its meaning from the indeed "dogmatic" episode of postwar French intellectual life. But the resistance to forced recruitment in "Nietzscheanism" takes, as we observe it, the grandiose form of a general theory of signs, with its ontology (there is nothing but interpretations, nothing to interpret that is not already an interpretation) and epistemology (there is no knowledge, nothing but discourses or dispositions of signs producing "truth effects").

Is this conception of language viable? If we take away the decorations around the way it is formulated, it boils down to a decision to homogenize the question of sense or meaning. It comes down to saying that there is one and only one passages from *signs* to *meaning*: interpretation. A crucial distinction is thereby lost: that between directly accessible meaning and meaning accessible only by inference. It is the difference between *understanding* and *interpreting*. The hermeneuticist whose philosophy is expressed by Foucault recognizes no difference between the *act* of interpreting, which is an intellectual operation by an active mind, and the fact of understanding, which is neither an act nor a performance but the possession of a *capacity*. This hermeneuticist takes a capacity to be an act and, like the fact of taking the Pireus to be a man, it is an error of category, therefore a metaphysical error. Or, as Wittgenstein would say, a grammatical misunderstanding. We may also note that the distinction in question is also overlooked by those hermeneuticists inspired not directly by Nietzsche but by Heidegger. For them, too, to understand is already to interpret.

The distinction in question will on the contrary be familiar to a reader of Wittgenstein. He will also see in this blindness to the difference between an act and a capacity of the mind the effect of an as yet unquestioned adherence to the Cartesian philosophy of *cogitatio*. For it is quite precisely in Cartesian philosophy of mind that the differences between acts, states, and capacities are erased in favor of the one and only *conscientia*.[9]

Is a person busy reading his ordinary newspaper, written in a normal fashion and in his mother tongue with a large readership in mind— is he thereby accomplishing a hermeneutical activity? In the normal case, one activity only is being carried out within this person: that of *reading,* in the ordinary, banal meaning of the term. There is no two-part process going on in this person: first, an activity of recognition of the printed signs, one after the other, on the printed page, and, then, accompanying this reading, a mental activity according meaning to these signs through interpretation.

But this double process does correspond rather well, at least as a first approximation, to what happens in the case of the decipherment of a text in a language the reader does not entirely master. The reader must, in that case, translate word for word and construct the sense. The hermeneuticist assimilates every understanding of what something means to the work we must do when, for instance, we have to translate into our language poems written in an ancient tongue, one we can therefore never really practice. A reading, to sum up, can take place in one of two ways: either through *understanding* (in the case of a nonhermetic text written in a language we read fluently, as the expression goes, by which is meant, quite precisely, without having to stop at every word) or through *interpreting*.

When we understand, understanding is not a mental episode parallel to the reading of the printed signs. It consists in the fact that we can, if we are asked to, summarize the article, react to its contents, comment on it, etc. If this capacity is missing, the reader has to simultaneously read the text and interpret it. Here, interpreting quite properly means formulating an explicative hypothesis about the text's organization. The philological interpretation of a text is an intellectually complex operation (as is its doctrinal or hermeneutic interpretation, the latter aiming at the text's application) that calls upon various competencies. In particularly difficult cases the interpreter will not hesitate to use colored crayons to mark up a sentence's possible constructions and aid him to make a choice among them. It's ridiculous to claim that such complex operations are always present even where they are not explicit, as in ordinary acts of conversation or reading.

We can easily verify that the rejection of the distinction between interpreting and understanding immediately brings about the appearance of those paradoxes that are "Nietzscheanism's" bread and butter. We would, for example, have to say that a text's author is, rather, its first translator and not really the author. Or we'd have to say that this translation comes from an original that is never at hand, that is always already lost, always already covered over with new strata.

This philosophy of omnipresent interpretation has yet another consequence. The same missed distinction between *reader* and *auditor* has also disappeared around *speakers*. When people talk about the *meaning* of their acts and gestures, they behave as if they were the inter-preters of a "text" that they are writing elsewhere by behaving as they do. Just like external observers, they are deciphering signs in order to sovereignly give them a meaning. At that point the very notion of anthropological knowledge is ruined. We cannot then, as a matter of fact, separate in what people say between what has to do with an under-standing of the rules (in other words, a *capacity* to follow them cor-rectly) and what manifests an attempt at interpretation on their part (dealing with aspects of their lives that remain obscure or strange to them). If we cannot make this distinction, we cannot seek to determine the meaning of human institutions either, whether they be our own in-stitutions or institutions foreign to our customs. Anthropological knowledge is obviously impossible if there isn't, in an ensemble of insti-tutions, something to understand, something we can call *the spirit of the laws*. Discerning this spirit means understanding the principles govern-ing the specific rules people follow. But for us to be able to aim at under-standing these principles, we have to presuppose that people *follow* those rules and that therefore they have a comprehensive knowledge of them. But the philosophy of endless interpretation is obligated to bring everything down to the same level: the apparent understanding that in-digenous peoples have of indigenous customs, the interpretation that indigenous theoreticians can give of these local customs, and finally the theories or interpretations that foreign visitors can give of the same as long as they have not understood them.

"Nietzscheanism" has on this matter forged an unnatural alliance in the 1960s with orthodox structuralism (an alliance that created what is called poststructuralism in the United States). Both schools of thought are as one in finding the point of view of the concerned subjects to be *suspect*. We may recall that orthodox structuralism, that of the early Lévi-Strauss, disqualified the indigenous viewpoint on institutions. Such a point of view expresses, according to Lévi-Strauss, only a "sub-jective incidence" of the social structure.[10] In philosophical terms, or-thodox structuralism criticized *consciousness* in the name of the *concept*. Indigenous peoples, it explained, have only theories about their institutions, of which they can grasp only fragments or effects. Only the scientific researcher can have access to the whole of the system and to its way of functioning.[11]

But poststructuralism disqualifies both indigenous explanations ("consciousness") and those of scientists (the "concept"). Within a positivist structuralist perspective, social actors do effectively meaningful things but they do not have an exact notion of what this meaning is. The meaning of their mores and customs is to be found in the system that the scientist reconstructs. The philosophy of interpretation is of course opposed to such positivism: no facts, nothing but interpretations. There is no sense or spirit to the institutions, but as many meanings as there are forces confronting one another in a struggle to take ahold of the system and give it a *dominant* signification. Yet, having given up on opposing concept to consciousness, the philosophy of interpretation maintains the separation between the subject of the action and the meaning of his action. The meaning of what people do is no longer to be found within social structures that are inaccessible to consciousness, and yet those people still don't know what they are doing nor why. They have only interpretations which they take to be veridical representations.

Poststructuralism extends orthodox structuralism on at least this: that there is no reason to take seriously what people have to say on what concerns them—which amounts to taking away their right to speak in order to give it to the experts. By the same token, the consequences of Nietzschean hermeneutics are not limited to epistemology. They reach as far as politics, and it has to be admitted that they are detestable. When he speaks of "war of interpretations," the philosopher acts as if there were a difference only in degree between armed conflict and a public debate. In the texts that have been influenced by "Nietzscheanism," we can observe an exaggerated use of heavily connoted words like *violence* and *terror.* Far from leading us to greater vigilance, the generalized use of such notions at every occasion in fact renders them banal.

We are, for example, told that every reading is interpretative and consequently "violent." But this "violence" of reading doesn't go any further than the impossibility of justifying a certain reading completely and on every point against a colleague's different reading. Thus, the philologist doing an explanation of a Heraclitus fragment will be said to be committing a "violent gesture" because he has decided that his text begins on this word and should be read in this way, which amounts to ("violently") excluding other possible readings. There will also be, for obvious reasons, a tendency to describe a lively public debate as if it were an embryonic civil war. But if there is supposed to be a continuity from learned controversy to public debate, and from the latter to war properly speaking, then why not acknowledge in civil war not the ruins of politics but their very essence, their most accomplished form, even?

RELATIONS OF FORCES

We can schematize "Nietzscheanism's" defining argument as follows. Its first movement is a critical one. Through (abusively) generalizing the notion of interpretation, this philosophy destroys the received idea that a meaning could, beyond orthodoxy, arrive at truth. All of a sudden, the fact of being the only one to hold a certain opinion, the fact of not subscribing to "authorized" doctrines, cease to be facts experienced as being mistakes or reasons for unhappiness. It is the orthodox and the partisans of the official line of the moment who look bad. Uniformity of views betrays, generally speaking, people's mental servitude, even if it is also the result of an efficient policy of mind control by an "organization" or "apparatus" that administers the true.

Then comes a positive movement aiming at rendering practical decisions possible. The problem is one of finding reasons to make a choice that go beyond the relativization of every assertion into a mere perspective. Here, "Nietzscheanism" calls upon a normative principle—the sovereignty of the individual—and hopes to ground not only a personal morality but a line of political conduct on this principle. Yet it would seem that, in this domain, "Nietzscheanism" does not improve upon philosophies expressing a more classical French individualism. "Nietzscheanism's" politics seems to be summarizable as a program of resistance to constituted powers and authorities: as Raymond Aron has pointed out many times, the philosopher Alain's position of "the citizen against the powers"[12] is, as such, a moral position. As a moral position it has its own dignity that we don't intend to dispute. The fact remains that it is devoid of political meaning. I mean by this that it does not allow us to undertake the political analysis of any given situation. We even have to say that it represents a fundamentally apolitical position, and that in this it is the only honorable stance that would be permissible in a situation in which political life had become impossible. If every political power is already corrupt due to, for example, foreign occupation of the country or a fragmentation of the social body politic, then true civic-mindedness will consist, for lack of a better solution, in abstaining from participation.

Some may object to me that the Nietzschean authors put force or power relations at the center of their analyses where traditional idealism knows only knowledge relations. But since when has the political domain been defined exclusively by the determination of power relations?

Political journalism, with its nose on the day's events, no doubt spends most of its time following the transfers of power: Who has it? Who loses and who gains it? Yet the notion of power is, as such, no more political than it is chemical or mechanical. What is political is not power, period: it is the way it is conferred, exercised, controlled, legitimized, etc. With relations of power we have the material with which to build a political structure, but a principle is still lacking. Or, to put it in scholastic terms, political thought finds in power only its *material object*. To arrive at its *formal object*, we have to specify the aspect or mode under which this power exists, is exercised, acknowledged, or contested. If power relations alone could define the political domain, we would have to describe as political the relation between human beings and rats among New York's inhabitants, and man's taming of the horse would likewise be a major political event in history. The conceptual schemata made use of in the writings of French "Nietzscheanism" do in fact often give the impression of having been invented to account for this very type of relation and not for studying the life of human beings in society.

The will to think the political domain of human actions outside of any philosophy of law or of justice comes under the heading, as we know, of positivism. There is positivism in thinking that scientific rigor demands a naturalistic attitude on the part of the observer, one that consists in treating social facts as if they were things stripped of the (anthropomorphic) significations people attach to them as social agents. Following this positivist conception, we would have to separate the reality of things (power relations) from the subjective interpretations supplied by the involved parties (the invocation of the rules of justice). Might "Nietzscheanism" be, in the final analysis, an unexpected version of positivism? It looks like it sometimes, but that is because its philosophy of justice is not expressed directly. We have to seek it where it is put forward in indirect form, as an a priori philosophy of history.

THE SOVEREIGN INDIVIDUAL

A philosophy of history consists in a determination of a sense/meaning to history beginning with a conceptual analysis. In Nietzsche, the concept that permits thinking of universal history as of a teleological process is that of culture, understood as a process of training and selection that, having as raw material the brutal and amoral animal of prehistory, shapes the sovereign individual of posthistory. "To breed an animal *with the right to make promises*—is not this the paradoxical task that nature has set itself in the case of man?"[13]

It is instructive to turn to the commentary Gilles Deleuze made of this text in his study of Nietzsche,[14] a study which played, as is well known, a major role in the gestation of French "Nietzscheanism." A meaningful gap can be observed between Nietzsche's text on culture and Deleuze's reading of it. In the second essay in *On The Genealogy of Morals,* Nietzsche writes that the "morality of mores" can be understood as a simple *means* to discipline, a means destined to disappear the day the *end* is reached. This end, the "fruit" of this "tree," is

the *sovereign individual,* like only to himself, liberated again from morality of custom, autonomous and supramoral (for "autonomous" and "moral" are mutually exclusive), in short, the man who has his own independent, protracted will and the *right to make promises.*[15]

Nietzsche then describes the superior man—the man raised to the perfection of his nature. If this man is freed from morality, it is because he no longer needs it to have an "own independent, protracted will." The end of morality is therefore to forge a firm will, one that will not bend under circumstances. The sovereign individual is sufficiently sure of himself, of his value and of the meaning of his word, to promise, that is, to *answer for himself.* Nietzsche, in other words, defines the sovereign individual's superiority as being the supreme form of responsibility. We can trust the superior man completely when he has given his word, for the power to keep his word has become a second nature in him, an instinct.

Deleuze's commentary, on the other hand, draws a very different lesson from all this. In Deleuze, the opposition is between the moral, therefore responsible, man and the superior individual liberated from morality and therefore irresponsible. By an antithesis more verbal than conceptual, responsibility for oneself is classified as belonging to the *heavy* things, to the burdens we take on, whereas sovereignty is on the side of the *light,* of becoming innocent, and therefore of irresponsibility. Deleuze writes:

The product of culture is not the man who obeys the law, but the sovereign law-making individual who defines himself through power over himself, over destiny, over the law: the free, the light-footed, the *irresponsible.* For Nietzsche the notion of responsibility, even in its superior form, has the limited value of a mere means: the autonomous individual is no longer responsible before justice for his reactive forces, he is their master, their sovereign, their legislator, their author and actor. It is he who speaks, he no longer has to *answer*.[16]

Deleuze builds up a philosophy of history (of which *Anti-Oedipus* will later give the complete version) on the basis of this opposition between a human being subject to the obligation to answer and a being delivered from this obligation. Universal history follows, or rather *should* follow, the logic of the concept of culture. For the end of culture (understood as a discipline) cannot be within culture itself. Culture, which is a means, presupposes an end. If history took place according to this logic, it should let us be witness to morality's self-destruction. (We might find that this logic to history has a dialectical aftertaste, a strange thing if we recall that Deleuze's whole book aims at showing that Nietzsche is the anti-Hegel.) The morality of the Law should vanish in favor of a supramorality of sovereignty. Were history to carry out the end inherent in the process of culture, we would have this result: "The morality of mores produces a man freed from the morality of mores, the spirit of the laws produces a man freed from the law."[17] In fact, Deleuze goes on to write, things happen differently: the reactive wins out over the active. Churches and states, the instruments of taming and rearing, do not accept their withering away. The means refuses to make way for the end. History, which should create the sovereign individual, culminates in the subjected human being. "Instead of the sovereign individual as product of history, history presents us with its own product, domesticated man, in which it finds the famous meaning of history."[18]

The diagnosis Deleuze puts forward is obscure because it takes cognizance of the limitation of individualist ideology in this ideology's own language. A distance is remarked upon between norm and fact, between the ideal of individual sovereignty and the incessant experience of dependence. It has to be admitted that the apperception of this distance is the strongest aspect of this version of "Nietzscheanism." But its conceptual articulation is not of the same quality as the sentiment expressed here of a discrepancy between modern culture's promises and every person's experience. What was promised was the individual's autonomy; what is experienced every day is, in many ways, the reverse. Never in fact have the members of a society been so dependent on one another. As Durkheim put it, solidarity has paradoxically become "organic" where it was only "mechanical" in traditional societies whose members did not grasp the idea that they were *individuals*. But mutual dependence, far from figuring among our culture's ideals, is held to be a fact we have to resign ourselves to or even as something undignified and degrading. The modern individual is thus inevitably divided against himself, since he will perpetually experience himself as being deprived of his human status or feel guilty about not yet being liberated.

The discrepancy between Nietzsche's text and Deleuze's commentary is in this respect a good indication of where the difficulty is to be found. The problem is one of knowing how *human autonomy* is to be understood. The concept of autonomy is a complex one, since it aims at uniting sovereignty and subjection. But the relation between sovereign and subject within autonomy remains nevertheless intelligible as long as we stay in the political order, which is, of course, the concept's native land. We conceptualize a country as being autonomous if it is not embedded in a larger political entity from which it would receive its laws. And we conceptualize that, in a democracy, the same people can be in turn sovereigns and subjects.

The difficulties begin with the notion, encouraged by the spread of Kantian thought, of an *individual* autonomy. Where here are sovereign and subject? In locating autonomy in the capacity to answer for oneself, Nietzsche no doubt sought to preserve the concept's equilibrium. There cannot, indeed, be a sovereignty without subjection. A sovereignty that is exercised over no one would be a joke. The autonomous individual according to Nietzsche, he who keeps his word, is therefore in a way the subject of himself. Nietzsche at this point only takes to its limits German philosophy's tendency to *interiorize* the relations constitutive of the human being. It is within the individual that we shall find legislator and subject. Supramorality would then be nothing other than morality totally interiorized, with neither obligations nor sanctions. Using a different vocabulary, we could say that social ethics (*Sittlichkeit*) is completely absorbed by personal morality (*Moralität*).

Deleuze's commentary brings out the bizarre aspect of this concept of individual autonomy when it is defined as responsibility before oneself alone. What is going to distinguish a superior man, responsible before himself, from a creature so well trained that it has become completely predictable and no longer needs to be controlled from the outside? What distinguishes individual autonomy from perfect conditioning? It will no doubt be objected that moral education, or even culture, should not have been defined as an animal-like training. The goal of an education cannot be reduced to the creation of a conformity to existing codes, nor to the conformity out of respect for the law that Kantians talk about. Deleuze is not wrong in wishing to restore spontaneity or "lightness" to the autonomous individual. To put it in different words (that Deleuze no doubt would not accept), we expect of an education not only that it should shape civilized, self-policing beings, or even trustworthy subjects, but also minds capable of evincing judgment and inventiveness in morally complex situations, where the difficulty is not one of making the moral motive prevail over the immoral one, but of knowing with exactitude whether a morally satisfactory solution exists.

But there is something else, which is that autonomy cannot be thought of in purely individual terms. Deleuze wants, it seems, to avoid the transition to supramorality being merely the exchange of an external or transcendent law (corresponding to the "morality of mores") for an internal, immanent one, keeping surveillance over the individual from within. This internal law looks too much like the old divine law for one to be able to seriously speak of autonomy. If that is Deleuze's reasoning on this point, it's hard not to agree with him. The will to keep one's word can be as strong as one wishes; it is not a *law* the individual promulgates for his own use. Moreover, we can't see very well what a law is if not a source for law in general. And the idea of a valid law without a judge to guarantee its application, to whom different parties can appeal, seems incoherent. In the case of the promise, we find neither law, nor arbitrator, nor judge. The concept of human individual, even a "superior" one, does not in general provide us with the internal articulation that would permit us to distinguish within it between sovereign and subject. If things are different in the political order, it is because a third term comes into it, that of the body politic. To speak as Rousseau does, we can say that in a democracy everyone is, as citizen, a *part* of the sovereign but, as *complete* individual, a subject under the law. Which is why we can't talk about autonomy in the case of the moral subject without being led to accord the source of the law, like it or not, a transcendent status. If this source is reason, it can't be *human* reason.

The solution put forward by Deleuze is not satisfying either. He, in order to eliminate any subjection of the superior individual, frees the latter from the weight of his responsibilities. The autonomous individual is nothing other than sovereign and legislator. The question is inevitably going to come up about whom this sovereign rules over, since it isn't over himself, and to whom he gives his laws. But since the internalization of the morality of mores, or collective discipline, has been rejected, these constitutive relations have to be found outside the individual. The autonomous individual would therefore not be able to do without heteronomous individuals. The sovereign individual would then be the one who managed to impose himself as master over people willing to obey him. The philosophy that chooses to understand autonomy as irresponsibility ends up in an apology of tyranny.

We can draw out a more general conclusion from this last point. When we look over "Nietzscheanism's" more philosophical expressions, we find an interrogation about the principles of modern philosophy that itself never goes outside the limits of this philosophy. Certain authors, such as Jürgen Habermas, have assigned Nietzsche (and the French philosophers inspired by him) the role of adversaries of the spirit of modern times within philosophical debate. But that is to confuse Nietzsche with Joseph de Maistre. No doubt Nietzsche never ceases denouncing the inconsistency of what he himself calls "modern ideas" (those of his time). But his criticism in no way calls for the restoration of a traditional order. To wish to intellectually define a "modern project" without including its Nietzschean extension is to be incomplete or inconsequential. "Nietzscheanism's" philosophy does not have principles other than those of the "modern project," only a different version of those principles. And every time we seek to give a philosophically articulate form to one of the Nietzschean themes—whether it be the critique of consciousness, suspiciousness, infinite interpretation, or suprahumanity—we are disappointed at finding familiar conceptual frameworks. The critique of consciousness doesn't go beyond Cartesian mind philosophy. The infinite task of interpretation in no way perturbs empiricist language philosophy. The superior individual is inconceivable outside the idealist philosophy of autonomy. The Nietzscheans introduce no new principle within the philosophical order. Their vigor is, if we may say so, ad hominem, purely dialectical. And we know that ad hominem reasoning is logically valid but incapable of establishing a conclusion. All we can ask of it is that it incite us to look for those among our premises responsible for the paradoxes, vicious circles, and infinite regressions the critic leads us to fall into. But what new principles should replace the faulty premises is something we will have to find out from an examination of the thing itself rather than from Nietzschean philosophers.

NOTES

1. In *Vocabulaire technique et critique de la philosophie*, S. V. Moment, Paris: Presses Universitaires de France, 1st ed., 1926.

2. Text in Denis Hollier, *Le Collège de sociologie*, Paris: Gallimard, 1979, pp. 103–4. Italics in the text.

3. See Maurice Blanchot, *La communauté impossible*, Paris: Éditions de Minuit, 1984; and Jean-Luc Nancy, *La communauté désoeuvrée*, Paris: Christian Bourgois, 1986. What I call millenarian existentialism is close to what Nancy designates in the latter book as a "literary communism."

4. The proceedings of this colloquium have been published in two volumes under the title *Nietzsche*, Paris, 1978.

5. *Conscienciosité* was the term with which Leibniz suggested translating into French the English *consciousness*; see *Nouveaux essais sur l'entendement humain*, II, XXVII, § 9.

6. Published as *Nietzsche: colloque de Royaumont*, Paris: Éditions de Minuit, 1967.

7. Ibid., p. 195.

8. Ibid., p. 189.

9. See A. Kenny, *The Metaphysics of Mind*, New York: Oxford University Press, 1989.

10. Marcel Mauss, *Sociologie et anthropologie*, Paris: Presses Universitaires de France, 1950, p. xxiii.

11. It should be noted here that Lévi-Strauss himself later criticized the "hard" structuralist position. He admits having been wrong in looking for "an unconscious genesis of matrimonial exchange": he should have made a distinction between practices of exchange, which are in the domain of the real, and ideal, and therefore conscious, rules worked out by the group to control those practices. See *La pensée sauvage*, Paris: Plon, 1962, p. 333.

12. Alain, *Le citoyen contre les pouvoirs*, Paris: Gallimard, 1926.

13. *On the Genealogy of Morals*, trans. Walter Kaufmann, New York: Vintage Books/Random House, 1967, II, § 1.

14. Gilles Deleuze, *Nietzsche et la philosophie*, Paris: Presses Universitaires de France, 1962, p. 157.

15. *On the Genealogy of Morals*, II, § 2.

16. Deleuze, p. 157. Italics in the text.

17. Ibid., p. 158.

18. Ibid., p. 159.

4 "What Must First Be Proved Is Worth Little"

LUC FERRY AND ALAIN RENAUT

The essence of modern societies, as Benjamin Constant and Alexis de Tocqueville had already seen, consists in the way the individual is progressively liberated from the supervision of traditions. In the societies quite rightly named "traditional," the weight of all that is inherited from the past predetermined individual behavior, limiting a priori the room for free choice; modernity, on the contrary, is characterized by the decision to conceive of the definition of norms as taking place in the present, through their free foundation by individual wills: this is, in any case, the way modern societies represent the origin of their norms to themselves, even if this representation, more often fictional than real, and much too easily taken apart by sociological analyses,[1] obviously has above all a legitimating function. And, when taking thus into account only the representations that societies create of themselves, how can one not be tempted to oppose *tradition* to *argumentation*, through the ideal-typical designation of the one as the *ancient* and of the other as the *modern* form of the determination of norms?

No one, of course, will ever be able to develop any kind of argument without inserting himself into a tradition and without recuperating certain τόποι, and certain values, for his own purposes: but what is unique to modernity is the very way in which the subject, *even though it quite obviously does not dispose of an absolute capacity to create its own norms,* does nevertheless claim a sovereign right to put them under free scrutiny and, in this moment of critical examination, posits itself and thinks of itself as the ultimate foundation of the argumentation through which it legitimizes or rejects those norms.[2] Lacking as we do the traditional signposts that have been eroded away by the democratic dynamic, living in societies that can no longer discern the law in any kind of transcendence (neither that of an order in the world, nor that of a divine will, nor even that of the past), how can we even conceive of the basis for a norm if it isn't through a process of discussion, real or supposed, between the concerned parties, seeking for an agreement among themselves?

All normativity, imposing as it does, by definition, a limit to individuality, requires a dimension of exteriority in relation to individual wills. It is this exteriority that previous cultural arrangements sought in a tradition whose authority was rooted in its supposed conformity to the divine word or to the order of the world. When this figure of exteriority progressively collapsed, in conformity with the logic of modernity, and exteriority could no longer be found in any kind of immemorial past still capable of regulating our conduct, the norm could be instituted only through the movement of transcendence, the going-beyond of self presupposed by the fact of looking for arguments, for "reasons," *within oneself* in order to justify a certain point of view, but "reasons" capable also of obtaining *for others*. This heretofore unimagined figure of exteriority, that of an internal exteriority or of a transcendence within immanence, is expressed at the juridical-political level by the idea of democracy: limits can now be imposed upon individuals only as a result of public decisions, themselves the result of public discussion and argumentation. In a word—and here we come upon a perspective that various philosophies seize upon as a theme today—only democracy can correct and regulate democracy. This means that what the democratic dynamic has undone forever, only democracy can put back together (therein its grandeur), but imperfectly and therefore infinitely (therein its fragility).

One can, truth be told, either be attracted to this grandeur or be driven to despair by that fragility. As one or another of these two attitudes toward the fact of democracy predominates, one of two rigorously opposed philosophical projects can be envisioned: either, on the one hand, the enlargement of the model of argumentative deliberation in its theoretical suppositions or in its practical aspects; or, on the other, the denunciation of the emptiness created by the collapse of the traditional reference points as insurmountable with the aid of any kind of ethics of argumentation, and an interrogation about the possibility of bringing about the emergence of a contemporary analogue to a traditional universe through the critique of democratic modernity. Habermas, Apel, Rawls, and various others illustrate today the first attitude in different ways; MacIntyre and the "communitarians" have, following Leo Strauss, gone along the second route.

Within the context of these two more and more clearly separate camps,[3] Nietzsche's case is an especially interesting one for whoever wishes to undertake a critical examination of the neotraditionalist path. Two main reasons justify this evaluation:

—Nietzsche's work, on the one hand, explicitly and in an exemplary manner articulates the critique of democratic modernity and the denunciation of the argumentative foundation of norms: in this way it permits us—better than does the work of other philosophers—to grasp all that is involved, within the choice between tradition and argumentation, in the rejection of the latter.

—on the other and perhaps more important hand, the way Nietzsche went about this rejection illustrates in a particularly significant fashion one of the main difficulties this type of philosophical project comes up against: the neotraditionalist avoidance of democratic modernity makes it necessary to look for—and we insist on this—whatever could be today's *analogue* of a traditional universe: the *analogue,* for (as Nietzsche knew better than anyone) it is out of the question that in a time when "God is dead," tradition should function as it does in theological cultures, in which whatever renders the value of tradition "sacred" and gives it its power is never unrelated to its rootedness in the divine will or in a world order supposed to express this will.

Situating as he does his reflection at the same time after the "death of God" and after the (inseparably associated) discovery that the world, once "dedivinized," appears to be devoid of any order and must be thought of as "chaos" (*The Gay Science,* § 109), Nietzsche takes into account the end of the cosmological and theological universe, an end that in general defines the intellectual and cultural location of the Moderns: we are thus dealing here, by definition and, we could say, at the stage of a working sketch (since Nietzsche is, in philosophy, the very man who declared the foundations of the traditional universe to be antiquated), with a very peculiar mixture of antimodernism and modernity, of tradition and novelty—which is why the expression "neotraditionalism" seems perfectly appropriate here, right down to the tension expressed within it. The question is of course one of knowing what such a "mixture" could consist of, both in its content and in its effects. Since, more than most of the representatives of ordinary conservatism, Nietzsche cannot contemplate a naive resumption of tradition, his *neo*-conservative approach permits us to submit the traditionalist option to an interrogation that can best examine its limitations and unintended consequences—namely: what would a modern analogue of tradition consist of?

ARGUMENTATION AND DEMOCRACY

The shortest route to get at the principles of the critique simultaneously of argumentation and of democracy—and therefore of the democratic aspect of rationality—that Nietzsche develops cannot fail to take as its starting point a key formulation found in *Twilight of the Idols* ("The Case of Socrates," § 5): "What must first be proved is worth little."[4]

To which, as always with Nietzsche, we would have to attach a series of indications that share in the same conviction: in the epilogue to *The Case of Wagner*, for instance, the suggestion that both "master morality" and "Christian evaluations" have their necessity and both constitute "ways of seeing not to be approached with arguments and refutations": you don't "refute Christianity" any more than you refute "an illness of the eyes," you simply fight it. And, in the preface to *Ecce Homo:* "I don't refute ideals; I simply put on my gloves in front of them." This is echoed in the third part of the same book, when the intentions of *Human, All-Too-Human* are evoked: "the ideal is not refuted: it is frozen." In a word: the insistent rejection of argument, in either its positive form (demonstration, use of proofs)[5] or its negative (refutation).[6]

This mistrust of argumentation is quite clearly inseparable in Nietzsche from his global attack on dialectics and dialecticians. We will only bring to mind here the main argument put forward in "The Case of Socrates": "With dialectics, the plebs come to the top" (§ 5). Before Socrates, the "ancient Hellenes" rejected dialectical procedures within an aristocratic society out of the conviction that what is great and noble imposes itself and does not need to be argued for: what takes place, on the other hand, with Socrates and his "sick men" (§ 10), "the hypertrophy of the logical faculty" (§ 4), is the project, characteristic of one "oppressed" and marked by "plebeian resentment," of "taking revenge on the aristocrats" (§ 7) through displacing the conflict towards the only terrain where differences level out, the one in which it is no longer sufficient merely to *assert* one's right, one has to *demonstrate* it. Whereas "in every place in which authority still exists, everywhere it is not reasoned, where it is ordered, the dialectician is a sort of clown," (§ 5), the "decadent" Socrates, through his promotion of the dialectic to the detriment of "all the instincts of the ancient Hellenes," made sacred the only instrument with which he was capable of winning: we see at work here, as Nietzsche so kindly points out, the "malignity of the phthisic" (§ 4), stabbing in the back, with "the knifeblade of the syllogism," everything that had made up the greatness of Greece until that time: we should even wonder whether Socrates really was Greek (§ 3).[7]

In other words, and using a distinction central to the Nietzschean corpus: from the "ancient Hellenes" to Socrates, the mutation that takes place consists in the transition from *active forces,* which are purely affirmative and capable of a maximum exertion without mutilating other forces, to *reactive forces,* which can exert themselves only through their opposition to and their attempt to negate other forces. Both are examples of forms of "life" (since life, as will to power, is force), but where the active forces correspond to an ascendant form of life, the reactive ones are guided by a logic of degeneration, since in them life can assert or at least maintain itself only at the expense of a part of itself.

It isn't necessary to insist further on the Nietzschean assault against the Socratic dialectic. We can at best point out that it has a significant effect on the statute granted the Sophists: in general, Nietzsche stresses what still differentiates the Sophists from what emerges with Socrates, and considers Greek philosophy after Socrates to be a "symptom of decadence," in which "anti-Hellenic instincts come to the top"; the Sophist is "still completely Hellenic"[8] but, since the Sophists "verge upon the first *critique of morality,*" since they "juxtapose the multiplicity . . . of the moral value judgments," "they let it be known that every morality can be dialectically justified"—and, because of that, it must be made clear that though sophism is still Greek, it constitutes a "transitional form" (*Übergangsform*): Sophism, indeed, for the first time asks *questions* about the meaning of existence, and therefore "the Sophists are already sick." We can thus confirm that two determinants of our democratic universe we would be inclined to identify as signs of progress should be read, from Nietzsche's point of view, as symptoms of decadence:

—the way in which, on the one hand, the dissolution of the signposts inherited from the past causes the emergence of a swarm of *questions* for the individual and for society whose answers went without saying in a universe structured by tradition, questions, in fact, that did not even come up;

—the way in which, on the other hand, in this domain of infinite questioning, once open, every form of legitimacy therein now has to ceaselessly *be demonstrated:* from *authority* to *argumentation,* what we would hold to be a positive process of autonomization identical to the dynamics of modernity Nietzsche perceives as the sign, through the Socratic emergence of the individual, of a regrettable decline of the instinct for solidarity that made for the cohesion and the health of the "ancient Hellenes."[9]

We do not need to go into great detail here to show how, beginning with the detection of such symptoms, decrying such a decline leads Nietzsche towards a triple critique: of *democracy,* of *science,* and finally of *modernity.*

Critique of democracy as, of course, "a form of the decay of political organization" (*Beyond Good and Evil,* § 203) in which, precisely because that which holds needs to be demonstrated, the argumentative foundation of norms "level[s] mountain and valley, and call[s] that morality" (*Twilight of the Idols,* "Skirmishes of an Untimely Man," § 38), in a word: the tyranny of equality. A very well known theme, even if the texts that could be rediscovered through a more detailed examination of this critique of democracy leave us, thanks to their rhetorical violence, somewhat whimsically perplexed as to how they did not prevent a generation of our philosophers—that of the 1960s—from professing Nietzscheanism: where Michel Foucault, in a celebrated interview, consigns Sartre to the nineteenth century and to Hegelianism (because of the latter's continued reference to dialectics) and proclaims himself to be close to Nietzsche and to his denunciation of the "divinized man the nineteenth century never ceased to dream of,"[10] how, today, can one not take a certain malicious pleasure in recalling that Nietzsche is also he who denounces "the poison of the doctrine of 'equal rights for all'" (*The Antichrist,* § 43) and proclaims that "a right is a privilege" or that "the *inequality* of rights is the first condition for the existence of any rights at all" (ibid., § 57)[11]—declarations all that should apparently have had the effect, all the same, of somewhat restraining the temptation to call oneself "simply a Nietzschean."

Critique of science,[12] in second place, both because science is at bottom the heir of the Socratic dialectic (being interrogation and argumentation),[13] which is itself strongly connected to democracy: the truth science aims at establishing is intended to be universal (it claims to be valid for all, at all times and in every place), and in this sense it expresses the "plebeian" point of view since the validity truth lays claim to presupposes that we reject the infinity of interpretations[14] and that, to further this negation of hermeneutics, we neutralize the plurality of differentiated perspectives through which the differences and distances between the diverse types of humanity find expression,[15] and because, just as much as the *ressentiment* of the plebs, whose triumph is assured by democracy, the scientific will to truth is reactive in that it rejects the forces of mendacity, illusion, and error. It is no doubt in sections 348 and 349 of *The Gay Science* that most of the ingredients of this criticism of science as being in solidarity with democratic valuations, and thus with the ethic of argumentation, are structured in the most striking fashion: scientists and scholars are described there as being concerned with proofs and demonstrations, as being therefore "representatives of the democratic idea," since "nothing is more democratic than logic; it is no respecter of persons and makes no distinction between crooked and straight noses"—an allusion of dubious taste that Nietzsche does not hesitate to clarify:

A Jew, on the other hand, in keeping with the business circles and the past of his people, is least of all used to being believed. Consider Jewish scholars in this light: all of them have a high regard for logic, that is for *compelling* agreement by force of reasons; they know, with that they are bound to win even where they encounter race and class prejudices and where one does not like to believe them.

From Socrates to Plato, "Judaized" pseudo-Greeks, to the modern Jewish scientist or scholar, it is, for Nietzsche, the same illness that has spread its ravages, to the extent that this denunciation of scientific-democratic rationality ends up taking the form of a critique of modernity.

Critique of modernity: that is moreover the title of one of the last aphorisms of *The Twilight of the Idols* ("Skirmishes of an Untimely Man," § 39), and it could be the title for a large part of Nietzsche's work. Since the Socratic dialectic seemed to him to have found its fulfillment in the modern cult of reason, since the "populist" obsession with neutralizing social distances, transmitted from Socrates to modernity through the mediation of Christianity, supposedly arrived at its zenith in Rousseau, in the declarations of human rights, and in socialism, Nietzsche could not but adopt a radical antimodernism—about the ramifications of which we will not go on, but whose vehemence has to be stressed, if only through this observation deliberately lacking the least nuance: "*All* that is modern can only serve posterity as a vomitive."

Despite the excessive and, at times, painful character of such formulations, we at least have to grant the Nietzschean attacks the merit of having brought out that which, in the establishing of norms, constitutes the dynamics of democratic culture: the shift from *authority* to *argumentation*. To illustrate the necessity of the argumentation that we are today constrained by, Hegel's formulation in the *Principles of the Philosophy of Right* is often cited: "The principle of the modern world requires that that which everyone accepts must appear to him to be legitimate." And it must be pointed out that, seen from this point of view, Nietzsche's diagnosis is just as precise and just as valid, even if its signs are inverted: inversion of the judgment made upon democratic rationality, which obviously leads him to wonder about the chances of producing an alternative to that whose emergence he interprets as a sign of decadence. But, along this second path, Nietzsche's project raises, it seems to us, a lot of questions.

TRADITION AND ARISTOCRACY

Even if, at first, the reference to the values of tradition seems to be out of sympathy with the spirit of a corpus suffused with the will to break with a two thousand–year–old degeneracy,[16] one can't be altogether surprised at discovering that there is in fact in Nietzsche a certain nostalgia for the traditional universe: how, indeed, could the critique of the dialectization of our relation to norms not incite towards retrospectively putting a high value on, or even idealizing, the tradition that the Socratic mania for argument is supposed to have enfeebled? Let us limit ourselves to detecting a few signs of such a nostalgia.

We can first of all observe that Nietzsche makes an explicit reference to the value of tradition to designate what has been lost with Socrates: the Greek philosophers (beginning with Socrates) were "the decadents of Greek culture, the countermovement to the ancient, noble taste (to the agonistic instinct, to the *polis,* to the value of race, to the authority of descent)" (*Twilight of the Idols,* "What I Owe to the Ancients," § 3)—an explicit elucidation of the notion of "authority" that "The Case of Socrates" opposes against dialectical ratiocination. We can also read in the sketches gathered together as *Wissenschaft und Weisheit im Kampfe* (Science and wisdom in conflict, 1875): "The older Greek culture made its forces manifest *in its continuous line of philosophers.* This manifestation comes to an end with Socrates: he attempts *to bring himself up* and repudiate all tradition (*Tradition*)" (§ 193, italics in original).

An equally unequivocal text, which is immediately corroborated by the indication (§ 196) that Socrates, in destroying "the naïveté of ethical judgment," "tore the individual away from his historical ties (*historischen Verbande*)": the argumentative dialectization of the relation to norms is thus part of a global process aiming at the subject's self-production or self-affirmation, and therefore at its becoming autonomous in relation to any kind of enlistment within a tradition. Nietzsche perceived perfectly well the close relationship between the irruption of the values of *subjectivity* and the repudiation of *tradition* as a principle.[17]

To bring this rapid survey to an end, we may add that when Nietzsche goes from the simple narrative of decadence to a deliberately normative discourse, this valorization of tradition is just as pervasive, as for example in this lapidary declaration from *Twilight of the Idols:* "All that is good is inherited: whatever is not inherited is imperfect, is a mere beginning" ("Skirmishes of an Untimely Man," § 47). We once again find here the primacy accorded the enlistment in a tradition or filiation over against Socrates' (already "modern") pretention to *found* or *inaugurate* values. But does that mean that Nietzsche seriously envisions the re-creation, supposing it is even imaginable, of a traditional universe whose norms would be purely and simply "handed down"? It is on this very point that his position is at its subtlest and most delicate to discern, since it cannot be unilaterally reduced to an effort to bring back, against Socratic argumentative practice, the "ancient Hellenes'" submission to the heritage of a tradition.

We come across a disconcerting aphorism when reading *Human, All-Too-Human* (I, 552):

The only human right.—Whoever turns away from his inheritance, becomes the victim of the exceptional; whoever remains in his inheritance is its slave. One will be led to one's perdition in either case.

A curious declaration, difficult, as so often with Nietzsche, to interpret with certainty. We can at least agree that it invites us to relativize a Nietzschean valorization of tradition whose reality is nonetheless confirmed by the aphorism's first part. This relativization takes place, moreover, in the name of an idea of liberty as autonomy whose historical emergence is, as we know, insistently assigned by Nietzsche to a logic of decadence: it's as if his critique of the idea of liberty does not exclude the possibility that, the idea having made its appearance, something of it must be conserved even in the attempts to find an alternative to the decadent universe it is in solidarity with (which is why Nietzsche, otherwise so critical of the very notion of "human rights," finds himself forced to consecrate as "the only human right" that which consists, for the individual, in not completely dissolving his freedom within a mechanical adherence to tradition).

It is obviously out of the question to establish any kind of interpretation upon such an enigmatic text, one likely to encourage projections on the part of the interpreter. Besides, these lines emanate from the period in Nietzsche's trajectory in which he rediscovered a certain proximity to the spirit of the Enlightenment (at the time of *The Dawn* and of *Human, All-Too-Human*), and what is thus expressed here could very well not affect Nietzsche's ultimate positions on the choice we are concerned with: tradition or argumentation? But it would be imprudent not to integrate into our analyses the warning given by this aphorism and not to deduce from it an incitement to ask ourselves whether Nietzsche's relation to the traditional universe isn't, beyond the nostalgia it inspires him with, more complex than it seems.

A complex relation indeed, for Nietzsche rules out the idea that the response to modernity should lie in the will to bring about a pure and simple return to a premodern phase of humanity's destiny. To convince ourselves of this we need only refer to the text in *Twilight of the Idols* ("Skirmishes of an Untimely Man," § 43) entitled, significantly, "Whispered to the Conservatives," because what Nietzsche warns the "conservatives" about is that "a reversion, a return in any sense or degree is simply not possible": we can only advance "step by step further into decadence," let, that is, "modern 'progress'" work itself out, perhaps "check[ing] this development," but it is out of the question that we could "be a crab" and "walk backwards." A position that, in its attitude towards the appearance of democratic rationality, mutatis mutandis evokes that of Tocqueville: whatever one may think of what is taking place (and Nietzsche is a lot more severe than Tocqueville is towards "modern progress"), it remains true that the process is irreversible, and that there are now certain "achievements" of modernity that are going to have to be taken into account. A lengthy analysis could be carried out here to determine what induces Nietzsche to represent history as a *destiny;* the key, we shall merely point out, is no doubt to be found in a text like this one: "How I fulfill fatalism: (1) through the Eternal Recurrence and preexistence, (2) through the elimination of the concept 'will'."[18]

More clearly put: the doctrine of the Eternal Recurrence is, in effect, "the extremest form of fatalism,"[19] since it implies that everything that happens has already happened an infinite number of times and will happen again, in the same way, an infinite number of times: it therefore excludes the possibility of a radical beginning or creation;[20] in this, it implies the "elimination of the concept of will," since freedom of the will, a key ingredient of the mythology inherent in the idea of "subject," makes sense only as the capacity radically to inaugurate a series of events—which is prohibited by the notion of Eternal Recurrence. Quite obviously, within such a perspective, in which, as the demon of section 341 of *The Gay Science* warns us, we have to learn to accept "living once more and innumerable times more . . . all in the same succession and sequence," the *voluntarist* project of canceling any stage of becoming is devoid of any meaning: if what has been must return, if pre-Socratic Greece is fated to be included in our future because it belonged to the past, it is not due to our will to return to it; it is, rather, through pursuing and carrying out what has emerged since then (in this case, the Moderns' democratic rationality) that the conditions for a "new beginning" will be put into place. Therefore neither "conservatism" *stricto sensu* nor what Nietzsche aims at under the name, that is to say the spirit of "reaction," animated as they are by the will, the former to petrify the future, the latter to cancel it out by walking backwards, has understood the true meaning of the present or of the passing instant: that this present "carries along after it all future things."[21]

Through this notion, the complexity of Nietzsche's relation to the traditional universe should become clearer. Naturally, the values he depends on in his opposition to democratic rationality and to the ethics of argumentation are singularly evocative of societies structured by tradition. This is particularly true of that essential component of the traditional universe, the intrinsically antimodern principle of *hierarchy*—whose importance in the definition of the aristocratic ideal that Nietzsche opposes to modern democracy is familiar,[22] even unto the most outrageous provocation.[23]

But on the other hand we can also discover without much trouble, in the Nietzschean corpus, a series of texts emitting frank reservations towards these "ancient Hellenes" whose virtues are nevertheless described as prototypical of the universe Socrates ruined: the great Hellenes were assuredly aristocrats (as opposed to the plebeian Socrates), but their purely "instinctive" aristocracy is "native" (or "natural") at the same time that it is "naïve"[24]—in the same sense as the "naïveté of the ethical judgment" that Socrates destroyed ("Science and Wisdom in Conflict"). Otherwise put: the Hellenes were spontaneously and totally noble, of a moral nobility which, "by its character of totality and simplicity," gives us an image of "simplified man," one without internal tensions—to such an extent that, as "Science and Wisdom . . ." does not hesitate to suggest, "they fill us with joy in the same way as the life of animals does." Simple and healthy, and practically simpletons as a result of so much health and absence of internal conflict, the ancient Hellenes could not but represent a fragile type of humanity, incapable of overcoming, by integrating them, the threats that Socrates' questions would bring to bear on their simplicity: since they practiced virtue "without asking themselves why,"[25] they were bound to be disconcerted and, finally, swept aside by the talent of the dialectician, who would find it easy to "laugh at the awkward incapacity of noble Athenians who, like all noble men, were men of instinct and never could give sufficient information about the reasons for their actions" (*Beyond Good and Evil,* § 191).

Under such conditions, once doubt and interrogation have substituted themselves for authority, bringing about the collapse of the aristocratic universe of tradition, it is out of the question that the naïve simplicity of the Hellenes could be found again: as soon as room for discussion and argument opens up, the quasi-animalistic spontaneity with which the native aristocrats adhere to a tradition that is as if incorporate with them disappears, and anarchy establishes itself amid instincts that are no longer, through their own doing, coordinated one with the other in a beautiful and immediate totality. It is thus no longer possible from that point on to go back and reestablish, in its archaic form, the absolute authority of a tradition that would now be experienced as slavery by a form of humanity in which the faculty of asking questions and of "wanting to know why" has developed itself. Because of this two possible paths presented themselves, at least retrospectively or apparently.[26]

The Socratic path, that of *asceticism,* consisted, when confronted with the anarchy of conflicting instinctual forces, of the suppression of all the instincts through their submission to reason and to the tyranny of truth: a radical gesture that was ratified by the Platonic invention of the intelligible world, but one that consists of the mutilation of certain forces (those of the sensible/sensual world) in the name of other forces (those of the intelligible). The Socratic path of argumentation is, in this, *reactive,* since, in it, certain forces are sacrificed to others, implying a diminishment of the global quantum of force and inaugurating a decadent form of life (a morbid form of the will to power) that manifests itself in Socrates' ugliness.

The other path, the one Nietzsche dreams about and which constituted his true ideal, would have consisted not in *mutilating* forces in the name of other forces, but in *hierarchizing* them. Where the Socratic dialectic is the prototype of reaction mutilating the instincts, and therefore of asceticism, the successful hierarchization of instincts corresponds to what Nietzsche calls the *"grand style"* and defines in these terms: "To become master of the chaos one is; to compel one's chaos to become form; to become logical, simple, unambiguous, mathematics, *law.*"[27]

We shall not analyze this well-known theme any further, nor shall we return here to the resemblances between the "grand style" and classicism:[28] briefly, it is clear that in Nietzsche's eyes only such a hierarchization of the instincts, integrating all of the forces of life—including reason and logic, once they have made their appearance—would truly escape from the "reactive" attitude inaugurated by Socrates; since if the reactive forces are those that cannot assert themselves without negating other forces, a critique of the argumentative dialectic and, more broadly, of democratic rationality that would consist of eliminating this rationality and the force it represents would remain prisoner of the reactive attitude, and thus weak and a begetter of ugliness. The hierarchization, on the contrary, of all of the forces of life presupposes a "victorious will," a "more intense coordination," a "harmonization of all violent desires": in a word, a self-mastery synonymous simultaneously with an intensification of life and with its "aesthetic improvement." *And it is in fact from the principles of such a harmonious hierarchization, obligat-*

ing the instincts to structure themselves within a new, well-ordered totality, that for a new aristocracy, less spontaneous, but also less animal-like than that of the "ancient Hellenes," the modern (or rather postmodern) analogue of a tradition should begin to emerge.

If such is indeed the specific content of the Nietzschean position—to the extent that we may pretend to grasp its consistency—in the debate between the ethics of argumentation and the ethics of tradition, it cannot help but raise, today, at least two series of interrogations.

(1) How, first of all, can one not be surprised at the singularly *dialectical* character, in the Hegelian sense of the term, of the logic in the sequence going from the "ancient Hellenes" to modernity (as it supposedly emerged with Socrates) and then to the postmodernity of the "grand style"? How, indeed, can one not see in the modern-Socratic reaction the negative moment, and in the conscious and thought-out recomposition of an aristocracy, the fulfillment of an *Aufhebung*, superseding the opposition between the Hellenes and Socrates (between action and reaction) within the appearance of a third term, integrating the moments of consciousness and of rationality,[29] and therefore going beyond not only mutilating asceticism but also the animal spontaneity of the original? An observation that raises many questions internal to Nietzschean exegesis: the historical one touching the complex and paradoxical relations between Hegel and Nietzsche; but also one of knowing how a dialectical logic, implying as it does the idea of progress, can integrate itself into a model such as that of the Eternal Recurrence, which by definition denies such an idea.

(2) Even if we accept leaving this first series of questions to one side, it becomes clear that the main difficulty with the type of position that Nietzsche elaborates has to do with the curious mixture of tradition and modernity that characterizes it and whose reasons for being, if not its formulation, we can now better understand. If we can, without any difficulty, conceive that a revalorization of traditional societies cannot completely put into brackets the values of consciousness, mastery, or reflection (in a word, of autonomy)[30] that the Moderns have brought to full development, then how do we reconcile this "moment" of modernity with what the denunciation of democratic rationality would decree must be reimported from the Ancients—to wit, the cult of natural hierarchy?

Even independently of the question of knowing whether such a mixture of modernity and tradition, in which many contemporary studies see the intellectual formula that defines fascism,[31] is truly desirable, we may simply ask whether such a mixture is possible—or, more precisely, whether the integration of what modernity has accomplished does not constrain to a definitive break, for now and forever, with the heritage of the Ancients. In which case traditionalism would come to look more *tragic* than, properly speaking, *reactionary*, to the extent that tradition is seen within it more as an irremediably lost value than as a pole to which we could return, even partially. This tragic tone, not always absent from Nietzsche's remarks, instills in him an undeniable grandeur: may we also point out that it underlines his limitations—just as it, more cruelly perhaps, also underlines the limitations of what the Nietzschean option in philosophy might have represented in the last few decades?

An entire current of our recent intellectual life thought it had learned from Nietzsche that one could not escape from the dissatisfactions of modernity without rejecting the logic of argumentative rationality in which modern consciousness, breaking with the traditional universe, has chosen to situate itself. It has thus been possible to believe that opening the way for a postmodernity meant above all ferreting out differences and their richness from the leveling tyranny of identity (and of the principle of identity).

Seduced less by the ethics of conviction than by that of responsibility, our philosophical generation is that which can no longer forget that *the hatred of argumentation means, principally, the return of authority*: thus, the moment has perhaps finally arrived to realize that, when we do not make a distinction between the public sphere of argumentation and the media sphere of performance, when we denounce the first because of the defects of the second, we open the way to a method of managing conflicts that risks leaving but one procedure to arrive at their resolution: that of lining up divisions on both sides.

NOTES

1. From this point of view, and even before the various sociological genealogies of norms, it has to be granted that the critiques of the Enlightenment formulated by the German Romanticists were not always baseless.

2. Karl-Otto Apel quite rightly, in this respect, designates this argumentative search for an ultimate foundation (*Letztbegründung*) as being inevitable for us moderns, even though it would be appropriate to interrogate ourselves about the status of this sought-for foundation more than he does.

3. On the logic of this separation, see Alain Renaut and Lucas Sosoé, *Philosophie du droit,* Paris: Presses Universitaires de France, 1991, introduction.

4. Let us note that, in this kind of formula, Nietzsche in no way distinguishes, contrary to current usage, between demonstration and argumentation, but covers both terms with the same opprobrium.

5. For example, in *The Will to Power,* § 431: "Positing proofs (*Beweisbarkeit*) as the presupposition for personal excellence in virtue signified nothing less than the disintegration of Greek instincts."

6. With the exception—which, in fact, is not one—of Socrates' ugliness, which constituted an "objection" and almost a "refutation" against him "among the Greeks." "The Case of Socrates," § 3.

7. To better understand what Nietzsche has in mind here, we have to recall that paragraph 6 ends by asserting that, in any case, "the Jews were dialecticians."

8. *The Will to Power,* § 427. Also, § 428:

The Greek culture of the Sophists had developed out of all the Greek instincts; it belongs to the culture of the Periclean age as necessarily as Plato does *not:* it has its predecessors in Heraclitus, in Democritus, in the scientific types of the old philosophy; it finds expression in, e.g., the high culture of Thucydides.

See also *Twilight of the Idols,* "What I Owe the Ancients," § 2.

9. See *The Will to Power,* § 428. See also: "Der letzte Philosoph: Der Philosoph: Betrachtungen über den Kampf von Kunst und Erkenntnis" ("The last philosopher: The philosopher: Observations on the struggle between art and knowledge." Unpublished essay from 1872), § 31: Socrates and his followers are limited by "*individual* concern about *living in happiness* . . . Before, the important thing was not *individuals,* but the *Hellenes.*" (italics in the original).

10. See *Magazine littéraire,* 1 March 1968. As well, of course, as the interview of 29 May, 1984, which appeared in *Les nouvelles littéraires,* 28 June—5 July 1984: "I am, quite simply, a Nietzschean."

11. It is, naturally, around this theme of the equalization of rights that Nietzsche establishes a lineage, that we will not deal with here, between Christianity, democracy, and socialism.

12. The critique of science gathers its greatest force in Nietzsche, as is well known, in his later writings: on his earlier period (that of *The Dawn* and of *Human, All-Too-Human*), cf. Philippe Raynaud's and Vincent Descombes's prefaces to the republications of Henri Albert's French translations of Nietzsche: éd. Hachette, collection «Pluriel».

13. On this parentage, see *The Birth of Tragedy,* § 16: "I shall speak only of the most eminent adversary of the tragic vision, by which I mean science,

which is essentially optimistic, beginning with its ancestor Socrates"; see also *The Will to Power*, § 68, in which the genesis of science is described in terms that repeat those used to describe the genesis of dialectics: because sureness of instinct has disappeared, because "we are practically as far as possible from perfection in being, doing, and willing," our desire to know, "symptom of a tremendous decadence," has developed itself; thus we "strive for the opposite of that which strong races, strong natures want—understanding is an ending." In a word: "That science is possible in this sense that is cultivated today is proof that all elementary instincts, life's instincts of self-defense and protection, no longer function."

14. From this point of view, the proclamation in the famous aphorism 374 of *The Gay Science* ("Our New 'Infinite'"), following which "the world has become infinite again for us, in that we cannot reject the possibility of an infinity of interpretations," is directed right at the "scientific prejudice."

15. On this "plebeian" character of science, through which it extends the Socratic dialectic, see *Beyond Good and Evil*, § 206: "What is the scientific man? To begin with, a type of man that is not noble, with the virtues of a type of man that is not noble, which is to say, a type that does not dominate and is neither authoritative nor self-sufficient."

16. Which is why Nietzsche is, to repeat, less a conservative than, properly speaking, a *neo*-conservative.

17. He simply locates the emergence of the idea of subject, and therefore of the philosophy of consciousness, before and at the origins of modernity, since, even if he credits the Moderns, since Descartes and *cogito* philosophy, with the radicalization of the process, he attaches its inauguration to Socrates: see, especially, *The Birth of Tragedy*, §§ 13–14 (the appearance of consciousness as a condition of virtue).

18. *Nietzsches Werke*, Kröner Ausgabe, vol. XIII, § 186.

19. Ibid., vol. XIV, 2nd part, p. 331, § 168.

20. *The Will to Power*, § 1066.

21. Ibid., IV, § 636.

22. It is, in this respect, peculiar that the "philosophy of '68" (*la "pensée 68"*), thinking it had found in Nietzsche one of its main inspirations, never really seemed to be embarrassed by declarations of intention such as this: "In the age of *suffrage universel*, i.e., when everyone may sit in judgment on everyone and everything, I feel impelled to reestablish *order of rank*" (*The Will to Power*, § 854). And see *Beyond Good and Evil*, §§ 257–58.

23. We are thinking of the—numerous—texts which, against the modern notion of equality of rights, explicitly defend slavery: see, for instance, *Beyond Good and Evil*, § 239 (slavery as the "condition for all superior civilization"); or this from the French version of *The Will to Power*:

Though it is true that the Greeks perished through slavery, it is even more certain that we shall perish from no longer having slavery; the latter never scandalized nor horrified the first Christians or the Germanic tribes. What a comfort it is for us to think upon the serf of the Middle Ages, with the vigourous and delicate legal and moral relations that united him with his lord, in the narrowness so rich with sense of his limited existence! What a comfort—and what a reproach! (*La volonté de puissance,* trans. Geneviève Bianquis, Paris: Gallimard, 1948, IV, 322).

And, in a similar vein, § 326: "Slavery must not be abolished; it is a necessity. We only need to see to it that the men emerge *for whom* one will work."

24. *Kröner,* vol. XIV, 1st part, § 237.

25. Ibid., vol. XIII, § 7.

26. At least apparently, for if we reflect on this situation from the point of view of an "extreme fatalism," no veritable choice was in fact given to "the will": the path Socrates rushed into, that of decadence, was itself an inevitable moment of our destiny—something Nietzsche never ceases to suggest when he insists on the way in which decadence is a phenomenon necessary to life (as will to power, which is to say as "the most intimate essence of being"). See, for example, *The Will to Power,* § 40; or: "In my first part, highlight decadence and its necessity."

27. *The Will to Power,* § 842.

28. See Luc Ferry, *Homo Aestheticus,* trans. Robert de Loaiza. Chicago: University of Chicago Press, 1993.

29. Another proof of this, if proof were still needed, is the way in which *Twilight of the Idols* ("Morality as Anti-Nature," § 3) insists that the true "spiritualization" which "triumphs over Christianity" is that which "consists in a profound appreciation of the value of having enemies": "The Church always wanted the destruction of its enemies; we, we immoralists and anti-Christians, find our advantage in this, that the Church exists."

30. In the definition of the "grand style" cited above, didn't Nietzsche invite the future aristocrat to "make himself . . . *law*"?

31. See notably Louis Dumont, *Essays on Individualism,* Chicago: University of Chicago Press, 1986, chap. 6, "The Totalitarian Disease: Individualism and Racism in Adolf Hitler's Representations."

5 The Nietzschean Metaphysics of Life

ROBERT LEGROS

To show the terrestrial roots of the most apparently celestial ideals, but also to suggest the vacuity of the distinction between terrestrial and celestial; to interpret values as signs of subterranean forces, but also to reject any interpretation that sees itself as unique; to reveal the self-interests hiding behind edifying proclamations, but also to question any revelation that pretends to be the ultimate one; to unveil the causes camouflaged by our certainties, but also to repudiate any cause that is presented as the first one. Such is the double path Nietzsche never ceases to follow: to demystify, on the one hand, and, to this end, show, demonstrate, take apart, explain, reveal, and, on the other hand, but indissociably, to make aware of an absence of foundation, of a principle of incomprehensibility of the world, of the abyss all evaluation rests on. To put it his way: to pull down the veils, but in the fashion of the artist—"cling[ing]," that is, "with rapt gaze to what still remains covering even after such uncovering" (*The Birth of Tragedy*, § 15). Which amounts to saying: bring to light, while allowing night to fall. Illuminate—while creating a crevice that makes us aware of bottomless caverns.

If it is thus, if Nietzsche is at the same time a demystifier (he who strikes down the idols) and a "genealogist" (he who know that one never arrives at a primordial origin), if he joins the swinging of the hammer to the art of "transvaluation," criticism with endless questioning, then there is no doubt that his two-sided project corresponds to the demands at the very heart of philosophy—of the philosophy, at least, that does not allow itself to be invaded by the contemplative, theoretical, explicative attitude, by, that is, the "monstrous absence of any mystical disposition" (ibid., § 13). To be more exact, there is no doubt that he radicalizes the demands that are at the heart of philosophy or, rather, and again to say it as he would, that are at the birth of philosophy: that come to light when the thinker still is a "physiologist" and an "artist," when he has not yet given in to the vision of a background-world built up into a true-world. Hegel used to like to say that every philosopher is, first of all, a Spinozist. If we had to take up the remark again today—but it's better not to rely on remarks except, as Hegel did, out of irony—we could say that every philosopher is, first of all, a Nietzschean. How could a philosopher not be Nietzschean, when all of Nietzsche's philosophy sets out to radicalize the two quests that are at the very birth of philosophy: to criticize the obvious tenets that carpet the world and, through creation, to evoke wonder at the irreducible enigma the world conceals? How to pretend to be a philosopher without feeling oneself to be Nietzschean?

On one side, the figure of a pedestrian demystifier, on the other, the halo of a prophet reciting myths issuing from the depths of the earth. At certain moments the free spirit striking down the idols, at others the intoxicated genius feeling himself imbued with a cosmic mission. At times the psychological analysis of beliefs, at others the mystical suggestion of being swallowed up in something inconceivable and unmasterable. Sometimes the Promethean tone of the man who conquers his autonomy and becomes master of his destiny, at other times the exalted, incoherent voice that echoes a loss of self in the world. At times a materialistic "physiologist," at others an artist in the guise of a mediator of the inexpressible: could Nietzsche be, without his knowing it, a romantic *Aufklärer?*

On the one hand a radical critique of metaphysics—of the way of thinking that seeks to establish or that presupposes a *separation* of the physical and the nonphysical, of the sensual and the nonsensual, of the not-intelligible and the intelligible, and which from the beginning attaches to this opposition a distinction between lesser beings and true beings, between appearances and truth, between fiction and reality. On the other a thinking that attempts to *separate* the physical (the body, drives, instincts, organism, life) from the nonphysical (superficial manifestations in the form of thinking within consciousness). On one side a radical critique of metaphysics—of the thinking that sets out to separate what is in the order of *substance,* what remains one and identical with itself, from what is of the order of the accidental, of the derivative, the multiple, what never ceases to differ. And on the other a thinking applied to uncovering one same terrestrial origin, one same human (all-too-human) foundation, one same vital, organic, instinctive basis *subsisting* under the diversity of ideals and undergirding the multiplicity of cultures.

On the one hand a radical critique of metaphysics: of the way of thinking that applies itself to separating the authentic from the inauthentic, the pure from the impure, the subject as *autonomous self,* as sovereign consciousness, from alienated, misled, distracted, overwhelmed, submissive man. And yet on the other hand a thinking that exalts *the autonomy and sovereignty of a fully affirmative "I."* Here, a radical critique of metaphysics: thought that aims at separating the *natural,* evident, undoubtable, given as immediately given, from what is artificial, doubtful, confused, lateral, hidden. There, a thinking that believes it finds in life, in the will to power, in the Dionysiac, the primitive purity of natural forces. On one side a radical critique of metaphysics as the thinking of separation, and on the other a thinking bent on separating the ideal (the overman) from the customary (man), the true (the true insofar as it is at once true and false, real and fictional) from the false (metaphysics). Does Nietzsche remain prisoner of the metaphysics he never stops struggling against?

A radicalization of the demands that are at the birth of philosophy: to reveal mystifications, but also to make aware of a mystery more original than any mysterious manifestation. But, at the very heart of this radicalization, the emergence of oppositions rendered manifest by the Enlightenment (free man and alienated man, individual autonomy and religious heteronomy) and oppositions created within Romanticism (primitive life and self-consciousness, the Self in harmony with the All and the individual who sets out to resemble his peers, the intoxication of union with life and the enslavement of an existence that subordinates itself to the Universal, the richness of singularities and the poverty of identical cases). The Nietzschean critique of metaphysics—the radicalization of the requirements at the birth of philosophy: is it not fated to get stuck in the very oppositions—in the metaphysics—it brings back to life? Does it not lead back to a new metaphysics (of, certainly, a peculiar and bizarre kind: an Enlightenment metaphysics melted into Romanticist metaphysics) that denies the most ancient requirements of philosophy?

Every philosopher is, first of all, a Nietzschean; he must, as a philosopher, take up again the spirit of a radical, Nietzschean critique of metaphysics. But isn't he by that very movement led to disavow Nietzsche: to question the massive return of the oppositions Nietzsche continually hangs on to?*

Let us begin by asking ourselves questions about the meaning of the Nietzschean critique of metaphysics. What could it mean to question the separation of the sensual/sensible and the nonsensible, of appearance and reality, of difference and identity, of the multiple and the one? What sense can one give to the denunciation of the "belief in the self" as illusory—as illusory as the "belief in logic"—without immediately falling into the liar's sophism (into what we call today performative contradictions)? In what sense can a path of thinking give up the separation between truth and fiction without denying itself?

Metaphysics resides for Nietzsche in a determination of the essence of truth: the being is true that appears without differing from itself or diversifying itself, that presents itself in the form of a stable given, that offers itself up while constantly remaining one and identical to itself. That which, on the contrary, never ceases changing, escaping from the grips of the concept, eluding all determinations: in a word, that which does not allow itself to be reduced to any identification is not really, or is only apparently, or is only a lesser, being. According to the Platonic structure of metaphysics: only the idea is true, for it alone constantly remains one and identical with itself. And the sensible being is a lesser being to the extent that it does not cease to differ from itself, to diversify itself into multiple appearances. Thus a bed, as Plato observes, "seems different but is not in any way different" (*Republic*, 598a): it seems different because it is not the same bed when I look at it from this side or from that side. But it does not differ because it is the same bed I'm looking at. The bed that remains the same is the only veritable bed, while the bed that never stops differing is only the appearance of *a* bed. The first is intelligible, the second sensible. The first is true, insofar as it remains one and identical with itself; the second false, since it has neither unity nor identity. Of course, in daily life, when I see the various appearances of *a* bed, I'm seeing the appearances of a bed, but I see them

---

*In this critique of Nietzsche, I have been very largely inspired by Eugen Fink's and Michel Haar's commentaries and interpretations. It is a pleasure for me to point out this debt.

thus to the extent that they already participate in the intelligible, are already perceived from the standpoint of the idea of which they are the appearances: in "themselves" they are not even the appearances of a bed, they are nothing but a pure chaotic multiplicity, a manifoldness in which nothing appears except to disappear. That, according to Nietzsche, is the separation operated by metaphysics: on one side what is purely and simply one and on the other a multiplicity with no intrinsic unity.

We know that empiricism carries out an inversion of Platonism: sensual experience can be true as long as it is not deformed by an interpretation or misshapen by our concepts. But the metaphysical structure remains unchanged, the sensual given (this whiteness, or this immediately perceived thing, or the fact that appears to a neutral and passive observation) being true to the extent that, in itself, it is one and identical with itself. Just as with the idea, the empirical object (sensation, thing, state of fact) is recognized as a source of knowledge to the extent that it is in itself what it is. The whiteness of this lily manifests itself as an *evidence,* according to Locke—therefore in the same way as the idea as conceived of by Plato—precisely because it remains one and identical with itself. It remains one because it is *one* whiteness I see when I look at a lily, and this whiteness, intrinsically one, remains the same since I recognize it, according to Locke, when I see it again. The thing conceived as an idea, on the other hand, is a lesser being than this concrete and immediate whiteness, according to the empiricist, because of its generality: because it is abstract (taken out of empirical data) and applies to a manifoldness (the distinct and different empirical givens it is taken from), this generality possesses a lesser substantial content, it is of a hypothetical nature, artificial, to be used with caution. The more universal the concept, the emptier.

Just as the sensible manifoldness conceived of by Plato cannot appear except to disappear into a confusion that leads to nonbeing, or at least if it is cut off from all participation in the intelligible, so the universal as it is understood by empiricism loses itself in emptiness the moment it is cut off from the sensible. Plato: if completely carried out, particularization towards a sensible cut off from all participation in the intelligible leads to the emptiness of night. The empiricists: if completely carried out, generalization towards a universal cut off from all sensible content leads to the emptiness of the heavens. Plato: between the unity of the idea and the sensible manifold, there is a multiplicity (for example a sensible thing) not devoid of all unity thanks to its participation in the intelligible. The empiricists: between the unity of the distinct empirical datum and the abstract universal, there is a multiplicity (for example a sensible thing) not devoid of unity thanks to associations based on habit. In the one as in the other case, stable and identifiable unity is at one end, emptiness at the other, and a multiplicity between the two extremes. In one as in the other case: outside unity and emptiness, a multiplicity that maintains a certain unity, but a unity exterior to it. The unity that a sensible thing manifests belongs not to the sensible realm, but either to the intelligible (Plato) or to a hypothetical or presupposed unity (empiricism).

Truth reduced to identity and to unity is a truth that gives itself up quite purely and simply. It gives itself up in the sense that its discovery involves, in principle, no invention, no putting into shape, no elaboration other that the act of unveiling and of directing one's gaze towards what is unveiled. Metaphysical truth—whether the idea in Plato's meaning or the brute empirical datum as empiricism means it—is a *naked* truth, meaning that it gives itself up in a native evidence. But evidence, as Nietzsche demonstrates, always carries an illusion with it: it requires a state of blindness. It indeed appears as an immediate and native evidence, as a given or datum that allows itself to be discovered, but it necessarily presupposes the act of separating identity from difference. The bed can give itself up as fully and immediately evident only to the extent that the veritable bed is reduced to the idea of a bed, held to be one and constantly the same, or to a sensual and distinct datum of a bed, held in its turn to be intrinsically one and identical with itself: in the one as in the other case, the evident *is conquered by an act* of disassociating what will be aimed at as a unity from what will be treated as subject to alterity, difference, and multiplicity. The evident is arrived at through a disassociation and an identification, but it gives itself out to be simply given and native in principle: it hides the action of separating and identifying what is presupposed by it. What is evident hides the fact that it hides: it is in this sense that it is much more deceitful that the confused and the obscure.

Nothing presents itself as identical with itself without an act of separating, without a separation that is an identification. But this identification brings about an illusion not only because it is destined to forget itself as identification, to let identity look like merely a given, native identity, but also because it is profoundly reductive: it makes for an am-

putation precisely to the extent that it rejects all that belongs to multiplicity, to mobility, to variation, to everything, in a word, that gives itself only by differentiating itself. It denies life itself—there being no life
without a diversification and a differentiation—and holds on only to an
illusion: a form that is flat (it is without depth because it hides nothing),
immobile (it remains constantly the same), and temporal (it remains
perpetually present).

The separation that is constitutive of metaphysics—of the comprehension of truth as identity—is not only the source of an illusion but
also the origin of a subjugation. For truth-identity (the reduction to
identity or reductionist identification) brings about the concept of
truth-adequacy: what *submits* itself to truth-identity is true. Not only
does truth reduced to identity make possible the idea of an adequateness
to truth (how could there be adequateness to a truth understood as infinite differentiation?), it demands it: if identity is truth (if it gives itself in
the form of an evidence, without differentiation), then we must con-
form to it. Whether we are dealing with logos or creation or action,
metaphysics imposes from the outset the criterion of a submission to
truth-identity (to an apparently preexisting and independent given that
seems to contain its truth in itself and presents itself as an originary evidence): submission of the logos to an independent reality (to a suprasensible idea or to a raw empirical fact), of creation to an (ideal or
empirical) model, and of action to external and given normative principles. Aimed as it is against the concept of truth-identity, the Nietzschean critique of metaphysics is by the same movement aimed against
the concept of truth-adequacy: therefore the radical questioning of the
theoretical or contemplative attitude (of the logos as submission to a
given reality), of art as imitation (of creation as submission to a model),
and of morality as obedience (as conformity to given principles).

The empiricist overturning of Platonism maintains its metaphysical structure (separation) and the Platonic understanding of truth (reduction of truth to identity), but it presupposes a new conception of the
sensible: the sensual or sensible datum (sensation as thought of by the
sensualists, or the fact as understood by those Nietzsche calls the *"fai-
talistes"*) is capable of giving itself up purely and simply, independently
of an infinite differentiation or of an irreducible diversification. Far
from dissipating itself in an obscure confusion, sensible appearance, according to empiricism, presents itself as the Platonic idea does: as a
datum or given that is immediately what it is, clear and distinct in itself,

and can appear as it is provided that it is discovered: that is, received without being deformed or obscured by an intermediary. The Nietzschean critique of metaphysics surely rests on an acknowledgment of the sensible, but not at all on this empiricist rehabilitation of the sensible: it grants to no sensual appearance the possibility of being able to be present without differentiation or diversification. The sensible is for Nietzsche the world of an infinite differentiation, of an infinite diversification; one will never find there a given that can offer itself up in the evidence of its simplicity and its identity, whether it be a sensual datum, a fact, or a thing.

Unlike empiricism, in other words, Nietzsche contests the Platonic interpretation of truth: the true is found neither in identity, nor in the identity of an idea, nor in the identity of a sensible appearance, but in an infinite differentiation-diversification. Nothing truly shows itself except through diversifying itself into multiple and mutually irreducible perspectives, be it idea, fact, or sensation. How can we understand this so radically new conception of the essence of truth?

To say that the idea never presents itself without diversifying itself is to say that it is in itself a differentiation of sensible appearances, that it is nothing outside of incarnation. To say that a sensible "thing" (sensation, empirical thing, or observable fact) never manifests itself without diversifying itself is to say that it is in itself a diversity of interpretations, of perspectives; that it is nothing outside of the various *comprehensions* that grasp at it: in a word, that it is itself animated by meanings. The idea is nothing outside of its incarnation, and the sensible in which it takes body is nothing outside of the meanings or the multiple senses that animate it: idea incarnate or animated body, the real is, in one word, *life*.

That the real is life means, in Nietzsche's conception of it, that it is never naked. The most simple color remains irreducibly veiled, since it never manifests itself otherwise than loaded with diverse senses and with meanings that nevertheless remain hidden to consciousness. The simplest idea remains irreducibly veiled since it never shows itself except under diverse sensible manifestations that escape unification. That amounts to saying that no sensation is simple, that no idea is simple, or that every sensation, and every idea, encloses an irreducible secret, that our ideas and sensations speak to us and escape us, that sensations cannot be separated from our intellection of them nor ideas from the sensual perceptions through which we grasp them. The sensible is itself nonsensible, since it is impregnated with multiple meanings, mutually hidden and irreducible, and the idea is itself sensual since it is itself diverse, scattered into multiple appearances from which it can never be separated. Such a rejection of the separation of the sensible from the intelligible forces us to conceive of the idea of a body that thinks— which is itself animate—and of an incarnate soul, one that is itself "mortal" and "multiple" (*Beyond Good and Evil*, § 12). How can we understand this essence of truth as life or as the original union of the sensible and the nonsensible, of the intelligible and the nonintelligible?

We could of course speak of a Nietzschean inversion of the way metaphysics (both Platonist and empiricist) understood truth: truth, claims Nietzsche, lies not in identity (truth-identity itself being a carrier of illusion), nor, therefore, in adequateness (truth-adequacy itself being the source of an enslavement), but, on the contrary, in an infinite differentiation, in the diversification of appearances, of interpretations, of perspectives. Yet it goes without saying that this inversion is not a mere inversion: it is not the sensible as it is interpreted by Plato which is for Nietzsche the manifestation of truth: such a sensible cannot be cut off from its participation in the intelligible without disappearing into the night of nonbeing. The bed that to Plato seems to differ from itself is for him a sensible/sense-perceptible bed, but its differentiation is still that of a bed to the extent that the sensible bed participates in the intelligible one. Torn away from all intelligibility, from all unity, the bed no longer differs. Or, rather, it is no longer *one* bed that differs: differentiation itself dissipates into a pure manifoldness that itself disappears as manifoldness. Nietzsche cannot envision referring to Plato's concept of the sensible as to a truth since it would then lose all relation to the sensible: Plato's sensible is no longer sensible when it is abstracted out of all intelligibility, it becomes rather nonbeing—that at least is how it goes in the logic of metaphysics. What is the sense of Nietzsche's return to the sensible, if the sensible he tends to rehabilitate is, on principle, not Plato's sensible?

The sensible Nietzsche speaks of when he evokes plurality, difference, diversity, alterity, is of course in no way the sensible of the empiricists, and this to the very extent that the latter claim to find at the very heart of sensual perception a given that is supposed to be clear and distinct because it is simply and immediately received: a naked sensation or a crude fact. The Nietzschean critique of metaphysics cannot refer to the empiricists' sensible as if to a manifestation of truth because that sensible is not sensible: in its being as clear and distinct given *(donnée),* the empiricists' sensual datum *(donnée)* knows no diversifications inherent to itself and no internal differentiation and therefore presents none of the traits that characterize the sensible.

Though it is true that Nietzsche claims that truth is found in the sensible, we have to understand that the "veritable" sensible cannot be, according to him, either Plato's sensible or the empiricists', since neither the one nor the other is the sensible (differentiation, diversification). We have, that is to say, to understand that the "true" sensible—"true" meaning according to the Nietzschean understanding of truth, not in the metaphysical meaning of truth-identity or truth-adequacy—cannot be that which appears *after* the separation. If indeed the sensible can be understood starting with the distinction between sensible and nonsensible, it disappears as sensible: it is no longer the sensible but "a" manifoldness that is swallowed up in nonbeing (Plato), or "a" manifoldness made up of a multiplicity of simple empirical data that put an end to diversification and differentiation (empiricism). Consequently, we need to understand, if we seek to follow the Nietzschean critique of metaphysics, that the sensible cannot be grasped as sensible except to the extent that it is more original that is the sensible of metaphysics, more original than the separation between the sensible and the nonsensible or of the intelligible and the nonintelligible. The metaphysical separation is nocuous in Nietzsche's eyes precisely because it cuts us off from contact with the sensible: with the sensible, that is *from before the separation,* which is the only sensible that is the sensible (insofar as it is also the nonsensible, or rather not yet separated from the nonsensible). Which amounts to saying that the separation deprives us of contact with the intelligible, with identity, with unity—with, that is, the intelligible, identity, unity from before the separation, and therefore with an intelligible that is "really" intelligible insofar as it is intrinsically sensible, with an identity which is in itself differentiation and not what Nietzsche calls fixed, frozen, immobilized identity, one that is no longer a "veritable" identity.

To sum up: it is not the cleft sensible that can, for Nietzsche, be a manifestation of truth, but the sensible from before the separation; and it is not the intelligible as such that is for Nietzsche an illusion, nor are identity, unity, or truth as such, but rather the intelligible separated from the sensible, and separated identity, unity, truth: all frozen, fixed. In what sense, a sensible and an intelligible realm before their separation? In what sense, an identity not frozen? In what sense, an original union of the one and the multiple? More precisely: in what sense are the "true" truth that is metaphysically false (truth not separated from fiction) and the "false" truth that is metaphysically true (that is, separated truth) not in a relation of opposition which, as such, would be a metaphysical relation? In a word: in what sense life?

"With the 'true world'," Nietzsche writes, "we have also abolished the apparent one" (*Twilight of the Idols:* "How the 'True World' Finally Became a Fable"). We may say: together with the concept of truth-identity or of truth-adequacy, we have abolished the world of appearances conceived of by Plato as the world of multiplicity without internal unity, as the world of unintelligible appearances; we have abolished truth-identity and appearance-difference, and we have inaugurated an appearance that is truth and fiction, identity and difference, or, what comes down to the same thing, truth as differentiation of identity, or identity as nonfrozen identity; we have abolished reductive identification, or reduction to identity, in order to inaugurate differentiated identity. To what extent can the abolition of truth-identity make way for truth as differentiation (of identity)?

The appearance that is truth and fiction is no longer appearance in Plato's sense: the truth that is in it is not external to it, does not consist of something of another nature in which appearance participates. Due to the very fact that truth is at the heart of appearances—that it is itself only truth through this incarnation in sensual appearance—appearances do not swallow each other up and sink into the night of nonbeing, but rather relay one another or transport us from the one to the other, one appearance opening up onto others, without ever converging in an ultimate appearance that would be the sole manifestation of truth. Every appearance refers us to another appearance, without any one ever clearly standing out from the others and presenting itself, like sensual appearances according to empiricism, as an atomic entity, clear and distinct in itself. Every appearance transports us to other appearances precisely because each one comprehends within itself other appearances and forms with them the unity of a differentiation, unity that escapes all fixation, all reductive identification, for it is in itself inherent to differentiation. Every appearance comprehends within itself other appearances, but each one is irreducible to the others: it is in that sense that the sensible is an infinite profusion, overabundance, overspilling, "richer" than any concepts. Mutually irreducible appearances which nevertheless endlessly point us towards other appearances: such is life, and according to Nietzsche such is also becoming, or at least becoming before metaphysical separation, before the distinction between immobility and mobility, between stability and change, between eternity and becoming.

Together with the "true world," Nietzsche claims to have abolished the "apparent world": that of appearances as shadows vanishing into confusion (Platonism) or of appearances as atomic entities that dissipate into discontinuity (empiricism). This abolition is for Nietzsche the precondition for a transfiguration of appearance, thanks to which appearance can become truth and fiction identity and difference. The abolition of the "true world" is a necessary condition for the inauguration of a transfigured appearance, of appearance before separation, but it is not a sufficient condition: it is not enough to abolish appearance in order to bring about the advent of sensual appearance before the separation, or of identity before separation. In other words: "total" nihilism (nothing is true, nothing is reducible to a truth-identity, no value has any meaning) is not yet the Dionysiac affirmation, the creation, that is, of the unity of opposites, of the identity of differences. There is no return to the "original"—to the world before separation—that is not also a creation: truth (as differentiation) is indissociable from art (as creation) because it is only in the arrival of the new that identity can establish itself as differentiation. In what sense is creation the advent of identity as differentiation—the inauguration of truth? Which is to ask: in what sense is "life" (as differentiation) *creation?*

Philosophy cannot break with metaphysics, Nietzsche suggests, it remains dependent on the separation, if it limits itself to abolishing said separation through critique, if it limits itself to rejecting metaphysics through deconstruction, even if it is done with a hammer. It must of course take up this work of criticism, reveal the illusion at the heart of all evidences, the error animating every interpretation that wishes to be, or thinks it is, unique, or of every revelation that claims to be the ultimate one, but it remains tied to metaphysics—to truth as reductive identification—if its questioning is not itself traversed by a creative force. Philosophy as critique of metaphysics denies itself if it isn't an art of turning language in on itself, of leading, that is, language, which as a shared language is a fabrication of false identities, to subvert itself by allowing fractured identities to emerge as irreconcilable fragments, if it doesn't forge concepts that escape the logic of the concept. Philosophy, in other words, denies itself if it isn't at the same time philosophy (critique of metaphysics) and nonphilosophy (art, creation, poetry). It cannot say the origin if it isn't creation, if it is identification, presentation of a given, description of a model: indeed, from the very circumstance that the origin is more original than the separation between the original and its copies, philosophy cannot be converted into an original—into a model, a fixed identity—without immediately disappearing as origin.

Thus summarized to its main themes, the Nietzschean critique of metaphysics naturally lends itself to various interpretations. It would moreover be in contradiction with itself if it claimed to be unequivocal. Because of this, we can legitimately ask what interpretations of this critique are suggested by Nietzsche himself. How does Nietzsche understand the rejection of dualism (of the evidence of ideas and the evidence of the senses) and the original union of the sensible and the nonsensible (of fiction and of truth), and what are his interpretations of the demand to fuse this critique of metaphysics with an art of allowing fragmented, differentiated identities to emerge? Let us try to present some of the interpretations through which Nietzsche claims to contest the principles of metaphysics.

The Nietzschean critique of metaphysics—of the separation between the "true world" and the world of appearances—implies a critical rejection of naturalism (or of the idea of a reality-in-itself) and of subjectivism (of man conceived of as a subject defined by consciousness and will). It leads, in other words, to a rejection of the nature-*nomos* opposition understood as opposition between a reality (or a norm) in itself, containing its truth in itself, or one whose basis is natural, and a reality (or a norm) stemming from man (from his decision, creation, elaboration, convention, will). But we may note that Nietzsche never follows up his critique of metaphysics without returning in a way to the nature-convention opposition. Even when his general aim seems to be animated by a subversion of metaphysics—of the ideas of truth-identity, of truth-adequacy—his way of proceeding seems to lead back to the opposition between nature and *nomos*, between in-itself and pure creation, between true and conventional.

His thought can of course be interpreted as an attempt to question the (metaphysical) opposition between nature and *nomos*, and it makes room for the idea of an original union of nature and the human, of the

nonconventional and the conventional, yet it never ceases to reintroduce, in the very heart of his analyses, either the presupposed notion
of a nature prior to the conventional or the affirmation of a convention
freed from the nonconventional.

The Nietzschean criticism of the reduction of truth to identity is inseparable from a critique of the in-itself or of what is generally called realism:
any reality conceived of as reality in itself—whether an idea, an empirical reality, an ideal or a value—is in fact a reality reduced to identity and
considered to be in itself separate from the various interpretations or
representations it can give rise to, from the partial perceptions it can
provide, and from the different languages that can express it. Rejecting
as he does any conception of a reality in itself, Nietzsche rejects also the
classical concept of nature as an independent reality— one which is
what it is independently of our interpretations, elaborations, languages,
conventions, creations—and consequently contests any ideas about a
natural foundation for our principles, values, and concepts, or about a
natural model that our creations, actions, languages, or conventions
could imitate.
    At the same time that it leads to questioning all forms of natural-
ism or of realism, the Nietzschean critique of metaphysics (of the separation of truth and appearance, of ideas and the sensual) leads to a
rejection of subjectivism or of any definition of the human being as consciousness or will. The human subject that is defined by consciousness is
metaphysical (it is based on the metaphysical separation) because it is
supposed to know fully what it is thinking, and, in consequence, to possess clear and distinct ideas, ideas therefore separated from the sensible
and freed from any internal differentiation; it is moreover supposed to
be the subject of its ideas, as if a subject one and identical with itself
could subsist while its ideas vary. And the human subject that is defined
by will is metaphysical to the same extent, to the extent at least to which
will is thought of as cause, since the human is taken to be master of the
situation (if will is cause, then the resulting effects have been willed),
and is therefore taken to be in touch with a sensual realm that is sensible
in a simple way (that is not secretly animated by different and mutually
irreducible meanings) and with ideas that are intelligible in a simple
manner (ones that come to the subject when the latter wills it), and because, furthermore, he is taken to be the subject of his actions, as if he
continued to be one and identical while his actions vary.

Truth to tell, Nietzsche pints out, the "I" is never the subject of its thoughts: it never fully knows what it thinks, nor what thinking means, and it is never master of its thoughts ("thoughts come to me when 'they' want and not when 'I' want"); and the self is not the subject of its actions either: it is never the first cause nor the master of action, the "self" being neither one nor identical with itself but rather plurality and differentiation. Individual unity is fictive because, first of all, the self is not behind (separate from) a multiplicity, it is nothing outside of a diversity of roles, of potentialities, and, second of all, because this multiplicity that certainly is one (the veritable multiplicity is the one prior to the separation between multiplicity and unity) is nevertheless not a totality that can be isolated but itself constitutes a "fragment": it is as a fragment that the (diversified and differentiated) self is always and irreducibly overwhelmed, absorbed, dispersed, without for all that ever being fully dissolved and lost (differentiation remains differentiation of a self), and it is also as a fragment that the (overwhelmed and dispersed) self is "cosmic."

Rejecting the ideas of a natural and of an individual foundation, the Nietzschean critique of metaphysics summons us to go beyond the opposition between nature (conceived of as reality in itself) and *nomos* (conceived of as law willed by men): (ideal) value, Nietzsche shows, can be understood neither as being natural nor as a product of conscious subjectivity. How does Nietzsche himself interpret the nonnatural, yet nonconventional (in the strict sense, according to which a convention is tied to consciousness and to will) character of values, of principles, of norms, of ideas, of words, of things?

Even as he is led to refuse the opposition of the natural and the conventional, or of nature (as foundation) and the individual (as foundation), Nietzsche never stops criticizing naturalism by referring to individual autonomy and to man as source of values, while simultaneously criticizing subjectivism by calling on a nature that is natural in a simple fashion. Man is on the one hand explicitly or tacitly constructed as sovereign and independent subject and on the other he is explicitly or tacitly interpreted as being an "organic" body whose "instrument" is consciousness, a body agitated by instincts and drives, absorbed in the flux of a purely natural life.

That the human being is "fundamentally" or "originally" or "primitively" an autonomous individual, the creator of his world, is a theme discernible throughout Nietzsche's work. We may call to mind the exaltation of the "free spirit" as it is developed around the time of *The Gay Science:* it always comes down to supposing that man has forgotten that he is the author of his principles, his ideas, his projects, and his world, that he thereafter wrongly imagined that the divine or the superhuman were outside of himself, and that he can consequently only liberate himself if he acknowledges being what he is, a creator, if he does not himself become what he is, a creator master over himself. The same theme comes up when Nietzsche wonders about the origin of religions: religion is born when man experiences "as a revelation" *(Offenbarung)* what is in fact only "his own opinion about things":

Then, one day, he suddenly acquires *his* new idea, and the happiness engendered by a great hypothesis encompassing the universe and all existence enters his consciousness with such force he does not dare to consider himself the creator of such happiness and ascribes the cause of it, and again the cause of the cause of this new idea to his god: as his god's revelation. *(The Dawn, § 62)*

Man is thought of as the foundation for his religion, but also for all the other "predicates" attributed to things.

We have long reflected and come to the conclusion that nothing is good, nothing beautiful, nothing sublime, nothing evil in itself; these are states of the soul in which we cover with words things that are outside and inside us. We have taken back the predicates we gave to things, or we have at least recalled that we gave them: let us see to it that, with this insight, we do not lose the capacity to give, and become at once richer and more miserly. (ibid., § 210)

Origin of his religion, source of the predicates that he attributes to things, man is the creator of his world: "What you have called world, you have to begin by creating it: your reason, your imagination, your will, your love must come from this world!" *(Zarathustra,* 2d part).

And the same theme of the creative and autonomous human being is the basis for the Nietzschean opposition of masters to slaves, since the latter rests on a distinction between the "sovereignty of the individual" and the "instincts of the herd," between the individual who is fully independent (of other individuals), incomparable (to other individuals), unique, irreducible to generality, that is to say, the master or "great individuality" (for example the Greeks before Socrates), and, at the other end, the human being that is absorbed by the species, become a "herd animal" attached to gregarious values. An idea of man as autonomous, sovereign, independent, original, unique creator is once again the basis for a conception of philosophy as creation of values: "*Genuine philosophers . . . are commanders and legislators:* they say, "*thus it shall* be!" They first determine the Whither *(das Wohin?)* and the For What *(das Wozu?)* of man" *(Beyond Good and Evil,* § 211).

The critique of the separation of the true and of appearances, of the supersensible and the sensible, or the critique of reductive identification no doubt implies criticism of the ideas of revelation and of a reality in itself, and, inseparably, the recognition of the human world as a human creation, as a creation founded on no previously given nature, on no natural order. But the critique of metaphysics also implies a critical examination of man as creator-subject: it forces us to envisage human creation as a creation of which man is not the sovereign subject, or that the world is a human creation (it is not of the order of *physis*) but not a creation produced by man (not of the order of *nomos*). To raise the individual up as the autonomous subject of his creations is to suppose that man is human by himself, that he is human prior to his giving shape and meaning to his world (prior to creation), and that he is therefore not "originally" sunk in differentiation (in a world before the separation of the sensible and the nonsensible) but finds himself faced with a purely sensible manifoldness, a shapeless and unintelligible multiplicity (things do not yet have the predicates man is going to attach to them, they do not yet have the meaning he will grant them, or the sense he will confer upon them, they are not yet in the order into whose hierarchy he will place them). Any critique of heteronomy (of a natural or divine reality as being the basis of ideals) of course constitutes a critique of metaphysics (of reductive identification), but it falls back into what it denounces (it restores the opposition between the same and the different, origin and derivative, the one and the multiple) the moment it calls upon the individual's sovereignty or on the autonomy of a human being supposed to be the creator/subject of his world's shape and meaning, the master of things and of sense.

By calling upon a man author of his creations, whose autonomy is radical, Nietzsche obliterates man's native insertion at the heart of what overwhelms him (within a world in which all apparent identity is the mask of an infinite differentiation); he thereby restores the concept of a naturally human human (human prior to insertion within a world) and in consequence reintroduces the opposition between the natural and the nonnatural and turns away from the interpretation his own thinking leads us to, the interpretation of the "self" as being originally "cosmic." What is the meaning of a fully independent, distinctive, unique, incomparable man, an individual in the strong sense of the word, if it is true that the "self" is an illusion, that individual unity is fictive, and that the individual (in the sense of *individuum*) "is an error"?

In bowing his head before meanings, ideals, and norms as if before revealed and superior realities, man in fact prostrates himself before his own creatures. In other words: every ideal (every truth-identity) is an idol (a representation worshipped as if it were the divinity itself), but it is in reality only a fetish (a human creation that is no longer recognized to be such, but is perceived as if it were a divine creation). Setting out from this critique of fetishism, Nietzsche sometimes concludes that there is something superhuman in man: doesn't the superhuman become human if man is the veritable creator of what appears to be superhuman? From this arise the themes of the free spirit, of autonomous sovereignty, of the individual master and creator of his world: it is by becoming the creator that he is, by acknowledging himself creator of his world, that man is on the road to the superhuman. But from this same critique of fetishism, Nietzsche also arrives at the human—all-too-human—quality of the superhuman: "There where you see the ideal, I see only human things, alas, too human!" *(Ecce Homo)*. That is: as the basis for everything that seems celestial, disinterested, moral, sacred, divine, we find only desires, instincts, vital forces, organic needs. Because he believes in "the opposition of values" *(an die Gegensätze der Werthe)*, the metaphysician asks, "How *could* anything originate out of its opposite *(aus seinem Gegensatz entstehen)*? for example, truth out of error? or the will to truth out of the will to deception? or selfless deeds out of selfishness? or the pure and sunlike gaze of the sage out of lust?" And he can only conclude: "Such origins are impossible" *(Beyond Good and Evil, § 2)*.

Because it questions the fundamental principle of the "opposition of values," the Nietzschean critique leads to the question: how do truth and error come to be separated? How is the will sundered into two distinct wills, the will to truth and the will to deceive? How do self-effacement and selfishness or looking and desiring come to be opposed to one another? And the critique can only conclude: opposites are born

as an effect of a forgetting or of a negation of a "life" that is more original than the oppositions. But Nietzsche is far from drawing only this
conclusion: he does not avoid the idea that truth may be born out of
error, the will to truth out of the will to deceive, or a pure vision out of
desire: "it would still be possible" he writes, in the conditional, "that a
higher and more fundamental value *(grundsätzlicherer Werth)* for life
might have to be ascribed to deception, selfishness, and lust" *(Beyond
Good and Evil,* § 2).

At times, man is shown to be conquering his sovereignty by going
beyond the human or on the way towards overcoming his humanity; at
others, he is shown as brought back to his selfishness, his self-interest,
his will to deceive, to the earthbound. Following the first branch of the
alternative, humanity is divided into two types or includes two extremes
which, at their limits, no longer belong to humanity: at one extreme, the
overman ("something that is no longer man," writes Nietzsche), and at
the other extreme, the "last man," the human being reduced to a "herd
animal" (therefore, we may ask, also something that is no longer human?). Shouldn't we then at this point understand how animality—
life—is also, for Nietzsche, sundered into two types: the fully affirmative life of the "human being" who has torn himself away from nihilism
(from all forms of negation of life), that is, the life of the overman, on the
one side, and, on the other, teeming humanity, life reduced to the herd's
life? Following the second branch of the alternative, humanity is also
divided into two types: the kind of life, on the one hand, that believes in
the consistency or independence of truth, or disinterestedness, of the
celestial, and the life, on the other hand, that has no illusions about human or celestial motives or about the world's ephemeral and deceitful
quality.

Nietzsche's way of thinking about life assuredly lends itself to various
interpretations. Led on as he is by his radical critique of metaphysics (of
dualism), Nietzsche is forced to think of human life as life which is not
lacking in characteristics that are generally assigned to the mind, and to
conceive of the human body as a body not separate from the soul (from
a soul that is itself "mortal" and "multiple"). The body that is the
"guiding thread" of the Nietzschean reflection on art is without a doubt
a "thinking body." It is, however, also certain that Nietzsche comes to
present life not only as a biological reality, as a combination of forces,
instincts, and inclinations, but also as an ultimate and natural founda-

tion. Is this a stratagem meant to tear down the illusions of a metaphysics of consciousness, or the naïveté of a kind of understanding that
is still prisoner of naturalist illusions?

We know that, for Nietzsche, our most apparently obvious judgments, our most certain evaluations, our most assured moral beliefs,
have an "instinctive" basis and rest upon "physiological requirements,"
stemming from a vital desire for preservation. A value judgment makes
sense, he maintains, only within the perspective of preservation
(whether of an individual, a culture, or a collectivity). Yet we cannot go
on from this explanation through instinct and conclude that this is a
biologism or a naturalism: Nietzsche, in fact, constantly tries to draw
out the cultural or historical origins of our "instincts," of our seemingly
most spontaneous inclinations.

For instance: metaphysical evaluations. "For example, that the
definite should be worth more than the indefinite, and mere appearance
worth less than 'truth'" (*Beyond Good and Evil,* § 3). Nietzsche calls
"instinctive" such evaluations that have become self-evident. They in
fact respond to a "physiological demand": they permit the conservation
of a certain way of living (one dominated by metaphysics). And they
express themselves with the spontaneity characteristic of instinct, with
the automaticity that any self-evidence calls forth. Yet it nevertheless
goes without saying that such "instinctive" evaluations have, in Nietzsche's eyes, no instinctive basis in any naturalistic sense of the word.

Example: the instincts undergirding either altruistic morality or
utilitarian prejudices, the instinct of pity, the social instincts, the instinct
of renunciation. It goes equally without saying that in Nietzsche's eyes
these "instincts" or "drives" are the products of history, or that they are
strictly tied to one culture: modern European culture. Nietzsche is one
with Tocqueville on this point: the feeling of pity and the desire for
equality, tied originally the one to the other, seem to be immediate,
spontaneous, nonreflexive, but they are in no wise embedded in a universal human nature; far from being founded upon a naturally human
sensibility, they represent a "symptom . . . of our European culture"
(*The Genealogy of Morals,* preface, 5); far from revealing a natural
inclination of the biological body, they are but the signs of one culture.
(Nietzsche, of course, is radically opposed to Tocqueville in his evaluation of the feeling of pity, since he sees in it "the most disquieting symptom of our European culture," and sees in the "instincts" that are
originally tied to it, the altruistic instincts and the desire for equality,

"humanity's great barrier reef"; ibid.) Does this mean that behind Nietzsche's naturalistic or vitalistic vocabulary a way of understanding freed from any naturalistic or biologistic vision comes to expression?

However attentive Nietzsche may be in tracing out the historical origins of inclinations that seem to be natural, or the cultural origin of "instinctive evaluations," he does not thereby renounce seeking, behind or underneath these cultural, historically arrived-at "drives," instincts he himself understands as natural: instincts preceding any insertion in a culture or in mores, more original than their diverse cultural expressions. He goes so far as to oppose instinct *in itself* and the "same" instinct covered over with a moral meaning, absorbed into the prevailing mores, become a "second nature":

> The same drive *(der selbe Trieb)* evolves into the painful feeling of *cowardice* under the impress of the reproach custom has imposed upon this drive: or into the pleasant feeling of *humility* if it happens that a custom such as the Christian has taken it to its heart and called it *good*. That is to say, it is attended by either a good or a bad conscience! In itself it has, *like every drive,* neither this moral character nor any moral character at all, nor even a definite attendant sensation of pleasure or displeasure: it acquires all this, as its second nature, only when it enters into relations with drives already baptized good or evil or is noted as a quality of beings the people has already evaluated and determined in a moral sense. *(Daybreak,* § 38; Nietzsche's italics)

How does Nietzsche interpret this opposition between an instinct "in itself," a natural one, and the "same" instinct *integrated* into the prevailing mores, given a moral meaning, become culture?

This opposition can of course receive an interpretation faithful to the Nietzschean critique of metaphysics. It can indeed be understood as an "opposition" whose terms are inseparable from one another; which are not merely opposed to one another. In this conception, the instinct "in itself" would be aimed at not as a distinct entity, graspable in itself, but rather as an empty unit, as an identity that is certainly *thinkable* but imperceptible outside its differentiation. We would then have to acknowledge—as does, for example, Tocqueville—that we can say nothing, except negatively, about a natural inclination inherent to human sensibility (about envy, about fear, about jealousy, about love, about hatred, about astonishment, about anger, about desire for power, etc.), that we can in no manner conceive of a natural inclination as such, inserted into a human nature (that would be to know a *"thing in itself"*), that we can reflect upon it only by referring to its various historical or cultural manifestations, to the expressions it takes on within distinct humanities, and that we cannot apprehend these diverse manifestations as specific cases of one same identity, as accidents of the same substance, precisely because their most essential "substance" is found not at all in what they have in common but rather in what differentiates them, or rather because their "common substance" cannot be separated from what differentiates them without being immediately emptied of all substantial content.

Such is the Nietzschean interpretation of the "opposition" (of the original nonseparation) between the in-itself and its manifestation, between nature and culture, between the universal and the historical, but such is nevertheless not the interpretation Nietzsche himself follows when he distinguishes between, on the one hand, the instinct that appears without as yet having received the least cultural connotation, the least moral evaluation, and, on the other hand, the "same" instinct as it is experienced and interpreted within a specific humanity. Nietzsche thus speaks of envy as a natural instinct devoid of any moral meaning and distinguishes it from envy as it is experienced by the Greeks (as being good and beneficent) and as experienced by Christian culture. If he praises Greek inclusiveness (the way in which Greek mores include natural envy), it is precisely to the extent to which it does not deny or deform the *nature* of envy, to which it respects envy as it is in itself as a natural instinct. In an 1875 text (*Nachlaß*, spring–summer 1875), Nietzsche wrote along the same lines: "The pleasure of drunkenness, of cunning, of vengeance, of envy, of insult, of obscenity—all of this was acknowledged by the Greeks as being human, and was consequently integrated *(darauf hin eingeordnet)* into the edifice of society and its mores." Nietzsche concludes: among the Greeks, "nature such as it manifests itself is not disavowed, but *integrated (nur eingeordnet)*." But in what sense could envy—a "natural" feeling certainly, if by that we understand that it is universal, that all human beings know it in the same way they know cunning, vengeance, insult, fear, anger, or jealousy—be grasped in its natural unity, in an identity distinct from its multiple and different historical expressions, if it is true, as Nietzsche never ceases to point out, that the opposition between the one and the multiple is a metaphysical illusion? How does Nietzsche conceptualize culture's natural side? To what extent does he restore the *opposition* between nature and *nomos*, the nonconventional and the cultural, at the very heart of his thought?

At the same time he is intent on making apparent the historical or cultural origin of "instincts" or "drives" that have become seemingly natural, or of evaluations that have become "instinctive" as a result of the domination of metaphysics' moral prejudices, Nietzsche also applies himself to the distinction between the apparently natural and the effectively natural life, or, if one likes, between the life that is not adapted to life's nature (the way of life ruled over by metaphysical or moral evaluations) and the life that is adapted to life's nature (that of the ancient Greek aristocracy). How should we understand this distinction?

When Nietzsche is led to make a distinction between natural instinct and its historical expressions, or instinct as neutral force and instinct become cultural, it can't be doubted that he gives in to a naturalist understanding of life and himself succumbs to the metaphysical concept of truth-identity. But the latter goes hand in hand with the concept of truth-adequacy: to believe that instincts can be grasped in their precultural truth is to raise those very instincts up into norms or models. Therefrom comes the inevitable distinction that secretes out of every naturalist understanding of life: life, on the one hand, that is adapted to the nature of life and, on the other, ways of life that do not adapt to life's nature or that are hostile to life's conditions. That, as we know, is the distinction at the basis of the Nietzschean differentiation between a master morality and a slave morality. But what is the meaning of a life adapted to life versus a life that denies life? Or, to use Nietzsche's expressions: an ascendant over against a decadent life? Or, again: a strong or affirmative will to power, against a weak or negative will to power?

Each culture, each particular humanity, has its own fundamental manner of making evaluations, its own ways of thinking, and its own "instincts." In each, Nietzsche shows, evaluations become "instinctive," "natural," that is to say obvious. Yet every culture is an "integration" of nature, either a way to integrate nature without disavowing it (the Greeks' way of life) or a way to absorb it through denying it. That the nature that is prior to culture is capable of making itself manifest, and of showing itself as it is, meaning divested of all cultural appreciation, of all metaphysical evaluation, of all moral judgment, in a word, of all form and meaning, or, in other words, that a "nonsymbolic" nature is for us accessible in principle, is what Nietzsche does not hesitate to affirm by maintaining that "all the concepts of ancient man were . . . at first incredibly uncouth, coarse, external, narrow, straightforward, and altogether *unsymbolical* in meaning to a degree that we can scarcely conceive" (*On the Genealogy of Morals*, first essay, § 6). How are we to understand a nature that manifests itself independently of all "instinctive" evaluation, of all appreciation, in a word, independent of all culture?

Let us note that by making reference to a "brute" nature, to a *physis* prior to the *nomos*, Nietzsche belies without ado his critique of metaphysics and reintroduces into his thought all of the metaphysical oppositions; at the same time he escapes from all of the historicist or relativistic understandings. He can state, the way the Greeks did but with a different meaning: *the way of living is good that is in conformity with nature* (that is, the way of life of the ancient aristocracy), and the way of living is bad that is not in conformity with nature, or which integrates nature while disavowing it (the way of life of the Christians or of any men subject to nihilism). Through forging a naturalist identity of nature—the idea of a preconventional nature—Nietzsche determines a natural criterion for truth (the concept is adequate to nature), a natural criterion for justice (an attitude faithful to life's nature), and a natural criterion for beauty (the work of art that brings about a certain state of the body or which brings to light a *physis* older than the artist's gestures). How does one understand this nature that is more original than any culture and that is liable to show itself such as it is, either through the concept (a concept whose sense is "nonsymbolic"), or through action (action adapted to the nature of life), or through art (a work that gives free play to those of nature's forces which gripped the artist)?

Every humanity has its own "instincts." Let us be clear: evaluations become "instinctive" because values become evident ("natural"). Though it is true that Nietzsche sometimes maintains that evaluations that have become "natural" ("instinctive," self-evident) can remain faithful (as the ancients' evaluation of envy) or hostile (for example, the Christian evaluation of envy) to nature (understood in a naturalist sense), it is equally true that he never ceases to stress that all values—all evaluations, all "systems of value"—emanate from a *creation*. Not of a creation that might be an individual's deed (of a will conceived of as a cause), nor of a creation that could be the imitation of a prior nature (of a nature conceived of in a naturalist sense), but of a *creation of life*.

What is the meaning of life if it is creation of values? And what meaning do values have if they are created by life?

The Nietzschean interpretation of life as creation of values subverts the metaphysical subjectivism Nietzsche gives in to when he exalts the sovereignty of the independent individual, the "great individuality," the unique and incomparable individual, the philosopher as creator of values. Or, perhaps: by interpreting life as creation of values, Nietzsche contributes a nonmetaphysical interpretation of the "great individuality," of the creator-philosopher, of the incomparable artist. For the idea that creation is what is carried out by life means for Nietzsche that the artist—the creator, the great individuality, the master—is all the more original (unique, innovative) in that he reveals what least belongs to him (as the subject of consciousness or of arbitrary will) or that he is all the more singular (irreducible to the general, different from socialized, gregarious individuals, liberated from "instinctive" evaluations) in that he allows universal life to flow through him (life as will to power, as creation), all the more individual (original, singular) in that he is less individual (that he effaces himself as consciousness or will). That creation is never the result of a conscious will, but of a force that of necessity imposes itself on the artist, that this force that commands the artist's gestures with a necessity he cannot dominate also brings the appearance of freedom within him (of an emancipation from "instinctive" evaluations), or that the unmasterable for him goes hand in hand with the greatest of masteries, is, Nietzsche specifies, what artists know very well:

Artists seem to have more sensitive noses in these matters, knowing only too well that precisely when they no longer do anything "voluntarily" (*willkürlich*) but do everything of necessity, their feeling of freedom, subtlety, full power, of creative placing, disposing (*Verfügung*), and forming reaches its peak—in short, that necessity and "freedom of the will" then become one in them. (*Beyond Good and Evil*, § 213; Nietzsche's quotation marks)

To say that life is creation is to say, from Nietzsche's perspective, that the artist is more an intermediary or a *medium* than he is the voluntary cause of his work. As far back as *The Birth of Tragedy* he wrote:

the subject, the willing individual that furthers his own egoistic ends, can be conceived of only as the antagonist, not as the origin of art. Insofar as the subject is the artist, however, he has already been released from his individual will, and has become, as it were, the medium through which the one truly existent subject celebrates his release in appearance. (§ 5)

To acknowledge that the artist or creator is a *medium* is surely to suggest that art is true art only to the extent that it allows a "nature" more original than subjectivity to speak. In conceptualizing life as creation of values, and the artist as the individuality that makes itself capable of letting the forces of a universal life flow through it, Nietzsche certainly does lead us to think that a nature is more original that the artist's consciousness or individual will or that a natural origin is more original than the artist as subject, but this idea of a nature more initial than the artist's subjectivity lends itself to an interpretation that not only rejects subjectivism but, moreover, concedes nothing to any kind of naturalist representation. It overcomes the subjectivist conception underlying Cartesianism to the very extent that it breaks with the image of man as master and possessor of nature; and it is liberated from the subjectivist conception at the basis of modern empiricism to the extent to which the artist through whom a "nature" comes to expression (and the spectator who feels the beauty of the work) experiences an "intoxication" not reducible to sensual pleasure (that is to say to passive sensations, to a sensibility that would imprison the subject in its bodily constitution, in its human or individual subjectivity). The artistic intoxication that is exalted by Nietzsche does not prolong the empiricists' subjectivism to the extent to which it can be interpreted as the feeling experienced by the individual who is taken beyond himself, ravished (swept away) by forces that captivate (capture) and liberate him (from his cultural "instincts"), subjugated as he is by a nature that transcends him and smashes away his imprisonment within established forms or self-evidences. And this idea of a transcendent, original, liberating nature does not lead back to a form of naturalism to the very extent to which it can be interpreted as the idea of an unmasterable, ungraspable force, as the reign of hidden powers where all forms that come to light (and tend to establish themselves and freeze into an order, to present themselves as originary, as ideals, as models and immutable truths) originate and are created.

It can't be doubted that the Nietzschean understanding of life as creation of values lends itself to an interpretation that distances itself from both naturalism and subjectivism. And it could certainly be argued that Nietzsche suggests this interpretation through the themes of the artist as mediator, of the created work as the union of necessity and freedom, of art as a force that erupts in the human being, transports him outside of his subjectivity, and opens him up to all that is beyond him, or, again, through the themes of "before culture," of historicity, or of an origin that is ungraspable yet more original than any graspable form, than any fixed or frozen identity, than any separated unity. But though we can acknowledge that Nietzsche suggests this interpretation that breaks away from both naturalist and subjectivist metaphysics, we have to note that he himself never stops negating this interpretation by going back to the idea of a raw and "merely physical" or "merely natural" nature, and by maintaining the idea of a fully sovereign creator. So that his conception of the artist as mediator never ceases to oscillate between the affirmation of an integral naturalism and the affirmation of an unbound Prometheanism. How are we to understand this strange alloy?

The Nietzschean critique of subjectivity (of the subject conceived of as consciousness and will) no doubt seems to prefigure a non-metaphysical (because not imprisoned by dualism) understanding of subjectivity. It indeed suggests that the human subject can be conceived of as neither a consciousness, an "I" that is either cause or foundation, nor as a body without a soul, but rather as a "thinking body." Yet Nietzsche never ceases being specific on this point: there is thinking inherent to the body in the same sense in which there is thinking at work in nature. And thought is a natural activity, according to Nietzsche, meaning, first of all, that there is a process of thought working at the very heart of inorganic nature: crystals are a form of thought in that they "realize forms." Meaning, thereafter, that organic life thinks: it is defined by a capacity for self-conservation and for growth. The "thinking body" as it is understood by Nietzsche is conceived of on the model of this natural thinking, of this "thinking" that is at work in nature, and it is precisely to that extent that we can discern in it a subject that could be the subject of the activity of thinking. Indeed, where there is a natural process, a realization of forms, or the maintenance of a vital process, we can speak, if we really wish to, of a form of thought at work, but there would also be anthropomorphism if we were to represent to ourselves a "something" that thinks, since nothing thinks that is outside of the process itself. Nietzsche denounces the idea of subject precisely to the extent to which he takes as a model of thought the kind of thinking that *coincides with a process;* the strong man, he maintains, acts the same way lightning flashes, meaning: there is no more subjectivity, or "substratum," behind the action or the display of force that is the strong man than there is behind the flash that is lightning (*On the Genealogy of Morals*, first essay, § 13).

But such an understanding of thought leads to a *metaphysical* challenge to subjectivity—it becomes vulnerable to the Nietzschean critique of metaphysics—for, under cover of a critique of dualism, of an opening up to the idea of a thinking body or of an incarnate thinking, it reintroduces Cartesian dualism in a massive way: the bodily, on the one hand (though of course as thinking body or as organism that, insofar as it is life, is thinking at work), and, on the other, the form of thought that thinks of itself as being that of a subject, of an "I," of a consciousness, and which, indissociably, "manifests itself in words." Either man as living creature—he "thinks unceasingly, but ignores this"— or man as "social" or "gregarious" animal—man communicating with his fellow humans through language, thereby acquiring self-consciousness and "knowledge" of what he thinks (*The Gay Science*, § 354).

Of course Nietzsche upsets the traditional oppositions: it is to the extent that the master thinks as nature does, and acts as an organism, being no more the author of his thoughts and his action than lightning is of its flash, it is to that extent, Nietzsche maintains, that his thought and his actions will be those of a unique individual, incomparable, independent, sovereign, autonomous, liberated from the "morality of mores" (*On the Genealogy of Morals*, second essay, § 2), and therefore the very opposite of every animal's behavior (because the animal species, as Nietzsche indicates, "believe in one normal type and ideal for their species, and they have translated the morality of mores definitively into their own flesh and blood" (*The Gay Science*, § 143). Conversely, the slave, the socialized human being, and in particular modern man or "the last man," has become in every way similar to a member of any animal species—he has assimilated the "morality of mores," he spontaneously adopts his (social) species's behavior and "instinctively" evaluates following the codifications of his (cultural) species—to the very extent that he has become consciousness and language. But however we may understand these strange associations between sovereignty and thought (and action) as natural processes, or between slavery and thought (and action) as consciousness and language, we are forced to acknowledge that they rest upon the opposition between natural thought (thinking and action as subjectless processes) and conscious thought and that this opposition leads back to all of the distinctions of metaphysics.

The Nietzschean idea of life as creation brings with it the notion of a thinking body, at times conceived of by Nietzsche in a way that calls for going beyond metaphysics and at other times in a way that presupposes a radical dualism. The same thing goes for the notion of intoxication: certainly, Nietzsche makes it understood that the latter transports whoever is its victim outside of himself, tearing him away from his subjectivity, from his sense-sensations, and from his individual will, yet he nevertheless provides an interpretation of it which in the end refers to a somatology. Intoxication, he explains, is strictly tied to the real increase of a vital or physical force. And a Nietzschean interpretation of the beautiful in biological terms derives from this: what permits a real increase of life is beautiful. This manner of understanding not only links up again with the empiricists' subjectivism: it radicalizes it. The artist's sensibility (or that of the spectator capable of feeling beauty) is for Nietzsche, as for the empiricists, a natural sensibility, an organic, animal one (of course it thinks, but in the way an organism thinks, like a process), but it is also in his eyes a singular sensibility, unique, incomparable, in such a way that artistic emotion is no longer conceivable in any way other than that of a sensation *at the same time sensory and personal*: it no longer imprisons in human subjectivity but in *individual* subjectivity. Whereas Nietzsche's naturalism—his conception of a precultural nature capable of manifesting itself as it is and of being "integrated" without being disavowed—can lead to the idea of a natural criterion for beauty, truth, and justice, his vitalism, on the contrary, leads us to a radical historicism: living matter thinks, interprets, chooses, but not only does its thinking, interpreting, and selective activity follow a process set up with the goal of self-conservation and self-increase, thus remaining locked into the perspective of life, but, besides, the perspective into which it is enclosed, life's, is a strictly individual perspective, in no way that of a living species. That is why Nietzsche calls the point of view of life an "illusion," using the term in its Platonic sense.

Nietzsche himself, certainly, never ceases interpreting life in a way which casts doubt on his vitalist affirmations, rejecting his conception of the beautiful in biological terms, his understanding of life as a vital process imprisoned within an individual perspective, and his definition of intoxication as the feeling of an increase in physical force. He contests his own "physiology" of art when he sees the artist's "grandeur" in his capacity for mastery, in his faculty for *becoming master over* the very chaos that he is, in his power to *give expression* to the vital forces that flow through him, in his ability to *hierarchize* the latter and extract forms from them, and in his *giving birth to forms* out of the potencies, however indomitable and undisciplined, that life contains. How does Nietzsche interpret this mastery over the unmasterable, this capacity to force a chaos into becoming form?

This manner of understanding surely lends itself to an interpretation that makes no concessions either to naturalism—art is the creation of forms that correspond to no prior natural model—or to subjectivism— the mastery the artist makes himself capable of is in no fashion that of a subject defined by consciousness or will, but of a "subject" that lest itself be penetrated by forces more primordial that its conscious decisions and which anticipate its own initiatives. In this perspective—which, con trary to what Nietzsche thinks, begins to emerge with Romanticism— the greatest self-domination (the greatest discipline) goes hand in hand with the greatest self-abandonment (the greatest effacement of the subject as consciousness and will, the greatest withholding of personal sensations), and this retreat of the subject itself goes hand in hand with the most "individual," the most "original," expression of the incomparable, of the unique. So it goes in the Romanticist hermeneutics of music: the interpreter abandons all initiative as conscious subject or isolated individual (the cadences are written down, the movements are strictly determined, all nuances are, in principle, indicated, tempos are noted, all improvisation banished, no further "embellishments" can be added by the interpreter), yet this self-effacement presupposes the greatest mastery (the greatest virtuosity) and makes the emergence of the most "individual," of the exceptional, of originality, possible.

It can't be denied that, against his will, Nietzsche rejoins this Romanticist hermeneutics: rejoins it even as he condemns the conception he attributes to the Romanticists (a sentimentalist conception) and praises the great classical art, or classicism, as the incarnation of "great art." Encountering again the Romanticist idea of creation as fusion (intoxication) of freedom and nature (of "mastery" and the forces of life), the Romanticist conception of freedom as a power more primordial than the faculties of a subject (defined by consciousness and will), and the Romanticist comprehension of nature as a force that is precultural, preconventional, but irreducible to a given, Nietzsche does indeed depart from subjectivism (from Cartesianism) and from naturalism (from the idea of a nature liable to manifest itself such as it is in itself). Nevertheless, and independent of the question of knowing whether or not Nietzsche's romanticism (what he calls his "classicism") leads to a new metaphysics (to a new form of naturalism, which would blend into a form of historicism), we have to acknowledge that Nietzsche never ceases interpreting mastery (which the artist must make himself capable of) in terms that lead back to a metaphysics of subjectivity and the subterranean and unmasterable forces (from which the artist must extract and create forms) as physical or vital forces, thereby falling back into a naturalist metaphysics. That, perhaps, is Nietzsche's most cunning strategy: to force us to recognize that we cannot be Nietzscheans (driven to subvert reductive identifications and the fundamental principle of an "opposition of values") without discovering in him, besides an inexhaustible source of inspiration, the (Nietzschean?) reasons to abandon all the paths he himself followed.

6 Nietzsche as Educator

Philippe Raynaud

> *Against the tyranny of the true. — Even if we were such
> fools as to hold all our opinions to be true, we would not
> wish for them to exist all alone — : I don't understand why
> we should desire the monarchical domination and
> omnipotence of the truth; it's enough for me that it enjoys
> great power. But it must be able to struggle so as to have
> opposition, and we must be able to relax away from it in
> the untrue — otherwise truth would become for us boring,
> without strength and taste, and it would make us into the
> same thing.*
>
> The Dawn, § 507

To the students of my generation, Nietzsche's oeuvre seemed to be at the
same time the *continuation* of "great philosophy" and the privileged
instrument of thought's emancipation from the entirety of the "metaphysical" tradition, and it was in this that it seemed to answer to the two
ambitions which dominated French philosophy in those days. Nietzsche was of course not the only reference among the thinkers who were
admired by France's post–high school *khâgne* students at that time;
Freud and Marx, as well as Spinoza and Mallarmé, had contributed to
the preparation of the "immense theoretical revolutions" (Althusser)
whose militants we were invited to be, but Nietzsche enjoyed a double
privilege nevertheless: having been often disdained by the preceding
generation, he was not compromised in the debates the latter had been
passionate about (such as the dialogue between phenomenology and
"Hegelian" or "humanist" Marxism), and he was the inventor of an
unprecedented form of "philosophical writing style" (*"écriture philo-*

sophique") which seemed destined to establish new links between thought and literature.

It does seem as though, whatever may be the quality of the books published by Deleuze, Foucault, and some others for the last fifteen years or so, something has been irrecoverably lost: the public may admire their virtuosity (or even their depth), but the feeling that French philosophy of the 1960s brought about an unprecedented upheaval in philosophical thinking seems to have disappeared. The prestige of " '68 philosophy" took two hits when the themes of "the death of man" and of "the end of the subject" lost their legitimacy, but also, and perhaps especially, when it became easier to see all that the antihumanist critique owed certain key ancestors, among whom Heidegger is the most prestigious, but also the most problematic, maybe even the heaviest burden. In these circumstances, the problem of our relation to Nietzsche has changed in meaning: Nietzsche has ceased to be an obvious reference in contemporary philosophical discussion, but, in compensation, we can now better discern his own thinking out of all that once seemed to us to be attached to it. But we have to add that that is possible only through understanding what we were looking for then and elucidating what the project that then motivated French philosophers could mean for us. No Nietzschean—or, better, no reader of Nietzsche—will be surprised: the interpretation of Nietzsche cannot consist merely in bringing to light a figure buried under the strata of learned or cultured commentary; it itself derives from a change of perspective and a new distribution of "forces."

Why were we Nietzscheans? It seems to me we could give three answers to this question, answers that would correspond respectively to Gilles Deleuze's work, to that of Michel Foucault, and, perhaps more radically, to the experience of contemporary *literature* or *art*.

For Deleuze, Nietzsche is he who led on the critical project in Kant's wake—but, mainly, against him. The meaning of this critical project is summed up in a simple formula:

The first thing the Copernican revolution teaches us is that it is we who are in command. There is here an overturning of the ancient conception of Wisdom: the wise man, the sage, was in a certain way defined by his own submissions, and in another way by his "ultimate" agreement with Nature. Kant opposed the critical image to wisdom: we, the legislators of Nature.[1]

Unfortunately, Kant only goes halfway through the "total and positive" critique that must spare nothing and that restrains the power of knowledge only "to liberate other, heretofore neglected powers":[2] he destroys the illusions of dogmatic metaphysics only in order to reintroduce them in a new, purified form, mutating them into *ideals;* making explicit, that is, what has in fact always been their veritable meaning.[3] Nietzsche's irreplaceable contribution was to go beyond this "criticism coming from a justice of the peace" and carry out a critique of *true morality, true religion,* and *true knowledge:*

Which is why Nietzsche . . . thinks he has found the only possible principle for a total critique in what he calls his "perspectivism." There are neither facts nor moral phenomena, but a moral interpretation of phenomena. There are no illusions of knowledge, knowledge itself being an illusion: knowledge is an error, worse, a falsification.[4]

Deleuze's *Nietzsche and Philosophy* thus put forward a *program* whose accomplishment could bring about infinite satisfactions as long as one understood the game that made it possible. Kantian moralism was vigorously rejected, but the aim of criticism remained the emancipation of the will ("it is we who are in command"), which led to an ironic, even parodic recuperation of the Kantian problematic of autonomy as well as its *redirection* against anything that was left of classical "naturalism" in Kant's philosophy. This ambivalent attitude towards criticism was itself an element within a general *strategy of circumventing (contournement)* the rationalist tradition: theatrics were substituted for discussion, and the new philosophy could at the same time oppose the "plurality" of forces over against the Subject's unity and base itself on subjectivity (autonomy) in its struggle against nature or tradition.[5]

At the same time as he defended an interpretation of Nietzsche that was quite close to Deleuze's, Michel Foucault situated it within the more general framework of a renewed history of the formation of the "human sciences" which also aimed to announce a global mutation of knowledge and of thought. The constitution of the "human sciences" and philosophy's hesitation between "positivism" and "phenomenology" were the adequate expression of the double dimension, empirical and transcendental, that the figure of "man" took when the reconstitution of the works of culture in their infinite diversity still seemed to call for a reference, in the last instance, to the *cogito,* even to a prereflexive one; the radical novelty of Nietzsche's thought came from the fact that, by linking the "death of God" to the appearance of "the last man," it opened the way to a new era of thought, when the "uprooting of Anthropology" should permit us "to find again a purified ontology and a radical thinking about Being,"6 while at the same time liberating new forms of knowledge (structural linguistics, ethnology, psychoanalysis).7

We can see here quite well what allowed Nietzsche to be given a central position in the working out of the French philosophers' "program": even before Heidegger, the author of *The Gay Science* had rendered possible the radicalization of phenomenology carried out by the former, and he alone permitted us to understand the newness of what the period's credo called "structuralism."8 But this incorporation of Nietzsche's work into the philosophical debate in those years would not have had the reverberation that it did had it not come up against a much wider and much deeper *cultural* experience. The "death of man," the "end of the subject," the "loss of meaning," the exhaustion of "grand narratives" secretly upheld by an "eschatology": all of these were first expressed in artistic and, most of all, in literary forms that in those days won over a public infinitely larger than that of the old "avant-gardes." The return of revolutionary passions in the 1970s paradoxically did nothing more than to radicalize these tendencies: if Artaud and Bataille did not at that time cease being legitimate references, it was well and truly because the goal for the new generation of militants was no longer so much the overcoming of the inherited alienation of class divisions as it was the creation of the conditions for an infinite upheaval, or for a generalized "transgression."9

That being so, the problem of our relation to Nietzsche is hard to separate from that of the judgment we can today make of the period when his glory was at its highest. That does not, all the same, mean that we ought to aim, through him, at his French admirers or commentators; it seems to me, on the contrary, more fertile to set out from his oeuvre in order to ask again, or to transform, the very questions it was once supposed to answer: about the kind of philosophy that is possible today, and also about the meaning of "modernity" or of "anthropology" for those living today. It is to bring some clarity to these points that I would like to begin with Nietzsche's highly ambivalent relation to the "Enlightenment" and come back later to what his critique of modern ideals can teach us.

NIETZSCHE AND THE ENLIGHTENMENT

It is well known that, between *Human, All-Too-Human* (1878–79) and *The Gay Science* (1882), Nietzsche carries out an apparently complete inversion of the arguments he had set forth in *The Birth of Tragedy* and in the *Unmodern Observations:* for the "irrationalism" of his youth, Nietzsche suddenly substitutes a fervid defense of French neoclassicism, the Enlightenment, and "positivism" whose place within his philosophy continues to intrigue his best interpreters. What I should like to show here is that Nietzsche at that time invented an exemplary "strategy" and, above all, that it is possible and legitimate to make of it the model for a reappropriation of his thought: if Nietzsche can make of the *Aufklärung* an instrument for his critique of Reason, then we in turn can make of his "irrationalism" the means to continue the liberation that began with the Enlightenment.

From his very first works, written under the influence of Schopenhauer and Wagner, Nietzsche sets out to bring to light, under the name of "Dionysian wisdom," a little-known *world* of which *music* is the most perfect expression and about which the metaphysics of *The World as Will and Representation* provides the deepest understanding. Plastic arts, Nietzsche writes at this time, are oriented towards the production of beautiful individual forms; music and tragedy, on the contrary, aim at the immediate presentation of what underlies these forms ("life," "will"), and this reproduction is possible only through the "elimination of the individual." This new aesthetic, which is directed against the traditional interpretation of Greek antiquity, is itself the propaedeutic to a general critique of the culture of the time (*Unmodern Observations*) and it presupposes a profound rupture with the heritage of German rationalism. Indeed, what the young Nietzsche violently denies is the idea of a possible harmony between theory and practice or of a continuity between knowledge and action: "Knowledge kills action; action requires the veils of illusion."[10] This thesis can moreover be indifferently understood as a critique of the illusions of action or, on the contrary, as a denunciation of the mutilating effects of knowledge. *The Birth of Tragedy* privileges the first theme:

In this sense the Dionysian man resembles Hamlet: both have once looked truly into the essence of things, they have *gained knowledge,* and nausea inhibits action; for their action could not change anything in the eternal nature of things; they feel it to be ridiculous or humiliating that they should be asked to set right a world that is out of joint.[11]

In the second unmodern observation it is, on the other hand, knowledge, under the figure of *historical science,* which is denounced because, in weakening our capacity to act, it endangers "life."

But these two apparently contradictory motifs in fact obey the same intention: the one and the other are directed against the two central concepts of German idealism that are *reflexivity* and the hope for a reconciliation between the subject and the world (or between the ideal and the real). In *The Birth of Tragedy,* the knowledge that leads to the "destruction of the individual" can come only from a direct access to the "horrible truth" which is different in every respect from the *calculation* carried out by reflective thinking; it is quite precisely the role played by reflection in the historical sciences that prevents us from seeing in them a form of knowledge and risks turning us away from both life and truth. In Nietzsche's first writings, the Schopenhauerian motif of the superiority of instinct over consciousness thus permits us at the same time to understand the necessity of leaving "the will to live" behind and to demonstrate the precedence of life over representation. In the same way, another theme borrowed from Schopenhauer makes it possible to link Dionysian "asceticism" to the polemic against the contemporary world; the quest for a reconciliation between individual and world in fact rests upon the same illusion which leads the "philistines" to identify success with culture:[12] the emancipation of thought presupposes, in both cases, the rejection of the Hegelian thesis about the identity between the real and the rational.

In Nietzsche's first works, the critique of the classical ("Apollonian") ideal and the analysis of the "Use and Disadvantage of History for Life" lead to rejecting the domination of the "principle of individuation," to devaluing reflection, and to contesting the merits of historical culture. Beginning with *Human, All-Too-Human,* on the contrary, Nietzsche puts himself forward as at once a defender of classicism against Romanticism, as a partisan of "positivism," and as a practitioner of historical science. An attentive study of the texts reveals, however, that there is a deeper continuity within Nietzsche's thought. The "classicism" of the second period remains faithful to the principal idea of *The Birth of Tragedy,* that of a *balance* between the "Apollonian" and the "Dionysian" instincts, and, in parallel fashion, the kind of history that is evoked in *Human, All-Too-Human* or in the *The Dawn* rests upon a generalized criticism of the various forms of historical rationalism.[13]

What appears to me, in fact, as most significant in the evolution leading from Nietzsche's "Schopenhauerian" period to what historians of philosophy sometimes call his "positivist" or "Voltairean" period[14] is that the modulation operated on Nietzsche's *arguments* goes hand in hand with the permanence of his philosophical *style* and that its effect is above all to make explicit the deeper meaning of the earlier polemics. Indeed, two ideas dominate the "classicism" and "positivism" of *Human, All-Too-Human* and *The Dawn*. The first concerns the disassociation between science and metaphysics, which makes the latter's ideal look like a substitute for religion:

Pneumatic explanation of nature.—Metaphysics explains the text of nature as pneumatically as the church and its learned men once did the Bible. A great deal of understanding is needed in order to apply to nature the same type of the strict art of explanation that philologists have achieved for all books: one whose intention is simply to understand what the text means to say, but not to scent out, indeed presuppose, a double sense.[15]

But this critique of the "need for metaphysics" is itself only the propaedeutic to what Nietzsche later calls his "campaign against morality." Metaphysical categories are indeed only "notions *auxiliary* to morality," and the privilege given to causal explanation, which permits a break with the magic spells of sacral history, has therefore as its real goal the preparation of the *"inversion of all values"*: the importance accorded the questions Why? and For What? "follows of necessity from the insight that humanity is *not* all by itself on the right way, that it is by no means governed divinely, that, on the contrary, it has been precisely among its holiest value concepts that the instinct of denial, corruption, and decadence has ruled seductively."[16] This genealogical orientation itself brings about a particular kind of philosophical argumentation and writing style. Categories and positions are not so much "discussed" as they are "evaluated" as a function of their capacity to increase or diminish the forces of life, and, because of this, the same cultural figures appear alternatively to be either means toward emancipation or, on the contrary, hindrances to the creative power of individuals, without there ever being a "dialectical" totalization of their sequence. The defense of the Enlightenment and of history to which Nietzsche dedicates himself during his positivist period does not therefore really contradict the inspiration of *The Birth of Tragedy* or of the *Unmodern Observations:* it is satisfied with modifying certain of their themes in order to reinforce whatever, in a given period's culture, is favorable to the active forces.

It is when we realize this that, it seems to me, we can understand what "good use" could be made of Nietzsche's work at a time when "Nietzscheanism" has ended up influencing large sectors of the culture and when, at the same time, his strictly philosophical legitimacy has been rather seriously weakened. I have already said that we should seek to put Nietzschean criticism at the service of Reason itself, just as Nietzsche managed to mobilize the Enlightenment in his struggle against the rationalist heritage; but this is possible only if we ourselves find a philosophical *style* as adapted to this task as Nietzsche's was to the task he set himself: that supposes that we know how to play, as the author of *The Dawn* could, upon the possible turnarounds in philosophical positions, but that also implies a *minimum* of systematic reconstruction that can only reduce the importance of the literary forms (aphorism, fable, etc.) in which Nietzsche's way of thinking expressed itself in a privileged way.

From Nietzsche to Weber: The Limits of Perspectivism

To illustrate what such a recuperation of the Nietzschean heritage might look like, the best thing seems to me to be to set out from the work of one of Nietzsche's greatest readers, Max Weber, whose line of thinking depends intimately on the *concepts* present in the former thinker (and not only in the "fin de siècle" *Stimmung* presiding over his books). Weber, in fact, is heir to four principal Nietzschean themes: "perspectivism"; the refusal of all "providentialist" interpretations of history; the disassociation between the ideal of autonomy and Kantian moral rationalism; and, finally, the impossibility of a rational foundation for ethical judgments. On each one of these points, of course, Weber proceeded to a *limitation* of the Nietzschean critique, which presupposes a certain fidelity to the rationalist heritage, but it nevertheless still seems that, decidedly, the work of undermining carried out by Nietzsche was not for him simply a given to be taken into account but also, in a way, the condition of survival for the ideals of the Enlightenment.

Nietzsche's perspectivism presupposes a *rupture* with the "positivist" idea of historical objectivity as expressed in Ranke's celebrated formula (the historian narrates "what really happened"). Nietzsche puts up a double objection to this ideal: the historian is not dealing with "real" events but with a continuous chain of interpretations to which his own discourse belongs, and, moreover, events have a *causal* effectiveness only to the extent that they are themselves taken up into *representations;*[17] but the real significance of perspectivism is above all, as Nietzsche puts it in *The Gay Science,*[18] that it opens up onto a "new 'infinite'" which prohibits us from according a privilege to the human point of view on the world.[19] In Max Weber, perspectivism has first of all an *epistemological* significance: it translates the heterogeneity *in principle*[20] between the sciences of nature, oriented toward the search for "laws," and the historical sciences, whose priority interest is that which is "significant" or "meaningful." The historical sciences are in effect inseparable from the "relation to values" which leads *a* specific scholar to privilege a *particular* set of problems and which also guides, within the scholarly research work itself, the determination of the questions to be solved and the selection of relevant information; like Nietzsche, Weber insists therefore on the idea that the scientific "fact" is not only "constructed" but is also dependent on the *point of view* of the scholar, who inserts himself into a preexisting chain of interpretations.

The Nietzschean aspect of Weber's thought is notably apparent in the way it transforms the notion of "relation to values" that he borrows from Rickert.[21] For the latter, the role of singularity in the constitution of historical discourse remains in effect rather narrowly confined: history is intelligible only if it is *one,* and this unity is thinkable only within the horizon of a *synthesis* between the various systems of values; for Weber on the contrary, the choice of "values" remains affected by an irrationality that cannot be entirely reduced, which prohibits both the taking up again of the Kantian point of view of "hope" and the illusion of a final synthesis among the different perspectives adopted by the scholars. We can, to that extent, consider that Weberian epistemology rests well and truly upon a Nietzschean bent given to his predecessors' neo-Kantian positions. But there is nevertheless a point at which Weber very firmly rejects Nietzsche's "perspectivist" radicalism; intent on establishing the possibility of an objective social science, Weber maintains that, despite the radical heterogeneity of the "values" orienting their

work, scholars and social scientists can arrive at an agreement as far as
the results of their researches are concerned:

The order (of significations) varies historically with the character of the civilization and of the thinking that dominates men. It does not therefore follow that
research in the domain of the sciences of culture could only lead to *results* that
the "subjective," meaning that they would hold for one person but not for another. What varies is rather the *degree of interest* they may have for one, and not
for another.[22]

It may perhaps be objected that this is an inconsistency on Weber's
part, one that translates itself, moreover, into a mere *displacement* of
the Nietzschean problem of truth; Weber does indeed absolutize the
"norms of our thinking" when he tries to demonstrate that there is a
universalizable element within historical knowledge, but he nevertheless implicitly acknowledges the aspect of nonrational decision that the
belief in objectivity brings to view: "Is scientific truth only that which
claims to be valid for all those who *want* the truth."[23] It nonetheless
seems to me that this argument can itself be turned around within the
very logic of Nietzsche's thought. If he chose, in *Human, All-Too-
Human,* to "bear the banner of the Enlightenment . . . further on-
ward,"[24] it is because, in order to carry out the critique of the "metaphysical need," and of the religious or moral illusion, it was imperative
that he posit the autonomy of the "true" in relation to the "good," leaving for later the task of applying critical genealogy against the will to
truth itself; there is, in that sense, even within Nietzsche's thought, the
need for a *minimal* distinction between the perspectivism of the questions and the objectivity of the results, even if the latter is ascribed (according to a formula Weber does not disavow) to the "will" of those
who seek the truth. Beyond Nietzsche's philosophical *style*—based
upon the indefinite displacement of conflict among the points of view
and the forces expressing themselves through them—the problem is one
of knowing whether the possibility of genealogy and of history is thinkable without a minimum of *foundation* for objectivity. Without being
able to discuss here the whole of Nietzsche's thought, I think it possible
to say that the ever more accented recourse in his last books to the idea
of a "scientific" or "objective" basis for the transvaluation of values
and for the Eternal Recurrence should be taken as the sign of a difficulty
which, for being trivial, is not any less important: the refusal of reflec-

tion undergirding "perspectivism's" skeptical interpretation seems to be paid for through the return of a rather flagrant *dogmatism* (even though today's Nietzscheans are most often silent on this point). If this is so, then Weber's apparently less "radical" position in fact expresses the return of a reflective and criticist problematic the Nietzschean radicalization of critique never really could go past since, in a way, it stumbles on the very questions Kant had tried to solve.

The analysis of the fate of the other Nietzschean themes in Max Weber's thought leads to similar remarks. Weber's polemic against the legacy of nineteenth-century philosophies of history in the social sciences of his day in many places joins up with Nietzsche's reflections: the point in both cases was to disassociate the historical sense from the speculative illusion of a *deduction* of diversity and, above all, from the consoling perspective of a final reconciliation beyond the antinomies that define the experience of becoming. But we should also notice that Weber's work remains dominated by a problematic of *rationalization* which no doubt owes as much to the heritage of German idealism as it does to Nietzschean critique. We may, in parallel fashion, notice that, in the way in which he poses the problem of the conditions for autonomy in the modern world, Weber proceeds to a subtle shift of Nietzsche's arguments. For the latter, the Enlightenment was of course to be rehabilitated, against Romanticism's critique of it, because the depoetization of the world that had been brought about by the diffusion of the determinist interpretation of nature had contributed to the emancipation of the will; but this seeming apology for Reason is inserted within a problematic that is "irrationalist" in its totality, one in which madness plays a major role in the destruction of the yoke of tradition[25] and, above all, one in which reason is prized only as the trace of a creativity that remains, at bottom, irremediably irrational. The Weberian typology of forms of activity and of domination, as well as the logic of rationalization that is reconstituted in *Economy and Society*, is here narrowly dependent on the Nietzschean problematic, as is evident notably in the role played by *"charisma"* in both the rupture with tradition and in the preservation of the chances for an authentic existence under modern bureaucracy.

It nevertheless remains true that Weber's *intention* is, in the final analysis, to save the heritage of the Enlightenment from its dialectical development and not, as it is for Nietzsche, to put it to use on the project of *going beyond* or *destroying* rationalism. This intent to reconstruct a minimal rationalism also comes through, despite Weber's hesitations, in his moral reflection; contrary to a much too widespread interpretation, the "ethics of responsibility" are *not* a choice among others: they express better than any other "acosmic" morality the tragic aspect of the human condition, as it becomes apparent in the reflection on the permanent antinomies of action.[26]

What gives Weber's oeuvre its great worth is that he dealt in the most serious manner possible with the *objections* Nietzsche made against modernity while being aware that those criticisms acquire real meaning only within the framework of a pursuit of the modern project. It is, moreover, not impossible that this apparent infidelity is the effect of a more secret, deeper faithfulness. It is, in any case, significant that the only problem in which Weberian "decisionism" cannot be overcome is that of the relation between grace and nature: we know that, when we are acting in the world, the acosmic forms of the "ethics of conviction" are pretenses, but nothing can guarantee us that our salvation happens in this world. Weber is here at once very far from and very close to Nietzsche: very far, since the latter takes for granted the possibility of a form of humanity superior to the highest incarnations of the Christian spirit, but also very close, since the *problem* of a possible deterioration of humanity as the outcome of the critique of religion is at the center of Nietzsche's thought.[27]

Weber's own greatness consisted in sensing the paths that remained open in an intellectual situation marked, on the one hand, by the constitution of the "human sciences," and, on the other, by the crisis of modern rationalism, in which what was philosophically at stake had been expressed by Nietzsche before the twentieth century took care to demonstrate its political significance. The division of Weber's posterity—from Carl Schmitt's decisionism to Habermas's renewed rationalism—indicates all the same that the problem of the relative importance to be assigned to the legacy of the Enlightenment and to its most radical critiques remains open. That being so, nothing can assure us that the disrepute "irrationalism" has fallen into today is definitive, and the eclipse Nietzsche's fame is going through today in France could well be temporary. But it seems to me that, even if our contemporaries should in the future once again become "Nietzscheans" in some form or another, it would be in a manner very different from that of the sixties or seventies: Nietzsche's oeuvre no longer seems today to be a *going beyond* modernity, but rather to be an element of a *discussion* that is no doubt destined to go on indefinitely. It seems to me to be particularly clear that we can no longer adopt the formulations, once so seductive, of Deleuze or Foucault. The radicalization of Kantian critique ("We are in command") exposes itself to a double objection: if its goal is to destroy the metaphysics of subjectivity, it's hard to see what could protect it from a Heideggerian criticism; if, on the contrary, its purpose is to complexify the problematic of autonomy, it must limit itself and once again make mini mal room for a practical philosophy of a Kantian tonality. In parallel fashion, the relative situations of the "human sciences" and of new discursive formations such as psychoanalysis cannot easily be described by the opposition between "man's" privilege (the "empirico-transcendental" doublet) and the arrival of some hitherto unknown figure that has been made possible by his "death"; it is, on the contrary, quite possible to consider that it is for essential reasons that the most radical critiques of "humanism" were formulated *within* the epistemology of "sciences of the mind" or of the "human sciences," as is shown by both Nietzsche's dependence on post-Kantian "historicism" and by Heidegger's debt toward Dilthey's work. What stays alive, on the other hand, is the obstinate feeling that something has been lost since the Enlightenment, and that a way of thinking like Nietzsche's can help us make of this loss a new opportunity.

If Nietzsche's writings have maintained a place of importance in contemporary philosophy, it is because they give expression to two *experiences* that are difficult to go beyond. The first is that of the loss of the "cosmos," or the fading away of the reference to a nature that is at the same time coherent and tending toward certain ends. This experience dominates the evolution of historical consciousness: if Weber's thought is once again exemplary here, it is because it liberates the preoccupation with an intelligibility to history from the reference to a privileged "center of perspective" that was still the "design of nature" as late as Kant—and Nietzsche's criticisms are well and truly at the center of this mutation.[28] This bursting apart of the "world" is also at the heart of contemporary *aesthetics*,[29] which is also one of the clearest manifestations of the other experience, once referred to as "the death of the subject," but which should rather be understood as the appearance of a new figure of subjectivity. We know the contribution psychoanalysis has made to this interpretation of extreme modernity: the model of the "split subject" *("sujet brisé")* seems to call for the abandonment of any idea of a *reappropriation* of the meaning of his work by the subject, in whom the cure could only produce a new arrangement of the elements of a "dynamic" unconscious;[30] on the other hand, it does seem as though the idea of a reconquered "autonomy," beyond the division of the subject, can be eliminated only with equal difficulty once we aim to show the meaning of the cure.[31] This debate seems to me to illustrate rather well what is at stake in the relations we have today with the "irrationalist" critics of subjectivity, who are often the conscious or unconscious heirs to Nietzsche. They have not only reminded us that the subject's full transparency to itself is an illusion: they have demonstrated that the development of the "for-itself" is itself sustained by a "creativity," or by an unconscious force that we cannot wish to eliminate; yet, on the other hand, we cannot give ourselves a subjectively intelligible project other than that of "autonomy," which presupposes our acceding to the condition of "subject." It is within this paradox that we must learn to live and to think.[32]

There is, finally, a last reason for the "contemporaneity" of this "unmodern" (or "untimely") author. Since the turn of the century, reflection on Nietzsche hasn't ceased being brought to life again by the discussions emanating from the development of modern democracy. Even without going back to the declared adversaries of democracy (who were not necessarily either mediocre spirits or fanatics),[33] we may recall first of all that the ideas and schemes underlying, in France, the great movement going from the sixties to today's "postmodernity" were created in a context (the thirties) which was precisely one of a *political* crisis for the Enlightenment, in the "classical" country of their "republican" realization:[34] the critique of the rationalist and "progressive" philosophical heritage was connected to the consciousness of this crisis. After a tortuous evolution, dialectical and paradoxical, including various round trips between Paris and California, the same ideas have curiously ended up as an integral part of the dominant culture and have been put to the service of democratic passions. This evolution is sometimes disapproved of for two types of opposing reasons: because it endangers democracy by promoting principles hostile to it, but also because it submits to reactive forces a kind of thinking which should, quite precisely, contain them.[35]

It seems to me to be more fruitful to consider that the task for democratic political thinking is analogous to that which I have tried to define for philosophy: as an antidote to the modern spirit, Nietzsche's thought should be taken by modernity as a privileged means for self-criticism. It is in that respect, more than as a master of truth, that Nietzsche is an *educator.*

NOTES

1. Gilles Deleuze, *La philosophie critique de Kant* (Kant's critical philosophy), Paris: Presses Universitaires de France, 1971, 3d ed., p. 23.
2. Gilles Deleuze, *Nietzsche et la philosophie,* Paris: Presses Universitaires de France, 2d ed., 1967, p. 102 (*Nietzsche and Philosophy,* trans. Hugh Tomlinson, New York: Columbia University Press, 1983).
3. See *On the Genealogy of Morals,* II, § 25; *Twilight of the Idols:* "How the 'True World' Became a Fable."
4. Deleuze, *Nietzsche et la philosophie,* p. 103.
5. On these aspects of Deleuze's thought, see Vincent Descombes, *Le même et l'autre: Quarante-cinq ans de philosophie française (1933–1978),* Paris: Éditions de Minuit, pp. 178–95.
6. Michel Foucault, *Les mots et les choses: Une archéologie des sciences humaines.* Paris: Gallimard, 1966, p. 353. *(The Order of Things).*
7. Ibid., pp. 385–98.
8. We know that Michel Foucault always rejected the ascription "structuralist": as an "archeologist" of knowledge, he placed himself outside the disciplines that incarnate its ongoing mutation. The reader may judge for himself the proportionate importance, in assuming such a stance, of the historian's modesty and of the philosopher's pride.
9. As Deleuze has shown, the "subversive" cinema of the 1960s and 1970s itself destroyed the optimistic myths that animated progressive aesthetics in those days ("the people are missing"): see Gilles Deleuze, *Cinéma II: L'image-temps,* Paris: Editions de Minuit, 1983–85, pp. 281–91. The same evolution took place in philosophy and in "avant-garde" criticism through the critique of Marxist "humanism." That opened up two possibilities: a recomposition of radical critical discourse (of which Deleuze's political writings are themselves a good example) or, on the contrary, a conservative position.
10. F. Nietzsche, *The Birth of Tragedy,* § 7 (trans. Walter Kaufmann).
11. Ibid.
12. See on this point the first unmodern observation, "David Strauss, the Confessor and Writer."
13. May I be allowed, on this point, to refer the reader to the preface I wrote for a French paperback edition of *The Dawn (Aurore,* Paris: Hachette, 1987).

14. Nietzsche dedicated *Human, All-Too-Human* to Voltaire, in order to "render personal homage . . . to one of the greatest liberators of the spirit" ("einem der grössten Befreier des Geistes . . . eine persönliche Huldigung darzubringen").

15. *Human, All-Too-Human*, part 1: "On First and Last Things," § 8.

16. Nietzsche, *Ecce Homo*, "Dawn," § 2. In *Basic Writings of Nietzsche*, trans. and ed. Walter Kaufmann, New York: Modern Library Editions, 1992 [1966], p. 747.

17. See especially *The Dawn*, § 307.

18. *The Gay Science*, § 346, 354, 374.

19. Ibid., § 374; Nietzschean perspectivism is therefore directed against Kant, who put the question "What is man?" at the center of philosophy.

20. Max Weber, *"Die 'Objektivität' sozialwissenschaftlicher und sozial-politischer Erkenntnis"* (The "objectivity" of knowledge in the social and political sciences), *Gesammelte Aufsätze zur Wissenschaftslehre*, 2d ed., Tübingen: Mohr, 1951, p. 176.

21. H. Rickert, *Grenzen der naturwissenschaftlichen Begriffsbildung*, Berlin, 1896, 1902.

22. M. Weber, pp. 183–84.

23. Ibid.

24. F. Nietzsche, *Human, All-Too-Human*, I, § 26.

25. See on this point *The Dawn*, § 14.

26. On all these points, allow me to refer back to my book *Max Weber et les dilemmes de la raison moderne* (Max Weber and the dilemmas of modern reason), Paris: Presses Universitaires de France, 1987.

27. See on this point how the Nietzschean description of the "last man" is taken up again at the end of *The Protestant Ethic and the Spirit of Capitalism*.

28. See on this Philippe Raynaud, *Max Weber et les dilemmes de la raison moderne*, pp. 62–67.

29. Luc Ferry, *Homo Aestheticus: The Invention of Taste in the Democratic Age*. Chicago: The University of Chicago Press, 1993 (trans. Robert de Loaiza). See also, in another perspective, Gilles Deleuze, *Cinéma I: L'image-mouvement. Cinéma II: L'image-temps*, Paris: Éditions de Minuit, 1983–85.

30. It could be shown that the distant origins for this model are to be found in the "romantic" overturning of Leibniz's problematic of the unconscious which weaves through the entire history of German idealism, from Kant's theory of the "genius" to the Heideggerian reconstruction of phenomenology, and which found one of its most powerful expressions in Nietzsche.

31. Luc Ferry and Alain Renaut, *French Philosophy of the Sixties*, Specially the chapter on "French Freudianism (Lacan)."

32. This problem is at the heart of Cornelius Castoriadis's work, and specially at the center of his reflections on psychoanalysis.

33. We need only think of Georges Sorel, or of the Thomas Mann of *Considerations of an Apolitical Man*.

34. This point has been quite well stressed by Vincent Descombes, *Phi-*

losophie par gros temps, Paris: Éditions de Minuit, 1989, chap. 4: "La crise française des Lumières," pp. 69–95.

35. Sometimes both critiques coexist, as is the case in Allan Bloom's writings, where they are integrated into a "Socratic" interrogation on the problem of education and culture *(The Decline of the American Mind).*

7 The Traditionalist Paradigm — Horror of Modernity and Antiliberalism

Nietzsche in Reactionary Rhetoric

PIERRE-ANDRÉ TAGUIEFF

No one should venture into the labyrinths of radically antimodern discourse without a thread of Ariadne, which should have a supplementary virtue: that of showing a way around the accumulations of clichés and commonplaces about the opposition between ancients and Moderns, or between tradition and modernity. There is a recurrent, yet little-known, theme among the various forms of antimodern traditionalism: the theme of modernity as the age of "perpetual discussion" (Donoso Cortés). A polemical theme, one that figures in a paradoxical manner: radical antimodern rhetoric defines the rhetorical activity as being the essential attribute of the modern phenomenon. By positing infinite discussion as being the royal instrument, value in itself, and absolute norm of modernity, the thinkers of antimodern traditionalism define their absolute enemy: liberal democracy, rejected, certainly, as political system or mode of government, but also and above all as way of life or mode of human existence. Commercial negotiations, financial speculation (which presupposes the use of verbal abstractions), and parliamentary debate: those are the activities typical of chattering modernity, which is rejected as "demo-liberal." The hunt for the rhetorical symptom of modern decadence brings together thinkers as different as Bonald or Donoso Cortés, Nietzsche, Spengler, or Julius Evola. Not to mention the multitude of reactionary polemicists who can be attached to one or another current of traditionalism—counterrevolutionaries and royalists, conservative revolutionaries and "fascists."

    If radical antimodern thought is a way of thinking about modernity as being decadent, we should, to understand Nietzsche's understanding of tradition, set out from a sketch of the idea of decadence as it is presupposed by all the forms of intransigent traditionalism. Only then can we show how, on the foundations of the same antiliberal axiom, the second traditionalism that is inaugurated by Nietzsche's thought overturns the hierarchy of the political and the theologico-religious to the benefit of the political. The result is that salvation no longer depends on Providence alone, and, in place of the ultrapessimistic involuntarism of the first traditionalism (Bonald, Donoso Cortés), we must substitute the most mobilizing form of all of political voluntarism in modernity: nationalism. The doctrine of the Action Française, "integral nationalism," is a very good illustration of this new synthesis of traditionalism and nationalist voluntarism, through which the radically antiliberal position carries out its first entry into the political. The reference to Nietzsche, despite certain appearances (Germanophobia's smoke screen), is not alien to it.

I. THE ANTIMODERN ARGUMENT AND THE VISION OF DECADENCE

The hypothesis directing the analyses we set forth here is that, in many respects, Nietzsche can be considered a traditionalist thinker. The first presupposition of nineteenth-century traditionalist thinking is the overall denunciation and total condemnation of the modern world. What is, more exactly, most intensely rejected in modernity is the mode of political organization that singles it out and stigmatizes it in antimodern eyes: the mixture of liberalism and democracy in which the primacy of liberty and the principle of sovereignty of the people are tied together in a problematic fashion. Before situating Nietzsche's thought within the traditionalist sphere, it would be fitting to reconstruct the logic of *antimodern* argumentation it presupposes, a recurrent argumentation that is established upon four fundamental propositions:

   —The modern world is in itself a process of *decadence*.

   —Decadence is, essentially, *loss* of supreme values, disappearance of absolute norms, whence it follows that no authority can be established and no hierarchy can be respected. Thus it is, for example, that in 1861 Antoine Blanc de Saint-Bonnet diagnoses the "forgetfulness of principles" through which France is "perishing."[1]

   —Decadence manifests itself and is accelerated through the general progression, in every field, of the *discussability* of principles and self-evident truths: that is, in the eyes of traditionalism, the most visible effect of the contagious force of "liberal" ideas that are perceived as being *destructive* of every order, every authority, every certainty.

—The modern process of decadence is *irreversible* and, because it is abnormal, untypical, or pathological, necessarily tends toward its own end, the fulfillment of a process of erosion or decomposition. The logic of a decadent time is that of a march toward general and final collapse. This inexorable march, which it would be vain to try to stop or reverse, cannot but go to its end: catastrophe. But this total and final upheaval can be diversely interpreted: the end of a world can be thought of as the end of the world, but also as the inauguration of a new one. The arc of interpretative attitudes stretches from radical pessimism to the most serene optimism. Such a conception of modern decadence certainly seems at first sight to imply a catastrophist pessimism based on the prophecy of the end of time. Bonald, for example, wrote to Joseph de Maistre in December 1817:

There are for me absolutely inexplicable things, whose outcome does not seem to me to be within the grasp of the power of men, in so far as they act guided by their own light and under the sole influence of their will; in truth, what I most clearly see in all of this . . . is the Apocalypse.[2]

But the endpoint of the final decadence, the point of no return, can also be interpreted as a new beginning, renaissance, creative rupture: the Nietzschean doctrine of an overturning of nihilism, of a conversion or transvaluation of values, demonstrates the possibility of a second kind of traditionalist thinking, in which the destruction caused by a decadence that has reached its endpoint opens the way for a counter-modernity very different from that of the counterrevolutionaries (who summarily link "reaction against" to "return to"). The antimodern reaction can be thought of either as seeking to halt the destructive process, thus authorizing a salutary return, or as a radicalization, making it possible for decadence to surpass and overcome itself (the transvaluation of all values designating this self-transcendence). According to whether it integrates the myth of redemption through return to the good origin or to the natural order before the fall, or that of metamorphosis or conversion of values through nihilism's self-transcendence, traditionalism is either counterrevolutionary and supernaturalist or untimely and super-humanist. The absolute revolt against the modern world can lead either to the name of God or to the name of the Overman. That is why we need to distinguish two traditionalist traditions in the nineteenth century: that founded by Bonald, Maistre, and Donoso Cortés, and that inaugurated by Nietzsche's later writings (1885–88).

This grand, radically antimodern argumentation was constituted in the first half of the nineteenth century, in reaction, of course, to the revolutionary event and to the irruption of the bourgeoisie as the dominant or managing class, but also to the trickling down of irreligiosity to the lower classes—this movement toward de-christianization, largely overestimated at its beginnings, being perceived as the progression of the barbarism specific to the modern world or as a regression toward primitive barbarity. It is in the latter writings of Juan Donoso Cortés (1808–53), following the "conversion" (in the summer of 1847) of this Spanish master of Catholic traditionalism, that we find the fully achieved expression of this radical antimodern vision: we shall call it the *traditionalist paradigm*. The traditionalist picture of modernity, as Donoso Cortés sketches it, puts in place a small number of critical notations from which a total condemnation is derived. We can make a brief presentation of its main motifs.

In the moral order, if we follow Donoso, the true and the good have become undefinable, hence inaccessible; in the political order, nothing escapes anymore from the "discussing class," the liberal bourgeoisie which from now on rules without contest, all of which enlarges and makes irreversible the reigning intellectual and moral an-archy. The modern, demo-liberal world is one in which there no longer are, or can no longer emerge, "absolute negations" nor "sovereign affirmations."[3] Moderation reigns, and the vacuum is filled by the agitations of commerce, both that of merchandises and that of words. The modern world has witnessed the triumph of "perpetual discussion." It is in this that the political expression of modernity is the rise and establishment of "bourgeois liberalism," the exclusive imposition of the liberal conception of democracy, which can see the world only as if it were an immense parliamentary assembly, where doubt encounters only doubt, where irresolution ever meets only with its mirror image, where lack of decision baptizes itself "tolerance," where the illegitimacy of the rulers is the echo of the mediocrity of all and reveals the baseness of the ruling ideals. Donoso Cortés sets forth his fundamental axiom in 1851, and immediately draws its main consequence: "Man is born to act, and perpetual discussion, incompatible with action, is too contrary to human nature"[4] The modernization of human existence is part of the process of denaturalization of man.

Nietzsche, especially in the posthumous fragments dating from 1885 to 1888, will find his way back to the principal motifs of this traditionalist impugnment of modernity. The modern world's degraded spirituality is, first of all, that of big words, of pompous labels stuck on pretended "ideals" and "higher feelings":[5] "The modern spirit's lack of discipline, dressed up in all sorts of moral fashions—The showy words are: tolerance (for 'the incapacity for Yes and No'); *la largeur de sympathie* (= one-third indifference, one-third curiosity, one-third pathological irritability); 'objectivity' (lack of personality, lack of will, incapacity for 'love')."[6]

A flabby and lukewarm logocracy, the modern world is also the world of negotiators and of intermediaries, of merchants and of parliamentarians—the world of "representatives." Nietzsche evaluates as being a symptom of decadence the double fact that in modernity, according to Carl Schmitt, "human society metamorphoses into an immense club,"[7] while the State becomes "a big company."[8] Nietzsche specifically stigmatizes modernity for being the world of "intermediaries" and "representatives": "The predominance of dealers and intermediaries [*Zwischenpersonen*] in spiritual matters, too: the scribbler, the "representative" [*Vertreter*], the historian (who fuses past and present), the exotician and cosmopolitan, the intermediaries between science and philosophy, the semitheologians."[9]

Modernity thus erects the in-between and the "neither this nor that," the neutral and the mixed, the at-home-nowhere and the at-home-everywhere, the nomad and the cosmopolitan, as normative types. Nietzsche stigmatizes political modernity quite precisely for being the organization of "representatives" into an oligarchy. Liberal democracy is the regime that favors social climbing and selects the "representative" type, he who is neither aristocrat nor worker:

Today, in our time when the state has an absurdly fat stomach, there are in all fields and departments, in addition to the real workers, also "representatives" [*Vertreter*]; e.g., besides the scholars also scribblers, besides the suffering classes also garrulous, boastful ne'er-do-wells who "represent" this suffering, not to speak of the professional politicians who are well off while "representing" distress with powerful lungs before a parliament. Our modern life is extremely expensive owing to the large number of intermediaries.[10]

If, therefore, parliamentary democracy incarnates modern decadence in the political sphere, in that it doesn't know how to say either yes or no, the shadow of decadence stretches as far as music, where Nietzsche analogically spots an incapacity or refusal to choose and affirm. But these partial decadences find their own analogue in all the domains of modern existence. If Nietzsche the pamphleteer treats Wagner's music or German culture the way he does, it is because he burdens them with all the losses, impotencies, and morbidities characteristic of modernity:

Of *what* do I suffer when I suffer of the fate of music? That music has been done out of its world-transfiguring, Yes-saying character, so that it is music of decadence and no longer the flute of Dionysus . . .

[This book is] an attack on the German nation, which is becoming ever lazier and more impoverished in its instincts, ever more *honest,* and which continues with an enviable appetite to feed on opposites, gobbling down without any digestive troubles "faith" as well as scientific manners, "Christian love" as well as anti-Semitism, the will to power (to the *Reich*) as well as the *évangile des humbles.*—Such a failure to take sides among the opposites! Such neutrality and "selflessness" of the stomach! This sense of justice of the German palate that finds all causes just and accords all equal rights—that finds everything tasty.[11]

We can see here, contrary to the lessons proffered by a certain orthodox interpretation of Nietzsche, that the denunciation of egalitarianism is not at the heart of his antimodern argumentation. If we read attentively the polemical phenomenology of the modern spirit in the last Nietzschean writings, we see that modernity is determined, rather, by the metaphor of a *mixture* of all nourishments, from the crudest to the most refined, and by a monstrous capacity to *assimilate* contraries. Modernity mixes and munches, it indifferently ingurgitates and digests everything. What characterizes it, above all, is the absence of aptitude to make distinctions that it manifests in all domains. Omnipotent digestion chases discrimination away from it. The sense of distinction is alien to it, which is why it is devoid of distinction. The egalitarian spirit is thus but an effect, the sign of a way of working that the Nietzschean texts describe using physiological metaphors. Modernity can thus be described as an immense digestive system or as a monstrous metabolism which, transforming all substances into equal elements, makes everything mediocre.

It is thus less the egalitarian spirit than its spirit of intermediation and assimilation that is characteristic of modernity in its negative essence. Nietzsche adds to this essential characteristic the exhaustion of the will and the rupture with traditions, themes abundantly commented upon in Paul Bourget's *Essays*, of which he said he was a good reader: "Toward a characterization of *"modernity"* [*Modernität*].—Overabundant development of intermediary forms [*Zwischengebilde*]; atrophy of types; traditions break off, schools; the overlordship of the instincts (prepared philosophically: the unconscious *worth more*) after the will to power, the willing of end *and* means, has been weakened.[12]

Yet Nietzsche, in his last fragmentary sketches, determines modernity not simply as a rupture with the past but as the *eradication* of all forms of the traditional element. Modernity is not simply loss, forgetfulness, or dissolution, it is, fundamentally, antitradition. More precisely: countertradition, destined never to be anything more than a new pseudotradition. The negative essence of modernity is to be a process of self-destruction. Power of destruction of traditions and omnipotent principle of disorganization, modernity produces something like a twilight of culture, what Nietzsche calls a "modern eclipse" [*moderne Verdüsterung*],[13] whose history he wants to write.[14] In a fragment written between November 1887 and March 1888, Nietzsche characterizes the antithesis between tradition (whichever it may be) and modernity:

What is attacked deep down today is the instinct and the will of tradition [*Tradition*]: all institutions that owe their origins to this instinct violate the taste of the modern spirit.—At bottom, nothing is thought and done without the purpose of eradicating this sense for tradition [*Sinn für Überlieferung*]. One considers tradition a fatality [*Fatalität*]; one studies it, recognizes it (as "heredity" [*Erblichkeit*]), but one does not *want* it. The tensing of a will over long temporal distances, the selection of the states and valuations that allow one to dispose of future centuries—precisely this is antimodern [*antimoderne*] in the highest degree. Which goes to show that it is the disorganizing principles that give our age its character.[15]

What we are attempting to show, against the dominant historiography, is that Nietzsche, smasher of idols, who deconstructed and held in contempt ascetic ideals in religion, morality, and science, Nietzsche then, with a reputation as a modern or even ultramodern due to his hypercritical and demystificatory perspectives, is also and above all an antimodern thinker, the thinker of modernity as the phenomenon of final decadence. It is in the evolution of Nietzsche's thinking in the direction of a growing antimodern radicalness, beginning in 1883–84, that he, knowingly or not, wanders down the paths laid down by the traditionalist critique of counterrevolutionary origins. And this until he finds again its main positive motifs: the value-norm of a hierarchical order, the vision of the Eternal Recurrence in which the theory of cycles finds a new life. The explicit rupture with the Christian tradition in no way turns Nietzsche into a thinker foreign to the traditionalist heritage, any more than the "death of God" diagnosis would make him inaccessible to theological constructs. Nietzsche appears rather to be the founder of a second tradition of radical traditionalist thought, whose intellectual and political heritage will only emerge in the first half of the twentieth century. The partial (in both senses) inheritors of this second antimodern traditionalism will be legion among philosophers and writers: Spengler and Evola, Édouard Berth and Drieu la Rochelle, Léon Chestov, Cioran . . . , and, of course, Heidegger.

This second traditionalism effected its transition into politics in the twentieth century either through "nationalist" mobilizations or through fascism. In every case, the dominant antimodern element was anti-demoliberalism; whereas socialism was not designated and treated as the absolute enemy as much as it was assimilated into various syntheses after due reinterpretation and reformulation. It is by taking such sociopolitical facts into consideration that we can, as a hypothesis, conceive of doctrinal nationalism (that of the nationalists) as a reinvention of traditionalism, and this not without a constitutive paradox: the nation, a properly modern invention, is defined, from the moment that it is posited as being origin and foundation, with the very attributes of tradition (transmission, meaning-conferring principle, foundational reference, the memory of a common origin, etc.). The integral nationalism of the Action Française, for example and par excellence, was a nationalist-traditionalism in which the ordering principle was the Catholic church (or "Christian civilization"), the incarnation of Tradition, as demonstrated by its very resistance to modernity's satanic seductions. But here the reference to the religious, unlike the constitutive usage the first traditionalism made of it, is functional and even instrumental ("Politics first!").

It is certainly due to the fact that twentieth-century traditionalist thinking was almost completely enmeshed with the Catholic counter-revolution, or with various currents of theocratic inspiration, that Nietzsche's pathetically declared anti-Christianity hindered the commentators from seeing in his last reflections the outline of a philosophy of tradition, one implied by his radical antimodernism but, at times, light, insouciant, ironic, at the opposite of the extreme spirit of seriousness of the dogmatic Catholic reactionaries.[16]

Present in all forms of traditionalism, perhaps the profoundest theological inheritance to be found in Nietzsche and also in Spengler is expressed by the scriptural proverb: God vomits out the lukewarm. If the modern spirit is what it is not, if it is neither hot nor cold, then salvation can be found only in "hardness" and the vocation to extremes.[17] Better death than an "entropy of feeling."[18] The traditionalist denunciation of modern decadence begins with the stigmatization of this lukewarmness, which is as incapable of negation as it is of affirmation. Out of the dogmatic inheritance Nietzsche keeps "hardness" in his neo-traditionalist style, but, through his anti-theological spirit, he breathes into traditionalism a positive passion the latter had not known before: he made traditionalism merry. But this merriness consists, nevertheless, in the joy of destruction. And to destroy first of all means, in literature, to indulge in writing pamphlets. The halfway secret motivation for Nietzsche's "untimeliness" was an incurable contempt for the present, brought to its highest intensity by a complete hatred of modernity, hatred whose privileged target is, quite precisely, political modernity, without cease denounced and unmasked by Nietzsche. The lesson will be heard not only by the "masses" but also by characters Nietzsche would have refused to shake hands with.

II. MODERN DECADENCE AND ITS SYMPTOM: "LIBERALISM"

We shall presuppose Nietzsche's diagnosis: "Disintegration characterizes this time, and thus uncertainty: nothing stands firmly on its feet or on a hard faith in itself; one lives for tomorrow, as the day after tomorrow is dubious."[19]

There is nothing new about the obvious state of things that has been worrying Western thought for the last two centuries: we—the "Moderns"—discuss everything, the principles we follow as well as those we reject. We are absolutely convinced that truth is the daughter of discussion and not of sympathy toward the legacy of words and ideas. The existence of such an absolute conviction during the age of the decline of absolutes is a strange paradox. Or so it seems at first sight, since it is really only the logical implication of radical relativism, which professes the new truth produced by the very movement of the modern world: "There is only one absolute—that everything is relative." The most widely shared self-evident idea is that truth, if it is possible, can be neither the gift of a Revelation, nor the fruit of the authority of tradition. The reference to an "eternal yesterday" has no foundational value any more: that is the now-trivial essential message of ideological modernity. It is in this that we moderns, insofar as we are modern, are all "liberals"—whether or not we are in favor of liberalism or followers of some form of liberalism. We are liberals, or bourgeois, if it is true that "the bourgeoisie is the class whose religion is freedom of speech and of the press"[20] or the "discussing class" *(clase discutidora)* in Donoso Cortés's expression.[21]

That is, perhaps, the main lesson given by the hypercritical philosophy of modernity as thought and rethought out by the nineteenth-century metaphysicians of counterrevolution—Maistre, Bonald, Donoso Cortés above all—and by the inspired polemicists who followed them—Louis Veuillot, the combatant against the "liberal illusion,"[22] the young Jules Barbey d'Aurevilly aligning himself with the arguments of the "prophets of the past,"[23] and Antoine Blanc de Saint-Bonnet.[24] We presume, following Carl Schmitt, but from a different perspective, that liberalism—or, more exactly, liberal metaphysics,[25]—grants an essential value to discussion. Liberal metaphysics, in fact, constructs discussion into the supreme value within a constellation in which negotiation and agreement (consensus) jointly reign over subsidiary values and norms. Let us specify the critical perspective on ever-discussing modernity: liberal institutions open up the specifically modern sphere of "perpetual discussion" which, on the one hand, shatters the absoluteness of the principles and self-evident beliefs stemming from tradition and, on the other hand, puts off indefinitely the moment of sovereign decision, of "absolute decision . . . a pure decision, not reasoning, not discussing."[26] The opening up of all values for discussion puts an end to the possibility of uttering "radical negations" and "sovereign affirmations." Liberal metaphysics instead constructs radical uncertainty and sovereign indecision as unquestionable norms. It is as a result of such an analysis of liberalism that Schmitt could declare himself to be antiliberal. As Julien Freud recalled recently, "Carl Schmitt was . . . antiliberal because he judged that liberal politics are antipolitics, the politics of yes and no at the same time."[27]

This critique of modernity seems to ape the dogmatic critique of skepticism: it does, indeed, take up again the theme of the self-refutational quality of the skeptical positions (the infinite swinging to and fro, the perpetual oscillation between positions inaugurates a world ruled by what is false, one in which skepticism cannot assert itself without paradox). But this is a post-Nietzschean critique of modernity: it does not reject skeptical doubt in the name of dogma so much as it refers to will as the power to decide. Although the first phase of traditionalism favored the dogmatic, theologico-political critique of the modern world as generalized skepticism, it was not for all that completely ignorant of the will-centered, decisionist critique that the second traditionalism brings forward beginning with Nietzsche.

Traditionalist thinkers have often acknowledged that their analyses of the modern world's negative logic concluded in a form of historical fatalism: the path the world follows being ruled by the logic of evil or by that of the worst case, what is to be done, except wait for the end while condemning reality? An ancient paradox in the criticism of the present: since he who carries it out is himself part of what he is criticizing, he perforce denounces himself. From that situation derives a modernized version of a Pascalian kind of argument ("We are caught in the boat . . ."). Because for something to be arguable, it must be doubtable: modernity thus defines itself as the era of inevitable doubt. More profoundly: the moment of doubt is at once irreversible and normal. Uncertainty is our destiny. That is how we must recognize ourselves, we who are embarked upon the modern boat as heirs of the "discussing classes," the unstoppable tidal movement whose inevitable consequences had been seen by Donoso Cortés in the middle of the nineteenth century. He also determined the ultimate outcome of this tide, the latter days of the sovereign uncertainty that was not yet designated by the name of nihilism: "When, under the pressure of newspapers, discussion, the fruit of civilization, arrives at a certain extreme, it kills books and plunges minds into an abyss of doubt much more terrible than ignorance."[28]

It truly is a negative dialectics of civilization, a way of thinking consisting of paradoxical consequences, whose first phase in the diagnosis of an illness (or an evil) that announces the emergence of a new barbarism, issuing from modern civilization, this perversely perfect counterfeit of civilization "in which the pile of writings and documents ends up making it more difficult to learn the truth that it is to discover it."[29] Here, we have to bring into the discussion certain axioms formulated by Donoso the traditionalist, in which a Manichaean dualism that structures his political theology of modern history finds expression: "I believe Catholic civilization contains the good with no admixture of evil, and that philosophical civilization contains evil with no mixture of good"[30]

The opposition is immediately normative in its radicalness. But we should pay special attention to the style of thinking, characterized as it is by the obsessive fear of mixture and by the rejection of all that is hybrid, in which we can see a manifestation of the idea, typical of "nineteenth-century Catholic philosophy," "that a great alternative imposes itself, leaving no place for any mediation."[31] The absolute self-evidence of the exclusive disjunction ("either . . . or . . . ," with no third alternative) chases away any kind of ideal involving a dialectical reconciliation. The roads to synthesis and to the overcoming of contradictions are paved with the counterideal of "tolerance," placing good and evil, true and false at the same level. Thus it is that Veuillot's untiring attacks against the "liberal gnosis"[32] derive from the fundamental certainty that "liberal Catholicism" is a contradiction in terms; an absurd fiction like a "deer-goat." Schmitt illustrated this manner of thinking of the irremediable alternative with a very explicit formulation of Cardinal Newman's: "No medium between Catholicism and atheism."[33] To reflect upon this great exclusive disjunction is to reflect upon the obligation of choosing; it is to rehabilitate, against the negotiating and dialectical spirit, the unconditional moment of decision. But, for traditionalist thought, decision remains subordinate to an assured knowledge of the hierarchy of values or, to be more precise, of the absolute opposition of values and antivalues. It is in this that the decision is not arbitrary, even at a time when the principles of tolerance and free inquiry, allied to a taste for "perpetual discussion," have led to the confusion of good and evil, of true and false, through their equalization or inversion.

The confusion begins with liberal laxity about words, the very image of the "unlimited freedom" defended by tolerant modernity, the "freedom of perdition" that is denounced by Veuillot in the first place because of its power of seduction:

> In today's atmosphere, the song of the siren finds dangerous echoes. Many of the maxims that are called liberal are specious and more than embarrassing for whoever does not oppose an absolute contradiction to them. But faith alone furnishes these absolutely victorious contradictions . . . There is a danger merely in prevaricating over words. Treason to words accomplishes the ruin of principles in a mind that is secretly tempted . . . A few liberal propositions are accepted, a few "intolerant" ones repudiated, even less, a hooray for one of the former, a grunt toward one of the latter, is all that is needed: the liberal church requires no other profession of faith . . . As soon as an adroit advocate appears who can throw a veil of beautiful illusions over the naked limbs of a consciousness that is now interested in deceiving itself, the liberal position triumphs. The true is found to be the false, and reciprocally.[34]

The modern world has made normal the mode of existence and the form of thought of sophists, professional chatterers, and mercenaries of verbal illusions who are now working for themselves. The "liberal" politician, that poisonous flower of modern democracy, is the very example of this. That is why the only possible attitude to be taken toward demo-liberal modernity is absolute distance, total rejection, wholesale negation. Donoso Cortés was perhaps the one who best systematized the arguments of the traditionalists who held the modern world in contempt.

Modern or "philosophical" civilization is, according to Donoso, the only one that engenders barbarity through an excess of civilization. A very specific barbarity, devoid of a fertile spontaneity; something like a neobarbarism distinct from the creative barbarity Donoso says had "an advantage over civilization: that it is fecund" where "civilization is sterile."[35] The opposition is, once again, very clear here: on the one hand, the power of regeneration, on the other, the sign of degeneracy. We can observe in this thought of Donoso's an echo of Vico's conceptions, which affirmed that "all civilizations are mortal, that they all travel from the brutality of primitive barbarity to the perverse refinements of the second barbarity engendered by an excess of reflection.[36]

It is in the traditionalist descriptions of this infertile, so-to-speak devitalized neobarbarism that emerge the first characteristics of what will be called, later in the century, "nihilism": unsurpassable ineptitude at arriving at a meaning and to establish legitimacy, disappearance of all absolute authority, a paralyzing fatigue in the quest for truth, which itself tends to be dissolved in the cult of majority opinion, of subjective certainty, or of the useful idea. The death of God, or the decline of absolute values, is inseparable from the positive valorization of inferior forms of existence and of thought, made into idols through the relativist principle of tolerance, the value of "equality," and the requirement of free inquiry. What the term *nihilism* conceptualizes, at least minimally, is quite precisely the observation that *there is nothing more* than what is left over when superior values, and the suprasensible principle from which they derive, have come to be valued at nothing. What is left are losses that are felt to be irreparable as well as corrosive substitutions, the indefinite multiplication of needs of a lower order, competition founded upon envy, and the desire to reduce everything to the lowest common denominator. The general disorder, or the dissolution of all hierarchical order that is absolutely legitimate, is but an effect, something like proof of the Fall. So maintains Joseph de Maistre: "All is bad, since nothing is in its place. The keynote of the system of our creation having been lowered, all the other ones have gone down in proportion, following the rules of harmony."[37]

The harmony being lost, or, more exactly, having become impossible, means that the dissonance now escapes the law of temperament,[38] that it becomes not only an independent force but also an expanding, unchained power. That is how the savageness specific to modern neobarbarism is perceived, savageness excellently illustrated by the revolutionary phenomenon. But no less well illustrated by the— now normal—state of social disorder as it is described by Bonald: "There are infinitely more inequalities between the pleasures that are available and the means of fortune to acquire them; there are therefore more desires than can be satisfied, there is more greed, there are more passions, more crimes, and the proof of all this is in front of our eyes."[39]

What remains, then, after the "irreparable losses"[40] is not nothing: it is the movement of infinite expansion of the forces of dissolution, it is the power of unlimited contamination proper to the lower passions, and the growing seduction of corrupt forms of existence. Where—to take up a distinction introduced by Gérard Gengembre—the "reassuring decadence" is the one that can be integrated as a phase in a providential history or in a cyclical temporality (decadence then being the prelude to a renaissance, figuring the transition toward regeneration), "terrifying decadence" is one that renders the explanatory categories useless, an unintegrable and disintegrating decadence, which can be described in its effects but remains unknown, even unknowable, in principle, a decadence that signals the beginning of the end and is equivalent to announcing death. The last sentence of the *Réflexions sur la Révolution de juillet 1830* (Reflections on the Revolution of 1830) throws out this unequivocal warning: "I shall not cease to repeat it: France as a republic would mean the end of monarchical Europe, and a republican Europe would be the end of civilization, of religion, of politics, the end of society, the end of everything."[41]

These portents and prophecies are uttered as if the original Fall, having opened up the tragic time of history, were closing it again definitively, as in a parenthesis, repeating itself as an echo in the final Fall. This monstrosity from top to bottom, the modern, postrevolutionary world, is incarnated in the form of life that is unstable by nature, one without a future. Society desocialized, politics deconstituted, men dehumanized: modernity is "a desocialization evolving toward chaos."[42] Modern decadence is interpreted as being the final decadence, and this especially by Bonald, who in certain texts abandons all idea of a reinsertion of decadent modernity in a metahistory that would go toward the better by passing through the worst. The absolute novelty of the modern monstrosity then becomes the sign that history has arrived at its last moment: the satanic inversion has been fully carried out, the regression toward the chaos of ante-Creation is, at the same time, the production of an anti-Creation. And it is true that, in the desperate and disillusioned eyes of the traditionalist thinker, the modern aberration is "literally unnamable":[43] "Never, I think, has anything like it been seen in the world. A nation as new by its name as it is by its origin, or rather a nation for which a name, as new as it itself, would have to be invented, a race of men outside humanity, to whom it would be impossible to form a society; a nation, one may say, that is without fathers, without god, and soon will be without men."[40]

III. Approaches to Nihilism

Death of the fathers, death of God, end of the human world: the diagnosis of the final decadence opens the way to the interpretation of decadent history as being transformed by nihilism, which comes to fulfillment within it. The chronology of texts and of philosophical constructions will be of no help to us in thinking our way through nihilism.[45] What should we understand by nihilism? First, and formally, it is the losses, the lacks, the absences that affect what is ordinarily called "the reasons to live." Second, it is the impossibility of answering the fundamental questions having to do with origins, final ends, the destiny of the human being and the "why" of what is, impossibility that destroys the bases of all science, all morality, and all religion. This can go to the point of bringing about the proof par excellence of nihilism: the questions that are said to be fundamental have no meaning themselves, being absurdities that reflect the unsurpassable absurdity of existence.

It is, finally, a fall, a process in which the "superior values" inescapably decline, disappearing and losing their value. Like decadence itself, nihilism can be said to be a process or a final state. But nihilism can, moreover, designate the experience of an unveiling, of an uncovering of essential nothingness, a new and final "truth" that destroys all truth. The extraordinary dissemination of various themes in Nietzsche's thought, or rather in Nietzscheanism, has rendered the main characterizations of nihilism trivial, "classical," and thereby not really thought out: the devaluation of all values, the waning of sublime ends, the disappearance of transcendence, and the dissipation of the meaning of existence. Let us return to the difficult clarity of Nietzsche's last texts: "What does nihilism mean? *That the highest values devaluate themselves.* The aim is lacking; 'why?' finds no answer."[46] The lack of finality leads to a lack of meaning: "any goal [*Ziel*] at least constitutes some meaning [*Sinn*]."[47]

This identification of nihilism can emerge—and so we hypothesize, as historians of ideas—only from within the limits of a theologically impregnated thinking. Which is why, behind the very obvious differences of vocabulary and of relation to context, Nietzsche's analysis of history as decadence and of nihilism as motor and truth of this decadent history is in no way foreign to absolute traditionalism's ultrapessimist theology of history. In a 15 April 1852 letter, Donoso characterizes the "liberal" position, the exemplary manifestation of the optimistic gnosis of Infinite Progress, as the conviction that *"discussion is to truth as means is to an end."*[48] A liberal belief, but also the first postulate of rationalism, and the constitutive principle of parliamentarianism. But the perverse effect of the specifically modern duty to discuss and debate had been well perceived by Donoso: the unwilled and unforeseen result of the "discussionist" imperative is irresolution and indecision; and, more profoundly, the beginning of the era of insurmountable uncertainties. Nietzsche will later, in his fashion, repeat the diagnosis about the heterotelic quality of the "modern" imperatives when he denounces "the modern spirit's lack of discipline, dressed up in all sorts of moral fashions": the first of the "showy words" he selects and deciphers, in a posthumous fragment from 1887, is, quite precisely, "tolerance (for 'the incapacity for Yes and No')."[49]

Here Nietzsche repeats Donoso's diagnosis and points to the same sign of decadence: the incapacity of the moderns, perpetual talkers, to deny and assert. Nietzsche spots this symptom of the modern illness in the most diverse domains, for the "road leading to a Yes and to a No" has been lost.[50] Modern man "sits between two chairs, he says Yes and No in the same breath":[51] we need only take a look at Wagner, or Tolstoy, or many other specimens (among whom Rousseau is one of the first historical types). This "innocence in moralistic mendaciousness,"[52] modern par excellence, expresses itself either by oscillating between the Yes and the No, or by illusory syntheses of Yes and No, or again by withdrawing into a neutral position (neither Yes nor No). The modern ineptitude at making "radical negations" and "sovereign affirmations" is reflected, so to speak, in a formulation that has become a commonplace: "The optimist says that the glass is half-full, the pessimist, that it is half-empty." The obviousness, for modern spirits, of such a proposition, which relativizes the optimist and pessimist positions and reduces them to simple opinions, as subjective as they are inconsistent, illustrates the reign of uncertainty and irresolution, as if even optimism and pessimism could not fully and firmly assert themselves.

In what sense can we consider the central thesis of the "liberal gnosis," in Donoso's intrasigent "Catholic" perspective, to be the "source of every possible error and the origin of every imaginable extravagance"?[53] The traditionalist thinker's analysis consists in positing and making explicit a fundamental distinction between "Catholic discussion" and "philosophical discussion."[54] It follows that modern verbal "speculations," as first denounced by Burke,[55] do not make up the totality of discussion: there are legitimate discussions diametrically opposite from "perpetual discussion." If we follow Donoso, Catholicism proceeds by "grasp[ing] a ray of light that comes from above and giv[ing] it to man to make it fertile with his reason."[56] For the Spanish philosopher, suffused as he was with Augustinianism, it is an absolute evidence that "in its infirmity, human understanding can neither invent truth nor discover it, but it can see it when it is shown to him."[57]

How, on the other hand, does "philosophism" proceed? It "begins by artfully veiling, under a thick veil, the truth and the light as they come to us from heaven; it then gives reason an insoluble problem whose terms are the following: through fertilization to extract truth and light out of doubt and obscurity, which is what it exposes to the fertilization of human reason."[58]

In this manner, the philosophical method comes up against an eternal law, which decrees that "fertilization has the power only to develop the fertile germ":[59] "Thus does the obscure emanate from the obscure, the luminous from the luminous, like from the like: *Deum de deo, lumen de lumine.*"[60] That is the terrible illusion of the "philosophical" conception of discussion: to believe that we can give birth to truth through the rational fecundation of doubt and obscurity. But this modern belief, as we have seen, clashes with the eternal law of begetting and, due to its inconsequence, cannot escape the heterogenesis of ends: "Human reason, in fertilizing doubt, has arrived at negation; and in fertilizing obscurity, has arrived at palpable gloom."[61] Human reason being impaired, it can gain access to truth only on condition that "an infallible and pedagogic authority . . . show it the way."[62] This authority which alone can show truth to reason, is the Church. That is why "when reason emancipates itself from the Church, error and evil reign without obstacles in the world."[63] Since human will is no less impaired than reason, Donoso authorizes himself to conclude, "It is clear that freedom of discussion necessarily leads to error, just as freedom of action necessarily leads to evil."[64] It follows that the peoples made up of "pure discussers"[65] become ungovernable, are ready for the worst tyrannies (beginning with the tyranny of opinion). It can be easily observed that "one of the traits that characterize the present epoch is that legitimacy shines by its absence. Those who govern have lost the faculty of governing, and the peoples have ceased being governable."[66]

The series of illegitimacies is thus: the discussability of the fundamental (truths, principles, absolute values, and unconditional norms) leads to the absence of all legitimate, which is to say absolute, authority, an absence that brings about a state of permanent irresolution, which transforms itself into "uncertainty, dilettantism, scepticism, pessimism—the contemporary forms of the 'mal du siècle.'"[67] Nietzsche's diagnosis of "disintegration" and "uncertainty"[68] will establish for a long time to come this vision of the modern world as one of continuous "crisis," one that is constitutive and therefore without resolution. Nietzsche had not overlooked the deeper affinities between liberal ideals, the spirit of tolerance, and the feeling of pity; he deciphered in them the triumph of the "weak" and the "mediocre" under various ideological pseudonyms: "The honorable term for mediocre is, of course, the word 'liberal.' "[69]

In the last two decades of the nineteenth century, that diagnosis travels from the philosophy of history to politics and constitutes the first premise of nationalist argumentation. Correlatively, the radical critique of parliamentarianism takes up this motif over and over again, justifying the complete devaluing of debate in the political sphere with an ideological self-evidence: from a symptom of chaos, only chaos can result. That is why the initiators of doctrinal nationalism in France at the end of the nineteenth century (Paul Bourget, Jules Lemaître, Maurice Barrès, Edouard Drumont, Charles Maurras) go over the same ground of the "observation" of a generalized "anarchy," incriminating the same signs and causes of the latter: individualism (always "dissolving"), the spirit of free inquiry, liberalism (and its alleged offshoot, socialism), and the "criticism of the nineteenth century."[70] In his study on "Monsieur Taine" published in 1882, Paul Bourget thus asserted:

We live in a time of religious and metaphysical collapse, when innumerable doctrines litter the ground. Not only do we no longer, as did those living in the seventeenth century, have a general credo regulating all consciences and, in principle, all actions, but we have lost even the force of negation that was the inside-out credo of the eighteenth century. All those who, from far and near, attached themselves to the movement of combat led by Voltaire at least had one certitude: they believed they were fighting error. An entire unconscious faith was wrapped within that certitude. To believe that an obvious sign separates that which is reasonable from that which is not is to assert, at the same time, that reason is infallible. Such is no longer the conviction of most of the cultivated spirits in our age of critique. We have so multiplied the points of view, so skillfully refined the interpretations, so patiently looked for the genesis, and thereby for the relative legitimacy of all doctrines, that we have come to think that a soul of truth can be found hidden within the most contradictory hypotheses on the nature of man and of the universe. And since, on the other hand, there is no supreme hypothesis that reconciles all the others and integrally imposes itself on the intelligence, an anarchy of a unique order has been elaborated in the intellectual world. A skepticism derives from this that is without analogue in the history of ideas . . . This disposition to put even doubt in doubt brings with it a procession of infirmities that we know only too well: vacillation of the will, sophistic compromises with conscience, a dilettantism that is always half-detached and ever indifferent.[71]

This extraordinary tableau of the nineteenth century's "perilous weaknesses,"[72] the other side of which is made up of so many irreparable losses, was almost certainly meditated upon at length by Nietzsche, reader of "Monsieur Taine"[73] and of the "inquisitive" and at the same time "delicate" "psychologist" Paul Bourget,[74] as well as being thought through again, in its essential points, in Nietzsche's last writings under the category of "European nihilism."[75] We also know that Nietzsche borrowed the term "nihilism" from the same Paul Bourget[76] who, in the preface to his 1885 *Essais de psychologie contemporaine* (Essays in contemporary psychology), introduced it in this way:

M. de Maupassant's *Bel-Ami*, although he is as nihilistic as *Obermann*, shows his nihilism in another fashion, and Baudelaire's extreme disciples celebrate their sentiment of decadence in rhythms very different from those of Sainte-Beuve. What does it matter if different kinds of speech communicate the same impression of an absolute, an irremediable discouragement? . . . For the psychologist, what is significant is that what lies behind, and the common background, here as well as there, is . . . a mortal fatigue with life, a dreary perception of every effort.[77]

We find also in Paul Bourget, between 1882 and 1885, an attempt to theorize a conjunction between the diagnosis of "degeneration" (*dégénérescence*) as a phenomenon of exhaustion, of aging, even of agony, and the new experience of the disappearance of all transcendence as something specific to modern Western culture (as incarnated in literary France of the nineteenth century). In the same way, in the last phase of Nietzsche's thinking, the "ruin of the sovereignty of the supersensible and of the 'ideals' stemming from it"[78] leaves "modern" humanity without "goals" in a world bereft of "superior values" and therefore devoid of "meaning." From this situation emerges, fatefully, the "exhausted" type, looking for rest at any price, acted upon by a "tremendous . . . *disease of the will*."[79] The "*present-day man.*"[80]

The disappearance of the "old French gaiety," added Bourget,[81] describing the effects of the "illness of the moral life come to its sharpest period"[82] in order, in the end, to ask about the causes of "this disappearance": "If the noble virtue of courage has been replaced by the useless and weary 'what for?,' if the conscience of the race seems to be troubled, should we not seek the reason for this visible problem?"[83] The *Essais de psychologie contemporaine* set out to try to answer this question.[84] But its explanations do not rise to the level of the problem and merely enumerate the symptoms once again. It is the minute description of the "intellectual illness"[85] that will provide a starting point for Maurras's doctrinal construction. From what, according to him, the "anarchy of the nineteenth century" had created, Maurras will note, paraphrasing Bourget: "A *What for?* was the universal settlement of accounts with people and with things, with substances and with ideas. It was nothingness itself, felt and lived through."[86] Such is the experience of the "nihilism" that will become a commonplace towards the end of the nineteenth century, descending from poets and philosophers to the literati and the journalists, to, at last, become a fashion, the "fin de siècle sensibility,"[87] an object of praise or blame.

We still need to understand how integral nationalism can define itself indifferently, by its own norms, as either an antinihilism or as an antiliberalism. For in the eyes of the young Maurras, calling against Taine for a return to classical order, the self-complacent "fin de siècle" pessimism is but a manifestation of Romanticism, a mixture of sentimentalism and idle chatter. And Romanticism is itself but the literary wing of the *"Clouds"* of which the revolutionary spirit is the political facet. Maurras could assert in 1922 that "friends and adversaries of Romanticism are in agreement about its profound identity with Revolution; it is a result of discussion."[88] The republican regime is the one founded upon discussion that goes nowhere. About the alleged affinity between the Republic and interminable discussion, Maurras wrote in 1912, The Republic is the regime of discussion for the sake of discussion and of criticism for the sake of criticism. Whoever ceases to discuss, whoever stops criticizing, offends the images of Liberty. The Republic means the preeminence of discussion, and of the most sterile discussion at that.[89]

Getting somewhere is the accomplishment of the will that judges clearly and decides and chooses firmly. Where in a "normal" political order speech is at the service of action, preparing it or explaining it, in the republican regime speech substitutes itself for action. This illness of language is inseparable from a weakening of the will. "Integral nationalism" invents a voluntaristic traditionalism. This is why the Action Française's doctrinal nationalism can, in its deepest intentions, be considered the attempt to rethink counterrevolutionary traditionalism outside of the limits imposed by historical fatalism, breaking therefore with the involuntarism of the earlier reactionary philosophy. That is the reason Maurras ended his introduction to *L'avenir de l'intelligence* (The future of intelligence), dated 1904–5, with this maxim: "Any political despair is an absolute imbecility."[90] It was an affirmation of traditionalism's change or conversion to voluntarism. And of the new alliance of authority and of decision against argumentation.

IV. THE DIALECTICAL POISON AND ITS REMEDY

Let us start out from the critical procedure through which traditionalist and antimodern thought is recognizable: the designation and denunciation of verbal abstraction, running on empty independently of any transcendent or suprasensible ideality, as a symptom of modern decadence and its accelerating factor. This symptom is most often considered to be literal and is explained as a pathological phenomenon. But this pathologization is itself projected either onto a long historical period, as in that of the history of Europe or of the West (the characteristic of Nietzschean thinking) or onto the shorter time period of modernity, or even of the author's contemporary period (as is the case in Bonald, Donoso, Bourget, or Norday, for example).

In a fragment dating from 1884, Nietzsche traced out a philosophical working program: "To describe the decadence of the modern soul in all its forms: to what extent *decadence* goes back to Socrates."[91] Four years later, Nietzsche began *Ecce Homo,* his ironic, peculiar, half-biographical, half-bibliographical spiritual self-presentation, with this reminder in the form of an allusion: "My readers know perhaps in what way I consider dialectic as a symptom of decadence; for example in the most famous case, the case of Socrates."[92] In a short interpretative essay, "The Problem of Socrates,"[93] Nietzsche characterized the "something [that] must be *sick,*"[94] the "physiological" disorder of the typical character: "Socrates's decadence is suggested not only by the admitted wantonness and anarchy of his instincts, but also by the hypertrophy of the logical faculty and that *sarcasm of the rachitic* which distinguishes him."[95] That is the essence of the diagnosis: the hypertrophy of the argumentative faculty, a "kind of degeneration" quite widespread during the decline of "old Athens,"[96] this sickness of the rational instinct, is called the dialectic. But of course "one chooses dialectic only when one has no other means."[97] Spengler will follow Nietzsche in his pathologization of the dreamer's optimism he thinks he discerns in most philosophers:

For the first time, we can see as a fact that all of the literature of "truths," all of the noble, good-natured, foolish inspirations, projects, and solutions, all of these books, pamphlets, and speeches, are a useless phenomenon, as all other cultures have learned and then forgotten again in corresponding epochs . . .

I would be ashamed to go through life with such cheap ideals ["the sonorous, noble, and abstract words that constitute the goal of our earthly existence"]. That is the cowardice of the born cringers and dreamers, who cannot stand to look straight at reality and set forth a true goal with a couple of sober words. They must always have great generalities, illuminating from afar. That calms the anxiety of those who are too spoiled to attempt taking on risks, challenges; for everything that requires enterprise, initiative, and superiority . . . he who is born only to talk, write, and dream, will suck his poison out of every book [this said about the supposed effects of the writings of Schopenhauer, of Nietzsche, and of Spengler himself, author of *The Decline of the West*].

What our contemplatives and idealists seek is a *comfortable* world-picture [*Weltanschauung*], a system, that demands nothing but to be convinced of it; a moral excuse for their fear of activity. They sit, debating, in the corners of life for which they were born. May they stay there.[98]

The opposition between decisionism and deliberationism rules out, in Spengler's thought, any third term: dialectical mediations and syntheses are not only foreign to a vision of history founded upon the difference in nature between "facts" and "truths" (an expression analogous to that of the absolute difference between "life" and "thought"),[99] they are designated as pathological illusions, denounced as harmful hallucinations by the "relativistic"[100] realist Spengler considers himself to be. And they are attributed, in conformity with the Nietzschean impulse, to a human type that is defined mainly by its weakness, its lack of energy, its quasi-physiological cowardliness: the exhausted type, he whom the forces of life have deserted.

Spengler had hopes only for a new "Roman hardness," he wished for the coming of a "Caesar," the only kind of politician corresponding to the destiny of twentieth-century Europe: "Politics, fine, but by statesmen, not world improvers."[101] It is as if he had meditated on the conclusions of a Donoso, who had acknowledged that "the time of monarchy has come to an end."[102] And "when face to face with radical evil, only dictatorship is left."[103] Going on to radicalize Joseph de Maistre's legitimization of political authority, Donoso finally posits the radical antithesis: chaos or dictatorship, which, as Carl Schmitt brilliantly demonstrated,[104] presupposes substituting "absolute decision" for the principle of legitimacy. Dictatorship becomes absolutely necessary as the only possible content of the counterrevolutionary idea form the moment that the unconditional political imperative is that of being opposed, without the least compromise, to anarchy, born out of the total destruction of all principles of legitimacy. The decisionist commitment presumes the inseparability of the two main manifestations of modern decadence: anarchy and "perpetual discussion." But "dictatorship is the contrary of discussion."[105] Therefore the new alternative: dictatorship or final decadence.

The counterrevolution can be thought of as either a reversal or a conversion. Reversal, inversion, subversion, contrary movement: these are all strictly modern schemas of the real negation, whereas to convert is not simply to turn over the "dunghill" of what is; it is to transmute, transform, and transubstantiate. Nietzsche had come upon the difficulty: how to think through the "revaluation of values"?[106] In certain texts, the axiological inversion seems to boil down to a mere overturning of the hierarchy of values or of their "principle":[107] overcoming decadence would mean placing at the top of the hierarchy of values those that the decadent morality par excellence ("Christian values, decadence values")[108] puts at the bottom of the ladder; it would be to radically devalue the values said to be superior and, correlatively, to erect as supreme values those that have been demeaned or disqualified by decadent axiology. The "new values" would be determined, in this perspective of overcoming, through the promotion of former negative values into eminently positive values, the "last" becoming the "first."[109] The reader will have recognized the Christian paradigm turned against historical Christianity. But in other texts Nietzsche thinks of the "inversion of values" in a quite different manner, as a transmutation following the alchemical analogy. He stresses the importance of the latter in a letter to Georg Brandes:

I have used these weeks to "revaluate values."—Do you understand this trope?—At bottom, the alchemist is the worthiest kind of man there is: I mean he who makes something valuable and even gold out of small and disdained things. Only he enriches us; the others merely give us change. My task is quite curious this time: I have asked myself what humanity has most hated, feared, and held in contempt:—and from those very things I have made my "gold."[110]

The alternative is clearly posited here: the inversion of values can be thought of as either "change" or exchange of values, or as conversion or transmutation. The recourse to the alchemical metaphor, the appeal to myth as a mode of presentation of a way of thinking unrepresentable in the conceptual framework accepted by the moderns (whether science or philosophy) are not in themselves devoid of undesirable consequences: the transmutation of values is not conceivable in any way other than as purification and sublimation, which brings us back to a Platonic-Christian heritage that was supposed to be eradicated.

The problem is that the great theoretical difficulty the various types of thinking in terms of decadence come up against, the speculative "cross" they must bear, arises whenever they try to go beyond diagnosis, where they excel, to indicate "remedies," to stipulate the way to salvation, and sketch out positive orientations. Through radical pessimism the problem of going beyond is avoided and the difficulty is abolished in its very principle. But for the "doctors of civilization," the double question persists and becomes unavoidable: What does one do? What does one hope for? As for those without hope and those in despair, they fall back on a state of waiting and apply themselves to perfecting the picture of what humanity may expect to find, in whole or in part, at the horizon of the process of decadence. Setting out from the presupposition of radical pessimism, two speculative and practical paths open up, neither of which is specific to ideological modernity: the expectation of the worst (Gobineau) and submission to destiny (Spengler). The Spenglerian position, should it need to be pointed out, is as distant from a pessimism that professes that the worst is certain as it is from progressivist optimism, settled into the certainty that we are heading for the better. The conversion of chance into destiny, whether or not it is tied to the "hypothesis" of the Eternal Recurrence, traces the path followed by most of those whose thinking sets out from the later Nietzsche: after identifying the figures of nihilism, one posits the problem of "healing"[111] and tries "to make way for a new order of life."[112] Only one path is absolutely excluded by the ways of thinking within the Nietzschean tradition: to want to overcome decadence by having recourse to the myth of Progress, that very definition of the modern illusion, that contradiction in terms and major inconsistency, given that progressivist beliefs constitute one of the typical manifestations of modern decadence.

The philosophy of counterrevolution comes up against a dilemma: salvation can be conceived of only through a turning back, but it is highly probable that that will not happen in the empirical course of history. And the salvation that is thought of as possible is burdened with a high improbability index. Truth to tell, Donoso's last word on the subject was that "the great catastrophe" designates the most probable event. And the conviction that the worst will not be avoided in this world pierces through here and there in his texts. The diagnosis of decadence is the first premise of Donoso's pessimist ratiocinations, and the prognosis of final decadence is their ultimate conclusion. That is because the "religious reaction," the only one that would be "salutary," appears highly improbable in that it has no historical precedents: "I say it with the deepest sadness. I have seen, I have known a number of individuals who, after having left the faith, came back to it. I have never seen, on the other hand, any peoples who have returned to the faith once they have lost it."[113]

And everything links up, including the losses, from the religious to the political realms: "turning back," finding once again the absolute meaning of what has been lost (faith, legitimacy, truth), to find again, in a word, the lost meaning, is precisely what no longer seems possible for collectivities, peoples, and societies. The exceptions constituted by individual returns,[114] the miracle of personal conversion and reconversions, cannot change anything in the evolution of the whole, determined as it is by the irreparableness of the essential losses. Nothing is left but dictatorship once "the legitimist idea of hereditary succession becomes . . . empty quibbling":[115] when restoration can no longer be anything but an illusion, the future can no longer belong to anything but chaos or dictatorship—but the latter will only delay the moment of the final fall. At that point, salvation cannot be hoped for from the least bad political choice. Being cast into darkness is the greatest certainty on the horizon of decline, writes Donoso: "I know that the light of truth is disappearing from the horizon of a world that will soon be entirely immersed in darkness. I know that shall soon rise over the societies the gloomy night that announces the Divine Wisdom."[116]

V. MODERN MEDIOCRITY AND CHRISTIAN DEGENERACY

The theoreticians of modern decadence posit strict alternatives, an operation characteristic of the maximalist style, which can be determined by the logic of the set of preferences it puts into place: maximalism consists in preferring the contrary to the intermediate, the most dangerous enemy over the mediocre one, the unhappy extreme to the happy medium—death rather than a "lukewarm life," voluntary death rather than mediocrity. Nietzsche notes, for example, in a fragment dating from 1885–86: "Prevention of reduction to mediocrity [*Vermittelmäßigung*]. Rather destruction [*Untergang*]!"[117] Alternatives are posited as if they were touchstones; they must function as a criterion: from the point of view of the symptomatologist, basic choices reveal, clear options discriminate.

Nietzsche was quite precise in his diagnosis: even unto cowardice, modern man is petty, small, minuscule.[118] And this mediocre cowardice is progressing, it "rises," which is to say it falls ever lower, it worsens through being institutionalized as a positive norm, as the modern substitute for the ancient "prudence": "Weakness of the will,"[119] "elimination of the choosing, judging, interpreting subject as a principle,"[120] are his diagnoses. Even more precisely: "*Cowardice when faced with the consequences*—the modern vice."[121] But there is, in modernity, no exercise in cowardice, whether political or not, without a self-legitimation of the rational kind: surrenders are always carried out in the name of rationality or reasonableness since, for the moderns, "before reason one may submit and acquiesce."[122] To the symptomatologist's eye, this normalization of cowardice is but the expression of weariness, which is happy to dress itself up in humanitarian sentimentalism and moralizing postures, for the "herd animal" wishes to be "virtuous": "Reconciliation is a form of lassitude."[123] "To 'understand' is not a sign of force, but of *considerable decadence; moralization* is itself a *decadence.*"[124]

The modern decline of courage is noticeable above all in the refusal to make a choice, out of impotence, in the flight before confrontations, out of weariness, in the ruling classes' taking refuge in negotiation and compromise, and in the submission of all to majority or dominant opinions. This indecision is itself a symptom of the decline of an essential characteristic of the affirmative life: "*Ineptitude to struggle:* that is degeneration."[125] The "virtuous" cowardice of the directing instances in modernity is one of the symptoms of the latter's nature. Nietzsche often justifies its recognition or identification through recourse to the experience of historical precedents:

The degeneration [*Entartung*] of the rulers and the ruling classes has been the cause of the greatest mischief in history! Without the Roman Caesars and Roman society, the insanity of Christianity would never have come to power.

When lesser men begin to doubt whether higher men exist, then the danger is great! And one ends by discovering that there is *virtue* also among the lowly and subjugated, the poor in spirit, and that *before* God men are equal— which has so far been the non plus ultra of nonsense on earth! For ultimately, the higher men measured themselves according to the standard of virtue of slaves— found they were "proud," etc., found all their higher qualities reprehensible.[126]

Nietzsche does not demur at utilizing the biomedical concept of degeneration (*Entartung*) typical of modern interpretations of decadence, which naturalize or biologize it while rendering it pathological. This Nietzschean inconsequence can be explained by the tendency to maximalism specific to the polemic: once the absolute enemy, "Christianity," has been designated in order to be stigmatized, everything is permitted. The rejection of modernity is for Nietzsche merely implied in the total war he has declared against Christianity, the paradigmatic harmful "error," the matrix of all the modern "errors." We know that Heidegger's interpretation of Nietzsche's thought, as Victor Goldschmidt has shown, "hangs, formally, upon the text on the 'History of an Error,' understood as the history of Western metaphysics, which is, in turn, the history of Platonism."[127] That text, "How the 'True World' Finally Became a Fable," in *Twilight of the Idols*,[128] is indeed of capital importance, and the understanding of the entirety of Nietzsche's last philosophical position depends on its correct interpretation.

To simplify and allegorize the problem, we may note that Nietzsche, in his last writings (including his letters), never confronted "Dionysus against Plato (or against Platonism)," but well and truly "Dionysus versus the Crucified."[129] Besides, in the "outline" of the planned book *(The Will to Power: Attempt at a Revaluation of All Values),* presented as "this gospel of the future,"[130] in the draft of an outline for "European Nihilism," Nietzsche specifies which "values" both reveal and "devaluate themselves"[131] in and through nihilism: "it is in one particular interpretation, the Christian-moral [*christlich-moralischen*] one, that nihilism is rooted."[132] The devaluing of the so-called superior values means that of Christian moral values, the death of God means that of the "Christian God"[133] and not, as in Heidegger's reading, "ruin of the domination of the suprasensual and of the 'ideals' that stem from it."[134] It then becomes advisable to follow a good philologist such as Victor Goldschmidt:

> The "History of an Error" is not the history of metaphysics. It isn't even, despite appearances, the history of Platonism. It is the history of Christianity and of Christian morals . . . Christianity is not, in the "History of an Error," the continuation of Platonism. It is, on the contrary, Plato who is placed at the top of the list as first Christian and as first symptom of decadence ["that Christian faith which was also the faith of Plato"].[135] Plato means "moral fanaticism,"[136] and it is because Kant is also a "moral fanatic,"[137] a "theologian,"[138] and, "in the end, an underhanded Christian"[139] that he is later cited.[140]

We are better prepared, after this much-needed observation, to read correctly the texts in which Nietzsche attacks Christianity or, more precisely, the "Christian-moral" phenomenon, by reducing it to manifestation of "degeneration":

> I regard Christianity as the most fatal seductive lie that has yet existed, as the great unholy lie: I draw out the after-growth and sprouting of its ideal from beneath every form of disguise, I reject every compromise position with respect to it—I force a war against it.
>
> Petty people's morality as the measure of things: this is the most disgusting degeneration [*Entartung*] culture [*Kultur*] has yet exhibited. And this kind of ideal still hanging over mankind as "God"!![141]

The genealogy of "the moral ideal of Christianity" does not in any way coincide with a history of Christianity: it takes into consideration the pre-Christian manifestations of "superior values" of a Christian type, as well as their neo- and para-Christian resurgences. Thus it is that "modern ideas" are stigmatized as being "insipid and cowardly" by being linked up to their Christian origins, which can be identified under their masks and disguises:

> *The more concealed forms of the cult of the Christian moral ideal.*—The insipid and cowardly concept "nature" devised by nature enthusiasts . . . as if "nature" were freedom, goodness, innocence, fairness, justice, an idyl—still a cult of Christian morality fundamentally . . .
>
> The insipid and cowardly concept "man" à la Comte and Stuart Mill, per-

haps even the object of a cult . . . The insipid and cowardly concept "art" as sympathy with all that suffers and is ill-constituted . . . And now, as for the entire socialist ideal: nothing but a clumsy misunderstanding of that Christian moral ideal.[142]

VI. DEMAGOGY, DEMOCRACY, CULTURAL DECADENCE

We can understand how Nietzsche's antisocialism could be implied, above all, in his anti-Christianism. But the entirety of Nietzschean antimodernism can be understood only if we presuppose the identification of modernity as a process—not necessarily Christian, or even expressly anti-Christian—of expansion and realization of Christian values. Thus it is that egalitarianism, herd mentality, and verbalism, characteristic of the axiological modern practices and orientations, should be recognized as Christian inheritances, all the more dynamic in that their certificates of vintage are missing:

I am opposed to (1) socialism, because it dreams quite naively of "the good, true, and beautiful" and of "equal rights" (—anarchism also desires the same ideal, but in a more brutal fashion); (2) parliamentary government and the press, because these are the means by which the herd animal becomes master.[143]

This fragment, with its remarkable traditionalist odor, is far from unique in Nietzsche's work. When the "solitary by instinct"[144] belatedly applies himself to redefining his "tempestuous" thought, he rediscovers the traditionalist alternatives: degeneration ("ineptitude to struggle") or war, mediocrity or despotism, as in this fragment from 1884–85:

Even in matters of the spirit, I want war and conflicts: I would rather have the most rigorous despotism (as school for flexibility of the spirit) than the humid and lukewarm atmosphere of an age of "freedom of the press," in which the mind fades away, becomes stupid, and relaxes. On this point I have remained as I was, "untimely."[145]

Beginning with the texts from the years of *The Birth of Tragedy* and *Unmodern Observations* (1871–76), one finds in Nietzsche the makings of a genealogy of modern mediocrity. The outbreak of the "plebeian," "talkative," Socratic type is its first symptom: "The most democratic, the most demagogic, is Socrates: sects are the result";[146] "Socrates' action: he advantaged logomachia and dialectical chatter."[147]

The gradual promotion of dialectics as the way to solve the fundamental problems of human existence, inseparable from the elevation of democratic values into supreme values through the secular vulgarization of Christian egalitarianism, has allegedly reached its climax in modernity. Modern mediocrity is thought of by Nietzsche in 1874 as decadence of culture, a process that must be understood as the "destruction . . . of culture":

The flood of religion recedes, leaving swamps or puddles behind; the nations veer apart once again in the most violent hostility, impatient to massacre one another. The various fields of learning, pursued without moderation and in the blindest laissez-faire, are fragmenting and dissolving every established belief. Educated classes and nations alike are being swept away by a gigantic and contemptible economy of money. Never has the world been more worldly, never has it been poorer in love and goodness. In all this secular turmoil, the educated are no longer a beacon or sanctuary; day by day they become increasingly restless, mindless, and loveless. Everything, contemporary art and scholarship included, serves the approaching barbarism. The educated man has degenerated into culture's greatest enemy by denying the general malaise with lies and thereby impeding the physicians. They take offense, these poor, spineless rascals, when you speak of their weakness and oppose their pernicious falsehood.[148]

The central idea here is that the modern destruction of culture is a self-destruction: the will to culture is inverted into a hatred of culture, the representatives of culture into enemies of culture, as if barbarism were using culture for its own purposes, as if it had succeeded in the feat of instrumentalizing its contrary par excellence, culture— *"Culture,"* writes Nietzsche in this, the third of his *Unmodern Observations,* gallicizing the German term *Kultur* in order to distance himself from the conception of *Kultur* then current in the Reich, one he despised without reservations.[149] Such is the picture of "the decadence of culture" as seen from on high, considered by the philosopher at an equal distance from the journalistic spirit, fascinated as it is by the anecdotal present (the misery of "the news") and subjected to public opinion, and from the servile thinking of the professors, respectfully subjected to the State.

The diagnosis of decadence is formulated here in the context of a hypercritical, sarcastic pessimism that owes much to Schopenhauer, the "good educator." The symptoms of decadence are interpreted as forebodings of the worst: "barbarism." The two fundamental schemata of *loss* (the observation that "no longer . . .") and of *reduction to the inferior* (the description "it is now nothing more than . . .") are both summed up in the logic of the becoming-worse (that the negative situation is destined to "always be greater"). The worse is culture's having become an active process of barbarization. It takes courage to say it, and to say it to oneself, when one is oneself a "cultivated spirit" in an age of counterfeiters of culture. The courage of untimely thought, which itself begins with courage, consists first of all in "acknowledging," in not refusing to see the debased state culture finds itself in at the very moment everyone talks a lot about culture, in an age in which it is intended that everyone should share in culture. The modern-plebeian spirit sees culture only as "cultural democracy," whose objective comes down to the production of a few mass-cultural "successes"; this is what Nietzsche has so much contempt for: "The pride that desires solitude and few admirers is quite beyond comprehension; a really "great" success is possible only through the masses, indeed one hardly grasps the fact any more that a success with the masses is always really a *petty* success: because *pulchrum ist paucorum hominum.*"[150] The massification of culture, "culture for all," is an imposture for all, which fact presupposes the emergence and the "success" of a new class of cultural impostors, become professional in and through modernity. In the face of this by-now standardized domination of cultural neobarbarism, a philosopher's, an untimely thinker's first task consists in pointing out the "symptoms of the complete destruction, the total extirpation of culture."[151]

What is today commonly referred to as the "democratization of culture," the voluntary and systematic vulgarizing dissemination of the peaks of "high culture," which has become intolerable in its "height," is quite precisely, Nietzsche wrote in 1871, the "barbaric" road that leads to communism:

The dissemination of culture is but a phase preparatory to communism. In this way, culture becomes weaker to the extent that it can no longer confer any privilege. The widest dissemination of culture, that is to say, barbarism, is quite precisely the preliminary condition for communism. From a culture adapted to the *present times* we go over to the extreme of a culture adapted to the *present instant,* a crude way of seizing a momentary utility. If one believes culture has any utility, one will rapidly confuse what is useful with culture. Generalized culture transforms itself into hatred of true culture.[152]

The domination of dialectical discourse, the reign of egalitarian values and the generalization of the "demand for equal rights,"[153] utilitarianism, the spread of herd ideals, hatred and destruction of a culture that is subjected to a barbarizing corruption, the establishment of communism as the fulfillment of barbarism: these are all factors, symptoms, and figures on one and the same complex and "progressive" process. For what is progressing is barbarity, proceeding along the road opened up by the decadence of culture. What is commonly referred to as "modern culture," once it has been reduced by the genealogical method, now appears to be a process of deculturing.

The earlier traditionalists had practiced this type of unmasking of modernity as being an anticivilization, and they had inserted a "pseudo-" before all authentic cultural forms, but they had presupposed that true civilization and higher culture could only be Christian. The identification of modernity as a gigantic counterfeit will become, after Nietzsche, the theme of many literary and politico-philosophical variations that converted an inexhaustible resentment into theory. After the European wave of militant right wings before 1914, Germany in the years from 1919 to 1933, with its "cultural pessimists" (a movement within the "conservative revolution"), and France in the thirties, with its "nonconformists," are witness to a tide of rebels and revolters against this or that aspect of modernity, and they will all "Nietzscheize." The dominant influence of Nietzschean thought will have been not doctrinal, but stylistic: the Nietzschean heritage means, most of all, the radicality of negations, the absoluteness of affirmations, the contemptuous tone, the unconditionality of commitments, and the "heroic" to-the-bitter-end attitude in action.

One cannot be a Nietzschean the way one can be a Kantian, a Hegelian, or a Marxist. Positions and analyses count less than the manner, or the style, which is led by the power to destroy and the capacity to assert with absoluteness. The destructive aim is directed first of all against pluralist/liberal democracy, the object of supreme detestation. Then it is turned against the socialist utopias that intend to fully realize the virtual possibilities of modern egalitarian democracy. After the devastating demystification that is effected by Nietzsche's philosophy, from the moment we attempt to follow it in its ultimate consequences on the political terrain, no expectations become possible that could be fulfilled within the limits of modern democracy. Nothing remains but the exalted call for the *"coup de force"* and the dream of a redemptive dictatorship. Various generations of Nietzscheanizing aesthetes and pious interpreters have made an effort not to see this terrible logical conclusion, to hide or mask it. It is time to recognize that Nietzsche's pluralism, his hyperrelativistic perspectivism, is, far from being consonant with the regulated pluralism implied by liberal democracy, its total negation. Radical relativism is for Nietzsche but a destructive weapon intended to completely disqualify the value systems and the beliefs of the modern world. Nietzsche does not call for us to settle down comfortably into skeptical doubt, cultural relativism, or doxic pluralism. The "hardness" that his thinking requires, at least in its prophetic mood, is of the kind implied by the assertion of irreducible differences or of hierarchical distances that are also destinies. Do we need to insist on the incompatibility of such an absoluteness of hierarchical difference with the foundational egalitarian requirements of the modern democratic sphere? To be convinced of this, we need to read in their entirety, without evading the letter of the text through this or that angelic reconstruction, fragments as explicit as the following one, of which there are plenty:

One of the tendencies of evolution is, necessarily, that which levels humanity . . . The other tendency, my tendency, on the contrary tends to accentuate differences, widen distances, suppress equality, and create monsters of power.[154]

The absolute affirmation of difference, the total negation of equality, the cult of hierarchies based on nature: these are the paths that lead to the heroic road, which lead us to the straight road thought out by the "immoralist." It is the only road pointed to by the radical, sovereign negations—the "no of the yes"—uttered against the modern world by the philosopher of the Will to Power. They hardly need to be added to.

It would be too easy, yet not very convincing in the eyes of convinced Nietzscheans, to illustrate, through outrageously "Nietzscheanizing" texts penned by doctrinal national socialists (to take a handy example), the hypotheses that we have put forward about the kind of politics implied by Nietzsche's philosophy (and not the politics that may

be inferred from this or that opinion held by Nietzsche, writer and polemicist). By taking a detour through the basic arguments made by the
nationalism of the Action Française we will, certainly, avoid making
things easy for ourselves, but we will not in any way be getting out of the
subject. It will be enough for the reader, in order to follow us, to keep in
mind the simple distinction between, on the one hand, the rather unfa-
vorable opinions on Nietzsche as a representative of German philosophy (the philosophy of the enemy!), opinions publicly put about by
certain violently Germanophobic master thinkers of "integral nationalism" (Charles Maurras first of all), and, on the other hand, the succession of arguments aiming at political-cultural modernity, in order to
radically disqualify it and to legitimize a "reaction." We should, moreover, be attentive to the fact that the testimony given by some nationalist
leaders about the influence, as decisive as it is hidden, of Nietzsche's
thought sound like confessions. The publicly anti-Nietzschean discourse of the Action Française turns out to be challenged by a "Nietzschean" or Nietzscheophilic discourse, one that is set aside for internal
use, praising a source of inspiration that is almost shameful and kept, as
it were, secret. In contrast to the Action Française's legal Nietzsche, one
that is hardly read and, when read, with malevolence, who is subjected
to conventional attacks, we distinguish a Nietzsche who is truly and ad-
miringly read, Nietzsche as the inspirer—together with Charles Péguy,
Edouard Drumont, and a few others—of the total revolt against the
modern world and against all of its political orientations (egalitarian
democracy, liberal pluralism, the various socialisms), revolt that constitutes the strictly traditionalist aspect of "integral nationalism."

VII. Integral Nationalism as Absolute Antiliberalism

The traditionalist critique of modern politics thus aims essentially at liberal democracy, which is most especially characterized by every citizen's
equal right to argumentative speech, which would install, according to
Donoso Cortés, the reign of "perpetual discussion." Demo-liberalism is
denounced by its traditionalist critics as being the regime of irresolution
and indecisiveness: if the word is sovereign there, it is because it has lost
all true legitimacy; the absence of an absolute foundation of power destroys the authority which should judge and decide in sovereign fashion. The traditionalist critique of liberal democracy turns on these few

motifs: the impotence to establish, the tendency to level, the propensity to mix and throw together what is different, and the flight into indefinite discussion.

Let us reformulate the founding axiom of traditionalism: *using arguments is the sign of irremediable weakness.* The modern opening up of the political domain as an argumentative one is interpreted and evaluated as a symptom of decadence. Now: one of the presuppositions of all argumentation is that no thesis should be rejected without examination, that is to say, without being discussed. The negative transcendental condition of argumentation is the rejection of any a priori or dogmatic rejection. Therefore the norm that excludes any exclusion not founded on arguments, which presupposes confronting contrary and contradictory arguments.

Shall we characterize this "demo-liberal" attitude as being "the exclusion of all exclusion," to take up a formulation of Renan's?[155] But how to understand this as applied to the political order? And, most of all, how do the committed enemies of liberal democracy understand it?

We can being by recalling that the multiple variants of socialism do not posit liberal democracy as being the absolute enemy; they integrate it as a necessary stage or phase in a progressive, linear, and universal evolution. It is part of the auto-foundational argumentative apparatus of "fin de siècle" French nationalism, and par excellence part of the Action Française's "integral nationalism," that "democrato-liberalism"—which is not differentiated from the Republic—is instituted as the absolute enemy, to the point of being demonized as it was in the earlier traditionalism. The main reason for this is that this nationalism was intellectually elaborated outside any reference to the evolutionist conception of progress; it follows that liberal democracy loses its relative value, and its own dignity, as a necessary stage toward a superior sociopolitical regime and is reduced to nothing more than an abnormal phenomenon, and an intrinsically pathological one. In nationalist eyes, liberal democracy is not a kind of regime that has become "outmoded" or "condemned" by the progressive march of history; it is a political antiregime, an unpolitical or pseudopolitical regime: not a precedent that is respectable in its own way, but a damnable perversion, a violation of the natural laws of political organization. It is in this that we may consider Maurras's doctrine, such as it appears in the first edition of *Enquête sur la monarchie* (An inquiry into monarchy) (1900), to illustrate simultaneously the creation of a new synthesis between political-religious traditionalism and the nationalism of identitarian self-preservation (meaning the duty of peoples to remain themselves) and the first of the transitions to the political sphere of what we have called the second traditionalism. In the rough description that follows, we shall strive only to show how Maurras's rejection of modern political "anarchism" derives from the definition of "democrato-liberalism" as the absolute enemy and from its interpretation as being an unnatural phenomenon, a deviation from the natural order.

In the journal *L'Action française* of 4 January 1932, Maurras believed he could take joy in a return to the normal state of things:

The liberal and democratic anomaly . . . is slowly withdrawing from the modern world. We foresaw it thirty years ago: the forecast is being clearly verified in a period of royal, princely, bourgeois, and popular dictatorships, which unceasingly rise from all the points of the compass of the new Europe . . . The bases of fascism—social, national, and not individualistic—are, we must concede, healthy. But it has to be added that the institutions that are being raised up and developed upon these healthy bases include a component of liberty, of arbitrary choices and contingent determinations in which it is difficult, even impossible, to recognize the characteristic of inviolability, of unassailability, which would legitimately eliminate any spirit of contradiction, of discussion, and of examination.[156]

The postulate on which such a positive evaluation of dictatorships of the fascist type is based is certainly the unavoidable alternative: "dictatorship or perpetual discussion." And it will have been noted that the only restriction formulated by Maurras concerning the return to political health that is incarnated by fascism aims, precisely, at the latter's incapacity to completely eliminate the remains of "demo-liberalism": the principle of free inquiry, critical discussion, and the spirit of contradiction.

Along the way, the Action Française's master thinker rejoins the logic of the total critique of political modernity as we have seen it in Bonald or Donoso Cortés and, more secretly, in Nietzsche. This total and radical critique rests upon a vitalistic naturalism that is applied to the political order, from which the imperative of a return to "health" derives. From this perspective, the absolute enemy is absolutely sick: the old notion of decadence is then burdened with images of illness, loaded with metaphors of the pathological. The ultimate criterion for any evaluation then becomes "health of sickness."

In his "New Letter to Monsieur Strauss" on 15 September 1871, Ernest Renan had characterized the "liberal" spirit through its antiexclusivity: "Everyone must be wary of all that is exclusive and absolute in his own mind. Let us never imagine that we are so right that our adversaries are completely in the wrong."[157] "Liberalism," as an intellectual attitude, is in fact often defended by its defenders as being a moderate skepticism, an inchoative effort to keep oneself from giving in to the temptation of a naive or dogmatic intransigence. But it is precisely this reasoned and reasonable moderation that the absolutist enemies of liberal democracy wish to denounce with the greatest possible violence as revealing a reduction, a weakening, a loss: incertitude, irresolution, and indecision. And, more profoundly, an impotence: therefrom the contempt that is so often added to hatred among the enemies of "demo-liberalism." There are, certainly, numerous varieties of maximalists who reject liberal democracy insofar as it has not been created in their image. But the rejection is maximal and the refusal total among those who base their antimodern position upon the sacredness of a tradition or of Tradition. From that point on, "demo-liberalism" is stigmatized not only as a type of political regime but as a global orientation of human existence. The object of this hatred lined with contempt is quite precisely constituted by the antitraditional orientation of "demo-liberal" existence, with its principal consequences: destructive as it is of hierarchies, instituting "anarchism, [which] is the logical form of democracy,"[158] a regime whose typical action consists in "disorganizing in order to equalize,"[159] as Maurras wrote, and a regime of the discussion without limits that incarnates the spirit of inquiry, liberal democracy favors, or privileges, the dialogue and argumentation which, by acknowledging fundamental disagreements as well as the contingent and provisory nature of every agreement, lead to the decline of absolute certainties and the infrequency of absolute decisions. Maurras observed, "A deadly rhetoric was then going to replace all philosophy; the ruling class, or the one which should have ruled, practiced or allowed itself to be subjected to a kind of obligatory anesthesia in front of the False, in politics or in sociology."[160]

Liberal democracy is the regime of the rhetors, of the perpetual debaters. That is the diagnosis made by the traditionalist nationalist doctors of modern political culture. Denouncing the "logical poverty" of modern Frenchmen, subjected as they are to the bad influence of democracy and of Romanticism, Maurras defined his logical ideal by referring to Catholic theology:

Unlike Protestant theology, its characteristic is to create a synthesis in which everything has been connected, settled, and coordinated for centuries by the subtlest and greatest human minds, so that we may say that it encloses, defines, distributes, and classifies everything. There is no useless discussion: everything leads somewhere. Doubts are resolved into affirmations; analyses, however far one wishes to take them, into brilliant and complete reconstitutions.[161]

Theo-logical discussion is the exact opposite of the perpetual discussion denounced by Donoso Cortés: correct logic makes distinctions, asserts, decides, and concludes—meaning it grounds decisions. And that is precisely what is unpardonable in the "spirit of mystical anarchism"[162] that is cultivated by demo-liberalism: neither acts of thought nor acts of will can be derived any longer from the lessons of an infallible tradition, and from the very start they lose themselves in irresolution and indecision. The self-confidence of the inheritor vanishes together with the inheritance of absolute declarations, values, and norms. The thus disinherited French are "the last of the French." When the "discussing class" rules, all action becomes impossible:

That is why all of the masters of political science, whether they belonged to the theological school, such as Maistre and Bonald, or to the positivist school, like Comte and his disciples, limit discussion to the theoretical sphere, to the domain of elaboration, but banish it from action. There is no Religion of discussion nor Morality of discussion, for from the moment one acts morally and religiously, one no longer discusses, one decides, one risks. To wait in such cases for "certainty" to be arrived at after a contradictory debate is to be resigned to perish. There is no *Government of Discussion:* to govern is, once again, to trust oneself, to take risks.[163]

A way of thinking that regards tradition or the continuity of the nation as being sacred can conceive of the "liberals'" liberty only as revolt and anarchy: "the systematic sedition of the individual against the species" or against such and such specific membership in a group, to take up an expression of Auguste Comte's that was dear to Maurras.[164] This freedom to tear themselves away from the given, this abandonment of inheritance, this rupture with traditions, this, in a word, disquieting liberty of the moderns could only provoke a stiffening among the partisans of protective continuities and of a rootedness guaranteeing the vital equilibria. Which is why the denunciation of demo-liberalism is so intense and so doctrinally elaborate in the texts of the Action Française, in which the traditionalist fear of the rupture with continuities comes to terms with the nationalist fear of the breakup of national unity. Maurras wrote along these lines, "To organize means to differentiate. To differentiate means the contrary of making equal. A *nation* is made up of people who are *born* here and not there. It implies birth, heredity, history, a past. It constitutes a first objection to the Babel-like dream of anarchy."[165]

If follows that Renan's antiexclusionist "liberalism" illustrates, in the eyes of fundamentalist nationalism, the double modern attitude, detestable par excellence: the lack of distinctness between true and false, and the confusion between liberty and "mystical anarchy." If "liberalism" is the incarnation of the "great derangement of the mind," it is because it is the exaltation of the skeptical, egalitarian, and moderate attitude which "kills military discipline"[166] and leaves the nation "directionless."[167] It follows that liberal pseudogovernment, an impossible "government of discussion," "forgets or neglects war, and . . . denies its repercussions," as Léon Daudet asserted.[168] If patriotism implies first and above all "the defense of the territory against the Foreigner,"[169] nationalism "is the preservation owed to all of the treasures that can be threatened without needing a foreign army to cross the border, without the territory being physically invaded."[170]

This distinction made by Maurras is of the utmost importance in defining the specificity of the "fin de siècle's" doctrinal nationalism of the "nationalists" (of those who call themselves that):[171] nationalism, Maurras adds, "defends the nation against the Foreigner within."[172] Therefore the redefinition that is distinctive of nationalism, explicitly breaking off from the revolutionary idea of the "principle of nationalities": nationalism is first and most of all a crusade directed against the interior. And a paradoxical crusade at that, since it merely proposes to reconquer the component elements of a collective identity that has been confiscated and polluted by foreign domination. It is not a case of

France being dominated by a foreign country, but of it being subjugated by "the Foreigner within" (*l'Étranger de l'intérieur*), one who is all the more powerful for not being visible. We are familiar with the Action Française's theory of the hidden action, inside the national body politic, of antinational forces, the forces of "anti-France": "These four oligarchies, of a profoundly international nature, all-powerful and now exercising their rule, have been called the *four confederated States.*"[173] Every government of the "demo-liberal" kind is "under the empire of their poison": the four confederated States (Jewish, Protestant, Freemason, and alien or "mongrel" [*métèque*])[174] are the agents of the loss of self from which France allegedly suffers. To reconquer France's identity means, first of all, to reassert its definition beginning with basic distinctions: France is, in its essence, neither Jewish, nor Protestant, nor Freemason, nor mixed (*métèque*). It is Catholic and monarchist.

"Liberalism," as mindset and as political regime, brings together all of the elements which, according to Maurras, are working together to undo France's identity, to change its nature, to replace it with a body of abstractions masking the actual omnipotence of the forces of "anti-France." The doctrinaire liberal lives in the "Clouds" and incarnates the mixture of moderation shot through with doubt and of pacifism in love with disorder that lends its visible aspect to France's decadence. Thematically and doctrinally elaborated antiliberalism concentrates its basic beliefs in the theory of the four confederated States. But we need also to consider the unthematic and unsystematic antiliberalism that surrounds the generally antimodern argumentation of fundamentalist nationalism. The decisive argument against demo-liberalism then becomes that the latter renders clear and fixed categories illegitimate, that it lowers barriers that were once insurmountable, that it makes no distinctions, that it refuses even to make distinctions and to differentiate, that it denies inequality, the precondition for any kind of political order. The path of demo-liberalism is one that leads to death through lack of differentiation. All of Maurras's antimodern criticism derives from a strict alternative posited in 1900 and from which he draws all the consequences that follow: "*Inequality or decadence, inequality or anarchy, inequality or death. The choice is up to the peoples: but, if they wish to live, the choice is dictated . . . Democracy is evil. Democracy is death.*"[175]

We will thus hardly be surprised to see that in 1937, when dealing with the problem of democracy, Maurras began with a short paragraph titled "Birth of Democracy: Liberalism":

The classic liberals and their anarchic and democratic progeny, descendants of 1789, profess that any man has the same value as any other and, from that starting point, also justify the elimination of social ranks, of professional guilds [*corps de métiers*], and the disappearance of all variety in the statutes of provinces, cities, and households. Where the ancien régime saw a combination of beings different through their value, their role, and their function, and who became equals only in the cemetery, the modern regime has dreamed of a juxtaposition of persons supposed to be equal and identical.[176]

Hatred of diversity and impotence to make clear distinctions: those are the essential characteristics of demo-liberalism in the eyes of the Action Française. It is against the sublimated version of this mixture of hatred and impotence that Léon Daudet draws, as is his wont, his sword:

It is a question of pointing out the emptiness of the beautiful spirits, those who have thought up the convenient balderdash that goes: "Above (or away from) the fray." These beautiful spirits are, to sum it up, the inheritors of the liberalism for which (in all questions of war or peace) no one is entirely right, nor entirely wrong. There is thus an allegedly moderate, arbiter's position, above the adversaries, where one can decide between hangmen and victims, arsonists and charred bodies, cutthroats and cut throats. I have denounced, in . . . *Le stupide XIXe siècle* [The stupid nineteenth century] liberalism as the plague of the times.[177]

"Liberalism's" great fault, the sign of its irremediable impotence, lies in not being decisive: it is, in this, the political expression par excellence of modern decadence. It follows that the fundamental dilemma of modern politics, the one that fundamentalist nationalism believes it overcomes through a decisive choice, can be formulated thus: nationalism or decadence, or, in other words, differentiation or democracy. That is why "cosmopolitanism," as it is called in nationalist rhetoric, designates not so much the universalist point of view as it does the ideal of nondifferentiation through mixing and egalitarian reductiveness, an ideal that is attributed to the modern regime of the demo-liberal type. That is the source of the analogy of proportionality that was developed in the Action Française's arguments: nationalism is to cosmopolitanism as difference is to mixture, as inequality is to democracy, as life is to death, as order is to disorder. In a 1904 text Maurras argued, basing himself on such analogies:

The synthesis of individualism and of collectivism is impossible if one places oneself on nationalist grounds, which *always* obligate us to establish differences between individuals: between, for example, citizens and resident aliens [*métèques*], Jews and native nationals, etc. which *always* brings about a certain degree of aristocracy. The same synthesis is very easy on cosmopolitan assumptions: it comes about through the idea of democracy.[178]

To the question, where do egalitarian doctrines come from?, Maurras answered in 1900, "From Israel, through the diffusion of biblical ideas."[179] And the spiritual guide of the Action Française, reasserting the traditionalist anti-Christianism based upon the distinction between Judeo-Christian disorder and Euro-Catholic order, added this commentary:

Instead of Catholicism's being able to powerfully organize these ideas and mitigate them . . . an inorganic and anarchical gospel spread from East to West and, parallel to the action of Gothic infiltrations (barbarian societies, where egalitarianism was also preached), it introduced individualism into the minds of the peoples and kept it there until the end of the Roman peace . . . The same phenomenon has repeated itself since the sixteenth century in Northern and Central Europe. The Reform, multiplying its Bibles, and making everyone read them, propagated the egalitarian mysticism of the prophets. Rousseau and Kant are, just like the French Revolution, the beneficiaries of the Jewish ideas that have been thus popularized.[180]

It is not without significance that certain radical "left-wing" anti-democrats were able to concur with the nationalist critique of the "modern regime" through the mediation of a literal reading of Nietzsche, and especially of *The Will to Power,* translated into French in 1903 by Henri Albert. In the thought of Édouard Berth, for example, the reference to Nietzsche joins the references to Marx, to Proudhon, and to Sorel, creating the syncretic space that gave birth to the Cercle Proudhon (December 1911 to 1913), "meeting point of the nationalist and syndicalist movements." A text of Berth's will allow us to measure the extent of Nietzsche's influence on the antidemocratic revolutionary milieux of the beginning of the century.

The final issue of the *Cahiers du Cercle Proudhon,* published in July 1913,[181] beings with an article by Jean Darville (a pseudonym for Édouard Berth) entitled "Satellites of Plutocracy," which is explicitly placed under Nietzsche's patronage. Denouncing the "bourgeois" pacifism of "plutocratized Europe," alarmed by the "irruption of the *fait guerrier* [the fact of war]," [182] George Sorel's disciple begins by quoting Nietzsche: "A society that turns away, definitively and out of *instinct*, from war and the spirit of conquest, is in decadence: it is ripe for democracy and the regime of shopkeepers." [183] This antiplutocratic and antiliberal "Nietzschean" pamphlet presupposes the antithesis between Gold and Force (or Blood), liberal democracy being reduced to the legal façade for Gold's real power:

France is so plutocratized and therefore so far along the road of decomposition and decadence that the very movements from which one could expect a reaction against the rule of Gold take no time at all in falling into the plutocratic rut: so for example this syndicalist movement which, instead of carrying out a reparatory and regenerative secession from the bourgeoisie, has hurried to borrow from bourgeois decadence all of its most corrupt ideologies, including the blandest and most inept humanitarian pacifism. There is no possible doubt about the interpretation we must make of this modern pacifism, and it has been known for a long time: (1) that democracy is the land of milk and honey for financiers, and (2) that State socialism, the natural, logical, and fatal consequence of democracy, is a socialism for which the financiers have always felt, feel, and will eternally feel an extreme tenderness . . . "The power of the mediocre," writes Nietzsche (*Volonté de puissance*, t. II. p. 198), "is kept up by trade, *especially by the money trade*: the instinct of the great financiers directs itself against everything that is extreme; that is why the Jews are, at the moment, the most conservative power in our so threatened and uncertain Europe. If they wish to have power, if they need to have power over the revolutionary party, it is only a consequence of what I have just pointed out, it is not a contradiction."

The power of the mediocre: that is, of democratic mediocrity, bourgeois and liberal (the word used to qualify with dignity all that is mediocre is, as we know and as the same Nietzsche remarked, the word *"liberal"*): we can thus understand the enormous influence of Israel in the conservative as in the revolutionary world . . . when we have correctly grasped these tendencies of the modern world, entirely given over to the Judeo-conservative stupidity of a bourgeoisie which, quite comfortably seated around the State's table, sweats with fear and feels its teeth chatter at the mere vision of the specter of War or Revolution. [184]

Darville-Berth ends his article by recalling his definition of the

"*Jewish empire,* meaning the absolute and incontestable rule of the plutocracy,"[185] before calling for heroic values and warrior sentiments:

The double nationalist and syndicalist movement, parallel and synchronic, must lead to the complete eviction of the regime of gold and to the triumph of heroic values over the ignoble bourgeois materialism in which Europe is now suffocating. The awakening of Force and of Blood against Gold must, in other words . . . lead to the definitive rout of the Plutocracy.[186]

Berth has read, and read attentively, those texts of Nietzsche which, considered too "embarrassing," have been effaced, ignored, or overinterpreted by generations of commentators with the intention of euphemizing them.[187] Philological integrity is on his side, not on the side of the falsifiers who, often with the "best" intentions, have invented acceptable or desirable Nietzsches following the current literary or political-ideological fashions (we have thus discovered democratic Nietzsches, liberal, socialist, Christian, leftist, antiracist, philo-Semitic Nietzsches, etc.). But the very least we can say on this question, in the face of these Nietzsches dreamed up by tender Nietzschean souls (sometimes accompanied by tender Nietzschean minds), is that Nietzsche's political thought, as it is found in his texts, is based upon an unconditional rejection of both the aspiration towards equality and the principle of individual liberty (liberty being reserved to the "small number"). Which is why, if we feel we must defend democratic and liberal ideals, we cannot call ourselves "Nietzschean," merely as such and without any consequences. Whereas all of the determined adversaries of pluralist democracy (of the "parliamentary chattering"!), of political-juridical liberalism, and of social democracy, can quite legitimately, though in various different ways, lay claim to the Nietzschean heritage.

Which does not in any way mean that we need to abandon Nietzsche to the devout, militant, or practicing Nietzscheans, or to the superficial and ignorant anti-Nietzscheans, who have concluded before having read, and condemned the work without having gone through it. It means, rather, that a reading that is as polemical as it is philologically scrupulous becomes necessary, something that brings us back, after a few detours, to one of Karl Jaspers's conclusions: "To philosophize with Nietzsche means to be constantly taking issue with him."[188] Too many enthusiastic readers, scholars and nonscholars, have for over a century practiced Gide's singular hermeneutic prescription: "To understand

Nietzsche well, one must become enamored of him."[189] We would instead say that to understand him beyond the charm of his way of thinking, one must be wary of falling in love with him. Given the hardness of
Nietzsche's proposals, a hardness often forgotten or forgiven through
the seductiveness of his style, empathy is the worst method. The difficulty comes from the fact that the hardness of the message excludes
neither a spirit of refinement nor complexity in its conceptual constructions.

VIII. The Action Française's Sublegal Nietzsche: A Teacher of Energy and Antiliberalism

The Action Française's Nietzsche is not to be confused with the representative of an eternal Germany, or with the "Germanic spirit" that was
hated and stigmatized by Charles Maurras as well as by Henri Massis or
Pierre Lasserre.[190] That Nietzsche, officially denounced by the Germanophobic doctrinaire nationalists, shouldn't hide the Nietzsche who
was received in a positive manner by a Hugues Rebell[191] or by a
Georges Valois, a Nietzsche teacher of will, of energy, of revolt against
the modern world and of antibourgeoisism, of anti-demo-liberalism
and of "untimely" aristocratism. In order to fix the image of this hidden
master to the *Action Française,* we will begin with the testimony of a
young Maurrasian militant who, in 1911, honored the "German of genius" despite the official nationalists' anti-Germanism. We are referring
to Albert Bertrand-Mistral,[192] a young royalist who, in an article on
"Nietzsche's influence," published when he was twenty-one years old,
aimed to "show what influence, in fact, [Nietzsche's] writings . . . have
had on French youth and on today's young Catholics."[193] "Nietzsche's
influence," if we follow Maurras's young disciple and Nietzsche's ad-
mirer, was essentially that of "distancing young Frenchmen from Romanticism and from democracy,"[194] and therefore simultaneously
from skepticism and from the despair stemming from "foggy theories"
and debilitating philanthropy. Nietzsche, master of the affirmation of
life and of strong convictions, professor of realism and of energy, absolute enemy, in a word, of liberal lukewarmness and cloudiness:

In the middle of the intellectual anarchy romanticism had created, when minds,
incapable of tarrying and of devoting themselves completely to an ideal, sought

the ways to escape from an anguishing doubt, it was necessary that a doctrine emerge that could clear away the clouds of skepticism, that could insert into intelligent spirits a bit of clarity and of confidence in life, and which could thus aid stray minds in finding their way again . . . *Necessarily,* a return to life had to come forth as the result of a strong, sudden, and apparently fortuitous impulsion; and this impulsion, this "hazard that everything cried out for," was the influence of a German of genius, of the great realist named Friedrich Nietzsche.[195]

The encounter with Nietzsche took place under the double auspices of a necessary revitalization and of an absolute aloofness from the surrounding mediocrity. Reading Nietzsche was the so-long-awaited antidote to the "fin de siècle's" wasting languor, the way to climb back up the slope that leads from skepticism to pessimism and from there to nihilism. It was to this immediately curing function of Nietzsche that the young A. Bertrand-Mistral paid homage: in his eyes, "the first effect of reading Nietzsche is to fortify us," and "this force he communicates to us is first of all a very great confidence in ourselves, which is soon transformed into hope, which hope suggests and encourages activity . . . This intellectual and moral pride is a good hygiene for the soul."[196] The witness Albert Bertrand calls upon another witness, an already prestigious one, Georges Valois: "This is what we owe Nietzsche: at the end of the nineteenth century, he was the liberator of our energy; for this, we remain very grateful to him."[197] This realism of force[198] seems to be, in nationalist eyes, inseparable from a radical critique of democracy's humanitarian and egalitarian ideals: "The philosophy of the overman, which expresses the result of the struggle for life, is, through its realism, aristocratic. Thanks to it, many were separated from democracy, the way others had been separated from literary or moral romanticism."[199]

Nietzsche was a master thinker for the royalist fringe of the radical right in that he destroyed the seduction carried out by the modern political mystiques and in that he dissipated in particular the illusions imposed by the democratic mystique. His outstanding "fortifying" message is that the humanism proclaimed by modern, postrevolutionary democracy is only a mendacious offshoot of *ressentiment,* a mixture of hatred and envy accompanied by a feeling of irremediable impotence. Nietzsche is praised for having stripped bare of her charms the moderns' Circe: egalitarian and humanitarian democracy, expression and mask of jealous weakness and hateful impotence. It is this "liberating" message that Georges Valois praises in 1906:

To Nietzsche I owe my liberation. At the time when we were bogged down in the democratic and humanitarian swamps, where our good masters of petty science had plunged us . . . we received from Nietzsche a lash from his whip that led us to consider the true realities with sincerity. Nietzsche put a stop to our bleating with a certain brutality, stripped us bare of our miserable humanitarian monk's robe, and constrained us to look at ourselves without pity: it is through him that we saw for the first time what this love of humanity that we had been taught is: in truth, a false love,—a ruse invented by the impotent to *disarm* their competitors, take away all desire for elevation from them, and weaken their competition.[200]

Nietzsche is a "liberator" to the exact extent that he is a demystifier of the modern political ideals implied by democracy and political liberalism. He is the destroyer of all the modern idols who led, if we are to follow such direct testimony, so many young people "in rebellion" to a rediscovery of tradition, whether religious (intransigent Catholicism) or political (royalism), who oriented them to this or that variant of counterrevolution within the perspective of a total rejection of the modern world. Nietzsche, quite involuntarily, played the role of a paradoxical "prophet of the past" through the lessons logically drawn from his radical antimodernism; he contributed to bringing about the second great traditionalist reaction in the Europe of the end of the nineteenth century, a traditionalism more political than religious and of which the Action Française's fundamentalist nationalism was the first historical figure.

Nietzsche's radical or untimely critique of the present presupposes a diagnosis of the same present, which implies an evaluation. The present must be deciphered and judged in all of its aspects, including egalitarian democracy. A problem presents itself to the partisans of the "realism of force" in the form of a recurring objection, brought to mind by Valois at the end of his 1906 introduction to *The Man to Come:* "Since you submit yourself to facts, why do you not submit yourselves to the contemporary fact that is democracy?" To this naively anti-Nietzschean objection, Valois had no problem responding following Nietzschean orthodoxy: "It is true that democracy is a fact; *but it is a fact of decay:* that is why we cannot, we who seek life and growth, submit ourselves to it."[201] In a word, democracy is the main political figure of modern decadence: democracy is a phenomenon of "national disorganization," for it leads both to "political anarchy" and to "intellectual and moral anarchy," hence constituting "the very negation of the nation."[202] The democratic regime is satisfactory neither for the requirements of the vital values of conservation nor for the vital values of growth: it incarnates the double movement of dissolution and of regression towards mediocrity, towards equality, which is to say, towards death.[203] It is indeed the Nietzschean ontology of Life as will to power, or as power accrued with will to self-preservation and growth, it is this vitalist ontology that, transposed to the level of the nation conceived as first substance, permitted the elaboration of more than one doctrinal nationalism.

But Nietzsche's thought has, in neotraditionalist eyes, yet another unexpected merit: that of reinforcing the camp of the intransigent or "fundamentalist" Catholics. From this perspective, his radical critique of Christianity is received positively as being a healthy pruning-away operation: it is enough for this to consider the Nietzschean critique of Christianity as aiming only at its humanitarian or philanthropic tendencies, whose modern hypertrophy can be considered as a process of degeneration of the religion founded by the apostle Paul. The Christian "poison" must from that point on be identified within charitable sentimentalism, of which the Moderns' philanthropy is but a humanist interpretation. That is why the young royalist leader glorifies Nietzsche for having distanced young Frenchmen "from a certain conception of Christian morality,"[204] founded upon a false "liberal" and "romantic" interpretation of the idea of charity. For, as Albert Bertrand-Mistral specifies, "it is on an erroneous sense attributed to this term that lies the ambivalence that gives birth to the liberal sentiments of many Catholics," who reduce charity to "the purely human and secular thing called philanthropy."[205] But the church's teaching is that "we must love our neighbor only after God and for the love of God."[206] Here we find again the arguments of explicitly reactionary Catholicism, the arguments of Donoso Cortés and of Louis Veuillot, aiming most of all at Catholicism's modernizing "liberalization," which is denounced as the work of the devil. Tolerance, that "limp idea" (Nietzsche), the tolerance dear to liberal pseudo-Catholics, is nothing but cowardice and spinelessness, the expression of an enfeebled life; yet, in our modern decadence, it pretends to take the place of true charity. Nietzsche's antiliberal lesson, whatever his intentions may have been, thus addresses itself in a privileged manner to intransigent Catholics and should permit them to get rid of "the retinue of 'blessers.'"[207] The true opposition is not that between Christians and anti-Christians, but between liberals and "fundamentalists":

It little matters that the hardness of fundamentalist Catholics be blamed; they recall that, before Nietzsche, it was Father Lacordaire who said of himself that he was "hard as a diamond," and that goodness toward man out of simple love of man is valid only for the liberals, these eternal fools.[208]

Hardness will save the world, as long as it is carried forward by the sense of transcendence, a transcendence that liberalism, a contagious, strictly modern illness of the spirit, never ceases to obliterate, effacing the memory even of its loss. The liberal spirit is the spirit that wanders and stagnates between the yes and the no, that affirms and denies at the same time; it is the radical irresolution that opposes normal and healthy life. The liberal spirit is a dissolution of the spirit, the expression of an irremediable impotence—the incapacity to conclude, to judge, to decide. That is the Nietzschean diagnosis that was accepted by a number of young people in rebellion against the modern world, which oriented them toward antiliberal and antidemocratic forms of dissent against the established order, from Catholic traditionalism to fundamentalist nationalism, and from counterrevolution to fascism.

It will have been noticed that the axiom on which the entire argumentation is based is that liberalism, a properly modern vision of the world, is a symptom and a factor of decadence. It is a recurrent theme in reactionary thinking of the twentieth century. Let us take an example from the corpus of texts deriving from Maurras's thought. In December 1940, at Uriage, Henri Massis wrote a short text on "conditions for a French recovery" in which, after having expostulated, with explicit reference to Péguy (Péguy's French cultural legitimacy being, of course, infinitely stronger than Nietzsche's), a spiritualist explanation of France's decadence through "weakening of the soul" and the "failure" of thought, he specifies:

It is "through the weakening of the intellectual fiber that a great people's decadence always begins." The first signs are manifested in the enfeeblement of ideas, in the abandonment of the essential certainties on which feed man's basic sentiments. Did not the love of ideas end up, in too many heads, by being confused with the indifference, *with the mental apathy that can only wander between the yes and the no,* and which is most likely to irritate the taste for virile, fecund affirmation?[209]

The skeptical oscillation between affirmation and negation, the infinite balancing between contraries: that is what characterizes the mental state that both expresses and engenders decadence. An unvirile France is an unbrained France, now incapable of certainty, of the production of vital certitudes. An infallible indication of this follows: the corruption of language that Louis Veuillot had deplored in his days:

A disparagement of intelligence followed from all this, thanks to which this dishonesty of language, these betrayals of the spirit through the tongue, this lack of integrity towards *words,* which have done so much damage to France, were able to develop. The degradation of character had to be the natural result of this, for the confusion that is in words, in the expression of thought, leads imperceptibly to a sort of practical imposture in which all human relations are debased.[210]

If therefore the France of 1940 is in this state of degradation, it is first of all because it has forgotten what authentic Christian civilization had taught it. Massis's diagnosis joins with that of the Nietzschean Bertrand-Mistral, with other expressions and through other references: France's decadence is essentially determined by the incapacity to affirm and deny. For the one as for the other, French decadence is to be explained by a pathological ailment of Christian spirituality, whether it be that the liberal-humanitarian counterfeit of Christianity chased away its authentic forms (intransigent and fundamentalist), or that the national intelligence decreased with the dissolution of Christian civilization. If decadence is determined by an increase in disorder and a loss of force, the weakening of the Catholic idea incarnated by the Church is the exact measure of French decadence. In 1926, Jacques Bainville resumed this fundamental conviction of the Action Française this way:

Catholicism is a force . . . It is a truth the statesman cannot neglect . . . In the chaos is which old Europe was foundering, the Catholic idea became a natural bastion against anarchy. The Church has identified itself with order and it is order the world is most in need of. It is bursting with revolution and democracy. It is dying of dissolution. The Church represents unity and stability. Catholicism organizes. It is the stone on which we can build.[211]

H. Massis's and J. Bainville's protest against the "established disorder" walks down the same path the first traditionalism had taken, without its despair. But the second traditionalism, à la Nietzsche, voluntaristic and decisionist, never ceased to be a sort of doctrinal countersong within the Action Française's nationalism.[212] That is why the metaphysics of "fundamentalist nationalism" presents itself as a contradictory mixture of references to a historically incarnated transcendent order (the Church, the Monarchy) and of calls for a willed, decided, imposed order, one taken on "heroically." When the "counter-revolutionary revolutions" of the twentieth century thought about themselves, with the means at hand, they discovered, or rediscovered, this constitutive paradox, reflecting the hatred of the modern world within the shadow of modernity.

NOTES

1. Antoine Blanc de Saint-Bonnet, *L'infaillibilité* (1861), Paris: N.E.L., 1956, p. 31. The diagnosis made by the young Arthur de Gobineau is of the same type: "Our poor mother country [*patrie*] is at the stage of Roman decadence . . . I believe in nothing anymore, and I have no opinions . . . Gold has *killed everything* . . . and even religion, passing, though it be eternal, in its present form, into another hemisphere, is too detached from our spirits and our civilization to pull it out of the mire in which it sinks ever deeper every day . . . Good-bye, the times of belief, the days of hope, the radiant futures" (Letter to his sister, 20 February 1839; in Ludwig Schemann, *Quellen und Untersuchungen zum Leben Gobineaus*, vol. I, Strasbourg, 1914, pp. 299–300). The fatal illness afflicting royalism is one of the forerunners of "the end of legitimacy," inseparable from the waning of religious feeling (cf. Alain Néry, "Gobineau et la succession d'Henri V," *Mémoire* 2 (1985), pp. 68–69.

2. Louis de Bonald, in Joseph de Maistre, *Œuvres complètes*, Lyon: E. Vitte, 1884–87, vol. XIV (correspondence, 1816–1821). For a commentary, see Gérard Gengembre, *La contre-révolution ou l'histoire désespérante*, Paris: Éditions Imago, 1989, pp. 211ff., 253ff. One finds in Maistre and Bonald a theory of decadence as the effect of the composition of multiple perverse effects attributed to "Providence" ("this secret force that mocks human counsel," as Jo-

seph de Maistre characterizes it in *Les considérations sur la France* (1797), ch. IX, ed. Jean Tulard, Paris: Garnier, 1980, p. 84). Albert O. Hirschman rightly insists on the ultrapessimistic anthropology (implying a radical antihumanism) of the explanation through "Providence," one which "leads to seeing man . . . as half-stupid, half-criminal" in that "by agitating himself, he obtains the contrary of what he professed to seek" (*Deux siècles de rhétorique réactionnaire,* trans. into French by P. Andler, Paris: Fayard, 1991, pp. 38–39); for the romanticist version, which presupposes the joyous vision of an "irresponsible and imaginative power" freely disposing of men, cf. Carl Schmitt, *Politische Romantik* (Political Romanticism), 2d rev ed., Munich: Verlag von Duncker & Humblot, 1925 (1st ed. 1919). But, in this providentialist perspective, is everything definitely lost, or does it only seem so to infirm human spirits? The problem has been nicely set out by Stéphane Rials discussing Joseph de Maistre: "How does he reconcile his certitude about *Providence* with the barely contained feeling of an inexorable form of *decadence?*" (*Révolution et Contre-Révolution au XIXᵉ siècle,* Paris: Albatros et D.U.C., 1987, p. 39).

3. Expressions dear to Donoso Cortés; see, for example, *Essai sur le catholicisme, le libéralisme et le socialisme* (1851), Paris, 1859 (Bouère: Éditions Dominique Martin Morin, 1986, p. 223).

4. Ibid., p. 223.

5. Friedrich Nietzsche, *De Wille zur Macht* [WzM], Stuttgart: Alfred Kröner, 1964, § 80, p. 61 (1st German ed. 1901). *The Will to Power,* trans. Walter Kaufmann and R. J. Hollingdale. New York: Vintage Books, 1968.

6. Ibid., § 79, p. 60 (spring–fall 1887). First italics are mine.

7. Carl Schmitt, *Politische Theologie: Vier Kapitel zur Lehre von der Souveränität,* Munich: Verlag von Duncker & Humblot, 1922, p. 54.

8. Ibid., p. 56.

9. *WzM,* § 76, p. 59 (spring–fall 1887).

10. *WzM,* § 75.

11. F. Nietzsche, *Ecce Homo [EH],* "The Case of Wagner," 1. In *Basic Writings of Nietzsche,* trans. Walter Kaufmann, New York: Modern Library, 1992 [1966], pp. 773–74.

12. *WzM,* § 74.

13. *WzM,* § 59.

14. "Toward a History of the Modern Eclipse," *WzM,* § 59.

15. *WzM,* § 65. This fragment is partially cited by Michel Salomon in Paul Bourget and Michel Salomon, *Bonald,* Paris: Bloud, 1905, ch. V ("Tradition"), p. 157; the reference, which is apparently paradoxical in what is a specifically traditionalist context, is introduced this way: "One of our contemporaries, very different from Bonald the Christian, the philosopher of *Beyond Good and Evil,* regrets seeing modern humanity deprived of 'the sureness of *instinct . . .*'"

16. Eugen Fink, for example, firmly announces on the very first page of his book on Nietzsche's philosophy, "Nietzsche's is the implacable, cutting 'No' to the past, the dismissal of all tradition, the call for a radical turnaround"

(*Nietzsches Philosophie,* Stuttgart: Verlag W. Kohlhammer, 1979 [1960], p. 7). On the basis of such postulates, one can make of Nietzsche, as desired, a resolute modern, an ultramodern, or a hypermodern, and, in the end, a postmodern.

17. See the remarks by the traditionalist philosopher Gustave Thibon on Nietzsche and Saint John of the Cross as "magicians of the extreme" (*Nietzsche ou le déclin de l'Esprit,* Lyon: H. Lardanchet, 1948, p. 278–79); and, as a counterpoint, Karl Jaspers's notes on "the extremes and the measured" (*Nietzsche and Christianity*).

18. See Konrad Lorenz, *Civilized Man's Eight Deadly Sins,* New York: Harcourt, Brace, Jovanovich 1974. trans. Marjorie Kerr Wilson, ch. 5: "Entropy of Feeling," pp. 31–42. For a presentation of the theoretical foundations of such a biological conception of "civilization's pathological problems," cf. K. Lorenz, *L'homme dans le fleuve du vivant* (1978), trans. into French by J. Etoré, Paris: Flammarion, 1981, especially pp. 386ff., 397ff.

19. WzM, § 57.

20. Carl Schmitt, *Politische Theologie,* p. 54.

21. Ibid., pp. 52, 54. Julius Evola, "Donoso Cortés," in *Explorations: Hommes et problèmes* (1974), trans. into French by Ph. Baillet, Puiseaux: Pardès, 1989, p. 213.

22. Louis Veuillot, *L'illusion libérale,* Paris, 1866; new edition: Dion-Valmont, Belgium: Dismas, 1989.

23. Jules Barbey d'Aurevilly, *Les prophètes du passé,* Paris, Alphonse Lemerre, 1851. Here we come once again up against the difficult question of "political Romanticism," not merely as a reference to the German school or to the strictly German movement that is so designated, but as a category in the history of political ideas. Cf. these remarks by Carl Schmitt: "Political Romanticism appears as a 'Flight to the Past,' a glorification of ancient, long-past conditions, and a return to tradition. This leads to another generalization: whoever does not consider the present better, freer, and more progressive than earlier times will be branded as a Romanticist, because the latter is supposed to be a *'laudator temporis acti,'* or a *'prophète du passé.'* In that case, the French Royalists would be a textbook example of political Romanticism" (*Politische Romantik,* p. 13), We can imagine what Charles Maurras's reaction would have been, for whom the "reform-revolution-romanticism" triad designated the three key figures for modern intellectual and political anarchism.

24. Antoine Blanc de Saint-Bonnet, *Restauration française,* Paris, 1851 (new edition: Paris, 1872); id., *L'infaillibilité;* id., *La légitimité,* Paris, 1873. For an overall study, see especially, Marcel de la Bigne de Villeneuve, *Un grand philosophe et sociologue méconnu: Blanc de Saint-Bonnet,* Paris: Beauchesne, 1949 (rather hagiographical); on the basic "revolution/restoration" opposition, cf. J. Drouin, "Le mot 'Révolution' chez Blanc de Saint-Bonnet," *Cahiers de lexicologie,* vol. XV, 1969 (2), pp. 27–34.

25. C. Schmitt, *Politische Theologie,* p. 54.

26. Ibid., p. 56.

27. Julien Freund, *L'aventure du politique: Entretiens avec Charles Blanchet,* Paris: Critérion, 1991, p. 51.

28. Donoso Cortés, «Pensées diverses», § V, in Donoso Cortés, *Lettre au Cardinal Fornari et textes annexes,* trans. into French by André Coyné, Lausanne: L'Âge d'Homme, 1989, p. 125.

29. Ibid.

30. Donoso Cortés, "Lettre à Montalembert du 26 mai 1849," in *Œuvres,* ed. L. Veuillot, Lyon: Briday 1858–59, vol. II, p. 340.

31. C. Schmitt, *Polit. Theol.,* p. 49.

32. L. Veuillot, op. cit., 1989, p. 27.

33. C. Schmitt, *Polit. Theol.,* p. 49.

34. L. Veuillot, op. cit., pp. 22–23.

35. Donoso Cortés, "Pensées diverses," § I, in op. cit., 1989, p. 122.

36. Jules Chaix-Ruy, *Donoso Cortés: Théologien de l'histoire et prophète,* Paris: Beauchesne, 1956, p. 170.

37. J. de Maistre, *Considérations sur la France* (1797), op. cit., p. 49.

38. G. Gengembre, op. cit., p. 198.

39. Louis de Bonald, "Sur la liberté de la presse" in *Œuvres complètes* [OC], Paris: Leclère, 1847–54, vol. 7: *Mélanges,* p. 73; cf. G. Gengembre, op. cit., p. 274.

40. L. de Bonald, *Pensées sur divers sujets* (1817), in *OC,* vol. 3, p. 313; cf. G. Gengembre, op. cit., p. 286.

41. L. de Bonald, *Réflexions sur la Révolution de juillet 1830,* ed. Jean Bastier, Paris: D.U.C./Albatros, 1988, p. 105. See G. Gengembre, "Bonald: La doctrine pour et contre l'histoire," *Le Débat* 39, 1986, p. 99; id., pp. 253, 285–86.

42. G. Gengembre, *La contre-révolution,* p. 286.

43. Ibid., p. 287.

44. L. de Bonald, "Sur les derniers événements" (1822), in *OC,* vol. 7, pp. 362–63. See G. Gengembre, art. cit., p. 100; id., *La conre-révolution,* p. 287.

45. The appearance of a word is not, in this case, the best of indices. For the outline of a lexical history, see especially Charles Andler, *Nietzsche, sa vie et sa pensée,* 5th ed. Paris: Gallimard, 1958, vol. III, p. 418ff.; Martin Heidegger, *Nietzsche* (1961), Pfullingen: Verlag Günther Neske, 1961, p. 31ff.; Jean Granier, *Le problème de la vérité dans la philosophie de Nietzsche,* Paris: Le Seuil, 1966, p. 235ff.; Angele Kremer-Marietti, "Que signifie le nihilisme?" in F. Nietzsche, *Le nihilisme européen,* trans. into French by A. Kremer-Marietti, Paris: U.G.E., 1976, p. 9ff.

46. *WzM,* § 2 ("Warum").

47. *WzM* § 12.

48. Donoso Cortés, "Lettre du 15 avril 1852 au directeur de l'*Heraldo,*" in op. cit., 1989, p. 97.

49. *WzM* § 79.

50. *WzM* § 54.

51. F. Nietzsche, *The Case of Wagner,* epilogue, in *Basic Writings of Nietzsche,* trans. Walter Kaufmann, New York: Modern Library, 1992 (1966), p. 648. Cf. Georges Morel, *Nietzsche,* Paris: Aubier-Montaigne, 1971. vol. II, p. 252.

52. F. Nietzsche, *On the Genealogy of Morals* (1887), 3rd essay, § 19, in *Basic Writings of Nietzsche,* trans. Walter Kaufmann, New York: Modern Library, 1992 (1966), p. 573. See also *Twilight of the Idols* (1888) [*TI*], "Skirmishes of an Untimely Man," § 41 in *The Portable Nietzsche,* ed. and trans. Walter Kaufmann, New York: Penguin Books, 1982 (1954); *The Case of Wagner,* epilogue, p. 648 ("Biologically, modern man represents a *contradiction of values*").

53. Donoso Cortés, "Lettre du 15 avril 1852," in op. cit., 1989, p. 101.

54. Ibid., p. 101.

55. See G. Gengembre, op. cit., 1989, pp. 270-71.

56. Donoso Cortés, "Lettre du 15 avril 1852," in op. cit., 1989, p. 101.

57. Donoso Cortés, "Lettre du 26 mai 1849 à Montalembert," in *Œuvres,* vol II, p. 342. See Guy Augé's remarks in "Donoso Cortés, doctrinaire espagnol de la contre-révolution et théologien de l'Histoire," *Vu de Haut* 3, 1984, pp. 21–22.

58. Donoso Cortés, "Lettre du 15 avril 1852," in op. cit., 1989, pp. 101–2.

59. Ibid., p. 102.

60. Ibid.

61. Ibid.

62. Donoso Cortés, "Lettre du 26 mai 1849," in *Œuvres,* vol. II, p. 342.

63. Ibid.

64. Ibid.

65. Donoso Cortés, "Lettre du 15 avril 1852 au directeur de l'*Heraldo,*" in op. cit., 1989, p. 106.

66. Donoso Cortés, "Pensées diverses," in op. cit., 1989, p. 121. See Carl Schmitt's somewhat forced commentary in *Polit. Theol.,* p. 53.

67. Georges Guy-Grand, *La philosophie nationaliste,* Paris: Bernard Grasset, 1911, p. 18.

68. *WzM,* § 57. See G. Morel, op. cit., 1971, vol. II, p. 305.

69. *WzM,* § 864.

70. G. Guy-Grand, op. cit., p. 17.

71. Paul Bourget, *Essais de psychologie contemporaine* (1883 and 1885), definitive edition with appendices. Paris: Plon, 1901, vol. I, pp. 215–16.

72. Ibid., p. 216.

73. See F. Nietzsche, *Ecce Homo* [*EH*], trans. W. Kaufmann, in *Basic Writings,* pp. 700, 719.

74. Ibid., p. 699.

75. M. Heidegger, *Nietzsche.*

76. See C. Andler, op. cit., vol. III, p. 418; J. Granier, op. cit., p. 235.

77. Paul Bourget, op. cit., 1901, 1885 preface, pp. XXI–XXII.

78. M. Heidegger, *Nietzsche.*

79. F. Nietzsche, *The Gay Science,* § 347.

80. *The Gay Science,* § 382.

81. Paul Bourget, op. cit., 1901, p. XXIII.

82. Ibid., p. XXII.

83. Ibid., p. XXIII.

84. Ibid., see p. XXIV.

85. Ibid., p. XXVI.

86. Charles Maurras, quoted by G. Guy-Grand, in *La philosophie nationaliste,* p. 20.

87. See Keith G. Millward, *Pierre Loti et l'esprit fin de siècle,* Paris: Nizet, 1955.

88. Charles Maurras, *Romantisme et révolution,* definitive edition, Paris: Nouvelle Librairie Nationale, 1922, new preface (1922), p. 2.

89. Charles Maurras, in *L'Action française,* 22 novembre 1912; reprinted in C. Maurras, *Dictionnaire politique et critique* [*DPC*], Paris: A la Cité des Livres, 1932, fasc. 4, p. 367.

90. Charles Maurras, *L'avenir de l'intelligence* (1905), in *Romantisme et révolution,* preface (1904–5), p. 35; cf. *DPC,* fasc. 4, p. 358.

91. *La volonté de puissance* [*VP*] [*The Will to Power,* French compilation], trans. G. Bianquis, Paris: Gallimard, 1938, T. II, L. III, § 27, pp. 21–22.

92. *EH* I, § 1, p. 679.

93. *TI,* "The Problem of Socrates" (§§ 1–12), in *Portable Nietzsche,* pp. 473–79.

94. Ibid., § 1.

95. Ibid., § 4, p. 475. In paragraph 3, Nietzsche seriously asks: "Was Socrates a Greek at all? Ugliness is often enough the expression of a development that has been crossed, *thwarted* by crossing" (Ibid., § 3, p. 474.) Nietzsche does not escape a commonplace assumption of the second half of the nineteenth century which held it to be obvious that there is a substantial link between racial mixture and loquaciousness, between the convulsive simultaneous presence of "contradictory [racial] inheritances" and interminable discussion (and certain pamphlets preferred using expressions such as "talmudism" and "talmudic spirit"); see on this P.-A. Taguieff, "Doctrines de la race et hantise du métissage: Fragments d'une histoire de la mixophobie savante," *Nouvelle Revue d'Ethnopsychiatrie* 17, 1991.

96. *TI,* § 9, p. 477.

97. Ibid., § 6, p. 476.

98. Oswald Spengler, *Pessimismus?* Berlin: Verlag von George Stilke, 1921, pp. 13–16.

99. Ibid.

100. Ibid.

101. Ibid., p. 19.

102. C. Schmitt, *Politische Theologie,* p. 56.

103. Ibid. Julius Evola made this commentary on the Schmittian theory

of absolute decision: " 'Exceptional powers' and 'dictatorship' are the necessary means, the 'means at hand' so to speak, which become necessary in such a historical situation, when the expected awakening of the central power of the State does not take place. Under those conditions, dictatorship is not a 'revolutionary' phenomenon. It remains inside legitimacy" (*Les hommes au milieu des ruines* [1953, 1972], French translation [1972] revised, corrected, and completed by G. Boulanger, Paris: Guy Trédaniel/Éd. de la Maisnie; Puiseaux: Éd. Pardès, 1984, p. 31).

104. C. Schmitt, *Politische Theologie*, p. 56.

105. Ibid., p. 54.

106. See Nietzsche, Letter to Reinhart von Seydlitz, 12 February 1888: "and in my implacable and subterranean struggle against everything that has been honored and loved by humans heretofore (—my formulation for it is 'Revaluation of all values')." *Nietzsche Briefwechsel: Kritische Gesamtausgabe*, ed. Giorgio Colli and Mazzino Montinari, 3rd part, vol. 5, Berlin: Walter de Gruyter, 1984, p. 248.

107. *WzM*, § 1006.

108. Nietzsche, Letter to Georg Brandes, 20 November 1888. Cf. *EH*, "Why I Am a Destiny," § 4, p. 784ff.

109. On the "new values," see for example: *EH*, "Birth of Tragedy," § 2, p. 38ff.; *WzM*, preface, § 4, p. 4 ("We require, sometime, *new values*"). The dominant determination of these "new values" that have been produced by transmutation is that they are "affirmative"; see especially G. Morel, *Nietzsche*, 1971, vol. III, p. 17ff.; Paul Valadier, *Nietzsche et la critique du christianisme*, Paris: Les Éditions du Cerf, 1974, p. 558. Since this affirmativeness oscillates between platitudes (the "yes" against the "no") and an unfathomable—and therefore undefinable—profundity, Nietzsche most often has recourse to the Dionysiac symbol. Being essentially "affirmative," the "new" values are more precisely determined by two categories that are presupposed to be positive: difference (simultaneously opposed to unity, to uniqueness, and to confusion) and hierarchy (as opposed to equality, to downward leveling, and, more broadly, to the inversion of values that grounds "slave morality," the "morality of the herd").

110. Nietzsche, Letter to Georg Brandes, 23 May 1888, *Kritische Gesamtausgabe: Nietzsche Briefwechsel*, p. 318.

111. On the importance of the themes of illness and the concern with healing in Nietzsche, see Karl Jaspers, *Nietzsche: An Introduction to the Understanding of His Philosophical Activity*, Tucson: University of Arizona Press, 1965. "Healing" (as a metaphor for the experience of transvaluation) is essentially determined by the idea-symbol of the "innocence" of the "yes": cf. G. Morel, *Nietzsche*, vol. III, p. 18ff.

112. *WzM*, § 1055.

113. Donoso Cortés, quoted by A. Coyné, in op. cit., 1989, p. 35; see also J. Chaix-Ruy, op. cit., p. 165.

114. Beginning with Donoso's own reconversion after the death of one

of his brothers in 1847; cf. J. Chaix-Ruy, op. cit., p. 120, and G. Augé, op. cit., pp. 16, 19.

115. C. Schmitt, *Politische Theologie*, p. 56.

116. Donoso Cortés, quoted by J. Chaix-Ruy, op. cit., p. 20.

117. *WzM*, § 1054.

118. See F. Nietzsche, *Thus Spoke Zarathustra*, 1st part (1883), prologue, § 5 (on the figure of the "last man").

119. *WzM*, § 29.

120. *WzM*, § 95 (1887).

121. *VP*, t. II, L. III, § 133, p. 54 (1888).

122. *WzM*, § 95.

123. *VP*, t. II, L. III, § 52, p. 30.

124. Ibid., § 53, p. 31.

125. Ibid., § 64, p. 34.

126. *WzM*, § 874.

127. Victor Goldschmidt, *Platonisme et pensée contemporaine*, Paris: Aubier/Éditions Montaigne, 1970, p. 199.

128. See *TI*, p. 485.

129. Cf. V. Goldschmidt, op. cit., p. 202. See for example *TI*, "What I Owe to the Ancients," §§ 4, 5; *EH; WzM*, § 1052. On the falsely simple figure of Dionysus, see especially G. Morel, *Nietzsche*, vol. III, p. 280ff.; and more particularly, on its emergence in Nietzsche's last letters (with and against the "Crucified"): Pierre Klossowski, *Nietzsche et le cercle vicieux*, Paris: Mercure de France, 1969, p. 333ff. (although these glosses and brilliant variations are likely to be of interest above all to Klossowski's unconditional admirers).

130. *WzM*, preface, no. 4; the theme of the anti- and post-Christian) "good news" is common in Nietzsche's last texts: cf. for example *EH*, "Twilight of the Idols," § 2.

131. *WzM*, § 2.

132. *WzM*, § 1, "Toward an Outline."

133. Mention is made of the "Christian God" or "Moral God." See *WzM*, § 55. Cf. V. Goldschmidt, op. cit., p. 202.

134. M. Heidegger, *Nietzsche*, vol. II, p. 34.

135. F. Nietzsche, *The Gay Science*, Book V, § 344.

136. *WzM*, § 438.

137. Ibid., §§ 95, 382.

138. On Kant's "theological instinct," see *The Antichrist* (1888), §§ 10, 11.

139. *TI*, "Reason in Philosophy," § 6.

140. V. Goldschmidt, op. cit., 200–1.

141. *WzM*, § 200.

142. *WzM*, § 340.

143. *WzM*, § 753.

144. *WzM*, preface, § 3.

145. *VP*, t. II, L. III, § 265, p. 90 (1884–85).

146. *"Der Philosoph als Arzt der Kultur."*

147. *VP*, t. II, L. III, § 33, p. 23 (1875).

148. *Unzeitgemässe Betrachtungen*, III (1874): *"Schopenhauer als Erzieher"*, § 4. In English: *Unmodern Observations*. New Haven: Yale University Press, 1990. "Schopenhauer as Educator," trans. by William Arrowsmith, p. 185.

149. See Nietzsche's letter to August Strindberg on 18 December 1888: "There is no culture outside of French culture" (*Briefwechsel*).

150. *WzM*, § 783. Along the same lines, *The Antichrist* (1888), preface and § 57; *WzM*, § 864.

151. *Unmodern Observations*, III, p. 185.

152. *VP*, t. II, L. III, § 248, p. 85.

153. *WzM*, § 789.

154. *VP*, t. II, L. IV, § 194, 277 (1885).

155. Ernest Renan, *L'avenir de la Science* [1848–49; published in 1890], in *Œuvres complètes*, Paris: Calmann-Lévy, vol. III, 1949, p. 780. We use the expression "demo-liberalism" (*démolibéralisme*), drawn from the pamphleteering rhetoric of the radical right, because it clearly exemplifies the polemical amalgamation we are here analyzing. In the corpus of Action Française texts we also find, for instance, the expression "anti-libero-democratism" (*antilibéro-démocratisme*) (Pierre Chardon, in *DPC*, fasc. 12, s.v. "Nietzsche," p. 185, note).

156. Article reprinted in *DPC*, fasc. 12, s.v. "Nation," p. 158. An analogous demonstration could have been made from Julius Evola's integral traditionalism, whose political genealogy of modern decadence is in many ways close to that of Maurras: "The beginning of the dissolution of the traditional social-political structures . . . coincided with *liberalism* . . . Liberalism is thus at the origin of the sequence of the various forms of global subversion . . . The essence of liberalism is *individualism*" (*Les hommes au milieu des ruines*, p. 45).

157. Ernest Renan, «Nouvelle lettre à M. Strauss» (15 septembre 1871), in *Œuvres complètes*, op. cit., t. I, p. 459.

158. Charles Maurras, *Mes idées politiques*, Paris: Fayard, 1937, p. 151; cf. *DPC*, fasc. 1, 1931, p. 75.

159. C. Maurras, *Mes idées politiques*, preface, p. LVII; cf. *DPC*, fasc. 4, 1932, p. 342.

160. C. Maurras, *Mes idées politiques*, p. LXXXVI.

161. C. Maurras, *Trois idées politiques: Chateaubriand, Michelet, Sainte-Beuve*, Paris: Champion; 2d ed., 1912; reprinted in *Romantisme et révolution*, definitive edition, Paris, Nouvelle Librairie Nationale, 1922, note VI ("Misère logique"), p. 281.

162. Ibid., note X ("Rencontre des athées et des catholiques"), p. 288.

163. C. Maurras, *Mes idées politiques*, p. 131; cf. *DPC*, fasc. 4, 1932, p. 367 (*L'Action française*, 22 March 1913).

164. C. Maurras, *Romantisme et révolution*, preface to the definitive edition, p. 4: "Having defined the movement of the Reformation as 'a system-

atic sedition of the individual against the species,' Comte sensed the true revolutionary kinship . . . The fathers of the Revolution are to be found in Geneva, in Wittemberg, and, more anciently, in Jerusalem; they derive from the Jewish spirit and from the varieties of independent Christianity that raged in the Oriental deserts or in the Germanic forests, in, that is, the various roundabouts of barbarism."

165. C. Maurras, *Mes idées politiques*, p. 129.

166. Ibid., p. 115; cf. *DPC*, fasc. 5, 1932, p. 404.

167. C. Maurras, *Mes idées politiques*, preface, p. LXXXVII; cf. *DPC*, fasc. 10, 1932, p. 442 (s.v. "Libéralisme") : "Anarchism, liberalism: these words are really synonyms" (*Gazette de France*, 12 April 1902); ibid., p. 438: "The classical liberals and their anarchical and democratic posterity, descending from 1789, profess that a man is worth as much as another, and out of that justify suppressing social rankings" (*L'Action française*, 2 June 1925).

168. Léon Daudet, *Moloch et Minerve of l'après-guerre*, Paris: Nouvelle Librairie Nationale, 1924, p. 123.

169. C. Maurras, *Mes idées politiques*, p. 264; cf. *DPC*, fasc. 6, 1932, p. 13.

170. C. Maurras, *Mes idées politiques*, p. 264; cf. *DPC*, fasc. 12, 1932, p. 160.

171. See the methodological distinction introduced by Jean Touchard and adopted by Raoul Girardet in his work on French nationalism: the "nationalism of the nationalists" versus "society nationalism" (*nationalisme sociétal*); or: "nationalism of doctrine" versus "nationalism of feeling"; cf. R. Girardet, *Le nationalisme français, 1871–1914,* Paris: Armand Colin, 1966 (new ed. Paris: Le Seuil, 1983).

172. C. Maurras, *Mes idées politiques*, p. 264.

173. Ibid., p. 201, note 1; cf. *DPC*, fasc. 6, 1932, pp. 10–11.

174. C. Maurras, *Mes idées politiques*, p. 200.

175. Charles Maurras, *Enquête sur la monarchie* (1900, 1903, 1909), definitive edition (Paris: Nouvelle Librairie nationale, 1924), new ed., Paris: Fayard, 1937, p. 119 ("Réponse à M. Paul Bourget"); *DPC*, fasc. 4, 1932, p. 335 (s.v. "Démocratie"); *DPC*, fasc. 5, 1932, p. 404 (s.v. "Égalité"); id., *Mes idées politiques*, preface, p. LXIX. See also, in the last book mentioned, p. 97: "A society can tend toward equality, but, in biology, equality is found only in the graveyard."

176. C. Maurras, *Mes idées politiques*, p. 147. See also *DPC*, fasc. 10, 1932, p. 438; ibid., fasc. 2, 1931, p. 175.

177. Léon Daudet, op. cit., p. 124. Let us recall one of Daudet's witticisms the mention of which has become ritualized in the nationalist rhetoric expressed in the French language, as demonstrated by this conclusive remark excerpted from an article in the pro–Le Pen newspaper *Présent:* "Léon Daudet was right when he gave this definition of the liberal: 'Someone who thinks his adversary is right' " (Guy Rouvrais, "Petite prose présidentiable," *Présent*, 27–28 July 1991, p. 6).

178. *DPC,* fasc. 23, 1934, p. 220 (excerpted from the *L'Action française* monthly, 1904).

179. *DPC,* fasc. 5, 1932, p. 405 (excerpted from the *Gazette de France,* 23 January 1900).

180. Ibid.

181. Jean Darville [Édouard Berth], "Satellites de la Ploutacratie," *Cahiers du Cercle Proudhon,* July 1913, pp. 177–213 (facsimile reproduction, Paris: Centre d'Études de l'Agora, 1976).

182. Ibid., p. 177. Darville-Berth refers here notably to "Italy's boldness in setting out on its war on Tripoli."

183. F. Nietzsche, quoted by J. Darville, op. cit., p. 177 (the passage is quoted from *VP,* t. II, § 344, p. 122).

184. J. Darville, op. cit., pp. 177–80. The passage from Nietzsche is from *WzM,* § 864.

185. J. Darville, op. cit., p. 208. The "jewification" of the enemy is a common procedure in Berth's pamphlets: where the plutocracy is mainly Jewish, modern intellectualism or rationalism, and, in general, modern "alexandrinism," are of Jewish essence. Which is why the ideal-typical intellectual is the Jewish intellectual: "Do you want to know what a modern Intellectual is? Read *l'Ordination,* by Mr. Julien Benda, a metaphysical Jew [*Juif de métaphysique*] and eminent and highly distinguished representative of the intellectual, perfumed ghetto; you will find there the quintessence and the be-all and end-all of modern intellectualism" (É. Berth, *Les méfaits des intellectuels,* Paris: Marcel Rivière, 1914, pp. 37–38; work prefaced by Georges Sorel [pp. I–XXXVIII] and dedicated by Berth "To my master, Georges Sorel").

186. J. Darville, "Satellites," p. 209. On the opposition, fundamental in Berth's mind, between the values of decadence and "heroic" values, whose symbolic basis consists in the antithesis between "the theoretical man" Socrates, the prototype of the modern intellectual, and the Apollo-Dionysus couple, see especially *Les méfaits des intellectuels,* pp. 15, 19, 41, 55, etc. Berth's dualistic axiology explicitly refers to Nietzsche's analyses, whose antitheses are reinterpreted following Sorel's theory of the "sublime" and its (proletarian or bourgeois) degradations: democracy and the "humanitarian, pacifistic, and rationalist ideal" of the intellectuals incarnate the values of "degeneration," against which are raised the "heroic, religious, warlike, and national values," the affirmative and positive values of "war," and of "work" that are symbolized in the antidemocratic alliance of Maurras-Apollo and of Sorel-Dionysus. On the opposition between "alexandrine" or "Socratic" culture (a notion explicitly borrowed from *The Birth of Tragedy*) and the "culture of the producers" (a Sorelian notion par excellence), cf. op. cit., pp. 217ff., 288ff.

187. Even Georges Morel, the most faithful to Nietzsche's texts, and the most upright among recent French Nietzsche commentators, when he quotes the fragment Berth makes reference to (*WzM,* § 864 , skips over the passage concerning Jews: cf. G. Morel, *Nietzsche,* vol. II, p. 291 (the "big financiers" and "the Jews" become: "these new pseudo-masters"). We would never be done

enumerating the ways, subtle or crude, in which enthusiastic commentators have made an effort to "save" Nietzsche (cuts in inconvenient passages, euphemistic translations, overinterpretation, etc.).

188. Karl Jaspers, *Nietzsche: An Introduction to the Understanding of His Philosophical Activity,* trans. Charles F. Wallraff and Frederick J. Schmitz, Tucson: University of Arizona Press, 1965, p. 458.

189. André Gide, cited by Pierre Chardon, in *DPC,* fasc. 12, s.v. "Nietzsche," p. 185 (note). It is a remark made by Gide in an article published on 10 December 1898, in *L'Ermitage* ("Lettre à Angèle: Sur Nietzsche"), and then again in *Prétextes* (Paris, 1903, pp. 166–82). On Gide's reception of Nietzsche's œuvre, see especially Geneviève Bianquis, *Nietzsche en France: L'influence de Nietzsche sur la pensée française,* Paris, F. Alcan, 1929, pp. 13, 62–66.

190. It is nevertheless the case that Nietzsche's pronounced Francophilia in certain texts (after the break with Wagner, and specially after reading Paul Bourget's *Essais,* 1883 and 1885) embarrassed the Action Française's doctrinaire Germanophobes and led them to judgments that were sometimes quite nuanced, at any rate before the 1914–18 war. But, to put it in a formula, Nietzsche is, for the Action Française, only the exception that confirms the rule: Germany is a seat of "barbarism." In a note to the tale *Les serviteurs* (1892), note dating from 1895 (*Le chemin de paradis: Mythes et fabliaux,* Paris: Calmann-Lévy, 1895), Maurras wrote, "a strange writer of slavic race named Nietzsche . . . This Nietzsche is an ingenuous Sarmatian, eloquent and rather subtle. Although of a bizarre spirit, reading Plato has not been wasted on him. However, the atrocious disorder in his thought ends up leading him to a proud anarchism. His birth predestined him to it. Faithful to this barbarism, he even went mad. I have, on the contrary, attempted the triumphs of reason" (Cf. *DPC,* fasc. 12, p. 183, note 1). In an article that appeared on 2 March 1900 in the *Gazette de France,* Maurras comes back to the question of Nietzsche's influence:

> I do not in any way admit the debt that is sometimes indicated to me towards Friedrich Nietzsche, because I know I do not really owe him anything: all that this Germano-Slavic philosopher seems to be able to teach us about authority, about freedom and their relationship, he owes, in fact, to us, for he owes it to minds of our race or of our lineage, such as a Joseph de Maistre, a Voltaire, a Renan, a Lucan, an Aristotle, or a Thucydides (Cf. *DPC,* ibid., p. 183).

Maurras came back to the thorny question in 1903 due to a critical study of Pierre Lasserre's book, *La morale de Nietzsche* (Paris: Calmann-Lévy, 1902) :

> Towards 1890 and 1891 . . . morally, politically, literarily, appeared . . . a doctrine of force and of the natural discipline this force must receive to be rich in itself, to increase and shine . . . *The Case of Wagner* was translated [into French] in 1893. Without sympathizing with Nietzsche, we could perceive that the barbarian had some good aspects . . . M. Pierre Lasserre has appeared . . . I had, a priori, so much confidence in M. Pierre Lasserre that I

expected from him the answer to *the great problem my mind comes up against at the mere name Friedrich Nietzsche* [my italics, P. -A. T.]. All that is good, ordered, hierarchical [in Nietzsche] we can find before him, expressed in infinitely better terms, in the French, Latin, and Greek series: we had discovered it before he had . . . The good barbarian that is in Nietzsche sometimes makes us blush with the very high lessons he has taken from us of which he has understood only certain parts . . . Despite his outrageous statements, his coarseness, and his mischievous priggishness, this half-Slavic German will be welcome in the sacred enclosure of the ancient French School; but, if anyone tries to make of him a doctor, his advocates shall have to be reminded of the just sentiment of what is mine and what is yours. ("Le tien et le mien dans Nietzsche," *Gazette de France*, January 1903; reprinted in *Quand les Français ne s'aimaient pas: Chronique d'une renaissance, 1895–1905* [1st ed., 1916], new edition, Versailles: Bibliothèque des Œuvres Politiques, 1928, pp. 111–22; see also *DPC*, fasc. 12, 1932, pp. 186–91).

Nietzsche's works are, in a word, judged in these texts to be either "useless" or else "dangerous." Maurras often came back, later on, to the same theme, with increasing harshness. But he always formulated the same reserve concerning the positive role played by Nietzsche as demystifier of the revolutionary, liberal, and democratic illusions:

From 1894 onwards, we have multiplied against the author of *Zarathustra* the reproaches of barbarism and anarchy. Somewhat later on, we called him . . . mischievous. And although several of our friends and collaborators have at times had the opportunity of observing that the Nietzschean error has helped young Frenchmen to cleanse themselves of the revolutionary error, a fact that cannot be denied, Lucien Moreau and Pierre Lasserre have never failed to add that this useful error is a drug to be put under lock and key in the cabinet where the poisons are kept. (Criton [pseudonym], in *L'Action française*, 12 février 1909; *DPC*, fasc. 12, p. 186).

If, then, Nietzsche is a "barbarian" due to his origins, he can nevertheless be classified among "the great Barbarians," next to, for example, Goethe, in that he "found himself to be the declared enemy of Germania" (C. Maurras, *Quand les Français ne s'aimaient pas,* p. 34). The orthodox Maurrasian evaluation of Nietzscheism can thus be summed up in a denunciation of the "barbaric" and/or "anarchical" core of Nietzsche's philosophy, accompanied by an acknowledgement of the "services" rendered the nationalist cause by the reading of Nietzsche (a positive instrumental conception of Nietzsche's works, for its anti-German and anti-demo-liberal orientations). For an exposition of the Master's radical, polymorphous Germanophobia, see C. Maurras, *Devant l'Allemagne éternelle,* Paris: Éditions "A l'Etoile," 1937.

Pierre Lasserre's evolution is a good indicator of the Action Française's increasing Nietzschephobia: in the first edition of *La morale de Nietzsche* (1902), he proves to be rather favorable to Nietzsche's aristocratic way of thinking and quite receptive to his critique of European decadence as well as to his praise of hierarchy; but in the preface, dated January 1917, of the new edition (Paris: Calmann-Lévy, 1923) of the same book, he multiplies the criticisms and the warnings (pp. 1–37; see also Pierre Lasserre, *Le Germanisme et l'esprit humain,* Paris: E. Champion, 1915, pp. 23–24). For the anti-German use of Nietzsche's texts: Jacques Bainville, *Lectures,* Paris, Fayard, 1937, pp. 129, 132, 306; already, in his answer to an inquiry on the German influence upon France (*Mercure de France,* vol. XLIV, 1902), Bainville said he rejoiced in "the blows Nietzsche dealt the detestable species of the moralists, against the humanitarian church, and against the democratic gnosis" (cf. G. Bianquis, op. cit., p. 82). That is a positive aspect of Nietzsche's influence that Lucien Moreau himself acknowledges, he who was one of the most virulent anti-Nietzscheans of the Maurras school: Nietzsche is of course merely "a prophet of anarchy," but "we do not mean to deny the services that a Friedrich Nietzsche can render against the democratic and humanitarian rationalists" (L. Moreau, "Autour du nietz-schéisme," *L'Action française,* 1 June 1905, pp. 366ff., 372). Where Léon Daudet dared confess his admiration for the polemicist's style (*Flammes,* Paris: Grasset, 1930, pp. 34–41), Henri Massis manifested an unfailing hostility to Nietzsche's thought, a hostility not excluding clichéd and polemical associations, as in these observations from later years: "A nihilist, this Nietzsche who was claimed by Nazism, and who ended up the 'prophet of an eclipse, of a darkening such as the world has never known.' Didn't he say of himself, when defining his mission: 'I am a cataclysm'?" (*Allemagne d'hier et d'après-demain,* Paris: Éditions du Conquistador, 1949, pp. 20–21). But the same Massis also remembered reading "Nietzsche who, when we were eighteen years old, had given us such a high fever," after having observed: "Besides, we loved nothing but the extremes" (*Évocations,* vol. 1: *Souvenirs, 1905–1911,* Paris: Plon, 1931, pp. 160–61).

191. See Hugues Rebell [Georges Grassal, 1867–1905], "Sur une traduction collective de Nietzsche," *Mercure de France,* vol. XIII, no. 61, January 1895, pp. 98–102; id., "Le Nietzschisme" [*sic*] (1902), in *Le culte des idoles* (1929), new ed., Gouy: A l'Écart, 1980, pp. 79–94. Rebell finds in Nietzsche's works mostly arguments against Christianity, sentimental humanitarianism, and the "low socialism that threatens to ruin everything we hold dear" (1895); his rejection of egalitarian democracy and his praise of the aristocracy to come fuse into a search for "the great health," modern civilization, being "sick," not being curable except by "doctors of civilization." In 1894, Rebell published *l'union des trois aristocracies* (The union of the three aristocracies) (Paris: Bibliothèque Artistique et Littéraire), which ends with an antirevolutionary outcry: "Revolution, humanity's sickness! We call with loud shouts for the doctor, even a brutal one, who will purify the world of your stains. Enemy of beauty and of thought, may our curses be promptly heard: The era of the mediocre is finished, may an era of nobility begin again!" (p. 48). See also the "Lettre de M. Hugues Rebell," in C. Maurras, *Enquête sur la monarchie,* pp. 145–50. On Hugues Rebell, see mainly: Auriant, "Portrait d'Hugues Rebell," *La Nouvelle Revue Fran-*

çaise 350, 1 April 1943, pp. 630–40; Luc Tirenne [Michel Leroy], "Hugues Rebell: poète nietzschéen et précurseur du nationalisme français," *Défense de l'Occident* 121, June 1974, pp. 78–92; id., "Hugues Rebell: traducteur et interprète de Nietzsche," *Défense de l'Occident* 125, January 1975, pp. 52–63.

192. Albert Bertrand-Mistral (1890–1917), whose literary pseudonym was Albert Bréart, died in combat on 7 June 1917. See Albert Bertrand-Mistral, *Le signal*, preface by Pierre Laserre, Avignon: Librairie Roumainville, 1922 (posthumous anthology of texts by the author and of homages to him).

193. Albert Bertrand-Mistral, "L'influence de Nietzsche," *La plume littéraire et politique*, February 1911; reprinted in *Le signal*, [pp. 32–36], p. 32. The author notably refers to a survey made by Jean Viollis for the *Grande Revue* on "Nietzsche et la jeunesse d'aujourd'hui" (Nietzsche and today's youth).

194. Albert Bertrand-Mistral, "L'influence de Nietzsche," p. 34.

195. Ibid., p. 32.

196. Ibid., p. 33.

197. Georges Valois, *L'homme qui vient: Philosophie de l'autorité* (The man to come: Philosophy of authority), definitive edition (3rd ed.), Paris: Nouvelle Librairie Nationale, 1923, introduction to the first edition (1906), p. 33 (quoted by A. Bertrand-Mistral, "L'influence," p. 34).

198. See Alfred Fabre-Luce, *Anthologie de la nouvelle Europe*, Paris: Plon, 1942, preface, pp. XVI–XVII and ch. II, p. 19ff.

199. Albert Bertrand-Mistral, "L'influence," p. 33. Replying to Gide, who made Nietzsche out to be a strange "protestant," the ultraorthodox Maurras follower Pierre Chardon wrote along the same lines as Bertrand-Mistral: "That does not mean that there isn't antiprotestantism, as well as anti-Germanism or antiromanticism or anti-demo-liberalism scattered throughout Nietzsche's pages, and this was what made an impression on many young Frenchmen at the end of the nineteenth century, *to the extent of orienting them towards our side* [my italics, P.-A.T.]" (*DPC*, fasc. 12, 1932, p. 185, note).

200. Georges Valois, op. cit., 1923, 1906 introduction, p. 32 (incorrectly quoted by Albert Bertrand-Mistral, "L'influence," pp. 33–34; we have reestablished the quoted text). For a more nuanced testimony, see Georges Valois, *D'un siècle à l'autre: Chronique d'une génération, 1885–1920*, Paris Nouvelle Librairie Nationale, 1921, esp. pp. 134–35, 151–53, 155–56.

201. G. Valois, *L'Homme qui vient*, pp. 43–44 (italics in the text).

202. Ibid., ch. XXXVIII: "National Disorganization: Democracy," pp. 211–23, which develops three themes: "(1) Democracy leads to political anarchy . . . (2) Democracy leads to moral and intellectual anarchy . . . (3)Democracy is the very negation of the nation."

203. Charles Maurras, *Mes idées politiques*, preface ("La politique naturelle"), p. LVII (equality), p. LXIX ("democracy is evil, democracy is death").

204. Albert Bertrand-Mistral, "L'influence," p. 34.

205. Ibid., pp. 34–35.

206. Ibid., p. 35.

207. Ibid., p. 32.

208. Ibid., p. 35. Maurras's antiliberalism has been well brought out by Emmanuel Beau de Lomenie in his book *Maurras et son système,* Bourg (Ain): E.T.L., 1953, p. 98ff: the essential point consists in grasping the necessary concatenation   "Reform-Revolution-[Romanticism]-Liberalism-Democracy-Socialism": liberalism, thus understood, "is . . . essentially the revolutionary doctrine . . . by virtue of which the only acceptable type of society would be democratic society" (pp. 98–99).

209. Henri Massis, "Les conditions du redressement français," in H. Massis, *Au long d'une vie,* Paris: Plon, 1967, p. 148 (my italics).

210. Ibid., 1967, pp. 148–49.

211. Jacques Bainville, "Maximes et Jugements," in *1927. Almanach de l'Action française,* November 1926, p. 63. Note that the explicit reference to Nietzsche is to be found in contemporary traditionalist literature quite precisely within the perspective of a restoration of the Catholic order, as witness this conclusion to an article that appeared in the National Front's doctrinal review: "Since we must hope in order to continue, it is Nietzsche that we shall call on, Nietzsche, of whom Gustave Thibon liked to quote: 'When all the mutations are finished, order will return to the Church and the Church to order' " (Pierre and Catherine de Meuse, "L'Église désacralisée," *Identité: Revue d'Études Nationales* 12, March–May 1991, p. 19).

212. Cf. Georges Guy-Grand, *La philosophie syndicaliste,* Grasset, 1911, p. 82. See also a strange anti-Maurras pamphlet, quite erudite: Jules Pierre, *Avec Nietzsche à l'assaut du christianisme: Exposé des théories de l'Action française suivi de leur réfutation . . .* Limoges: Pierre Dumont, 1910, 253 pages. The thesis concerning Maurras's Nietzscheanism has been defended by the specialist in German culture, Geneviève Bianquis (*Nietzsche en France,* esp. pp. 11–12, 45–52: antidemocratism, anti-Christianity, antiromanticism; praise of force, order, hierarchy, aristocratism): "There are, on one hand, meetings of ideas, coincidences; on the other, more or less conscious borrowings" (G. Bianquis, quoted by Pierre Chardon, in *DPC,* fasc. 12, p. 184, note; P. Chardon dedicates his long note in the article "Nietzsche" of the *DPC* to replying to Bianquis's analyses: *DPC,* pp. 183–86, note 1).

Index

Absurdity, 173
Action
  discussion vs., 178, 196
  knowledge and, 145
Action Française, 159, 178–79,
    192–202, 205, 209, 220–
    22n.190
Aesthetics, 55–62, 145, 153
  creator as medium, 135–36
  Nietzsche's metaphysics, 134–36,
    138–39
  Romanticist hermeneutics of, 139
  truth and science vs., 59–60
Alain (Émile-Auguste Chartier), 75
Albert, Henri, 200
Alchemical analogies, 181–82
Anarchy, 176, 181, 195, 221
Anger, 76–77
Anglophobia, 47
Animal behavior, 137
Anthropological knowledge, 82
Antichrist, The, 33, 54
Antimodernism. *See* Modernity,
    Nietzschean critique of
Anti-Semitism, 32–33, 54, 98,
    219n.185
Apel, Karl-Otto, 12
Apocalypse, 160
Argumentation and discussion
  action vs., 178, 196

antimodern/antiliberal critiques,
    96–97, 158, 159–67, 169, 173,
    174, 178, 193
  authority vs., 106
  creation of norms in modern soci-
    ety, 93, 97, 99
  Nietzschean critique, 95–97
  opposed to tradition, 92
  philosophical conception of, 174–
    75
  rationality in, 12–13
  truth and, 175
Aristocratic culture (ancient Hel-
    lenes), 29, 95–97, 99–100, 103
Aristotle, 29
Aron, Raymond, 84
Art
  as the cult of error, 61
  illusion, 59, 62
  in the service of life, 59
  Nietzsche's metaphysics, 134–36,
    138–39
  philosophy as, 61
  science and, 59
  truth and, 59–60, 121
  see also Aesthetics
Artistic intoxication, 135, 138
Aryans, 34
Asceticism, 104, 146
Assimilation, 163–64

225

Poststructuralism, 82–83
Power relations, 84–85
Pragmatism, and truth, 7, 13–14
Progress, 6, 101–2, 182. *See also*
  Modernity, Nietzschean cri-
  tique of
Prophetism, 40–41
Providence, 209n.2
Psychoanalysis, 153
Pyrrhon, 47, 48

Racism, 32–38, 214n.95
Rationality, 12–13, 17
  cowardice and, 184
  Nietzschean vs. Weberian
    projects, 148, 151
  Nietzsche's critique of democracy
    and argumentation, 95
  rhetoric and, 74
Reactionary philosophy. *See* Mod-
  ernity, Nietzschean critique of;
  Nationalism; Tradition and tra-
  ditionalism
Realism, 15–16
Reality, rejection of, 123
Rebell, Hugues, 203, 222
Reformation, 217n.164
Relativism, 7, 46, 49–51, 167, 191
Religions, origins of, 125
Religious reaction, 183. *See also* Ca-
  tholicism
Renan, Ernest, 195
Representatives and intermediaries,
  162–63
Responsibility, 86–87, 152
Rhetoric, 73–74
Rickert, H., 149
Romanticism, 112, 139–40, 146,
  178
  political, 211n.23
Rosset, Clément, 27, 30, 40–41, 52–
  53

Saint-Bonnet, Antoine Blanc de,
  159, 167, 209n.1
Sartre, Jean-Paul, 75, 97

Schmitt, Carl, 162, 168, 180–81
Schopenhauer, A., 145–47, 189
Science, 6–9, 11, 14–15, 51,
  107n.13
  aesthetics and, 59–60
  reactive will to truth, 98
Self
  autonomous, 112
  death and, 72
  as illusion, 127
  Nietzschean rejection of subjec-
    tivity, 124
Self-contradiction, 21, 46–47, 51–
  53
Self-destruction, modernity's process
  of, 164, 188–90
Self-interest, 76
Self-referentiality, 11
Semiology, 79–82
Sensation and sensibility, 116–20
Sentiments, 76
Sexuality, 26, 28–29
Signs, 79–81
Simmel, Georg, 1
Skepticism, 6, 47–48, 168
Slave morality, 30–31, 44, 132, 137
Slavery, 32, 108n.23
Socialism, 34, 165, 187, 193
Social structures, 82–83
Socrates, 4, 95–96, 99–100, 103,
  179, 188, 214n.95
Solidarity, 87–88
Sophism, 48–51, 96
Soul and body, 128
Sovereign (or autonomous) individ-
  ual, 84–90, 124–27, 137
Spengler, O., 158, 179–80
Spinoza, B., 25–26, 43–45
Structuralism, 82–83, 144, 155n.8
Subjectivity, 54, 67n46, 100, 122–
  24, 135–37, 153–54

Ten Commandments, 38
Thought, nature and, 136
Tocqueville, Alexis de, 129
Tolerance, 161, 162, 174, 206